REVISING MOVES

REVISING MOVES

Writing Stories of (Re)making

EDITED BY
CHRISTINA M. LAVECCHIA,
ALLISON D. CARR,
LAURA R. MICCICHE,
HANNAH J. RULE,
AND JAYNE E. O. STONE

UTAH STATE UNIVERSITY PRESS
Logan

© 2024 by University Press of Colorado

Published by Utah State University Press
An imprint of University Press of Colorado
1580 North Logan Street, Suite 660
PMB 39883
Denver, Colorado 80203-1942

All rights reserved

 The University Press of Colorado is a proud member of the Association of University Presses.

The University Press of Colorado is a cooperative publishing enterprise supported, in part, by Adams State University, Colorado State University, Fort Lewis College, Metropolitan State University of Denver, University of Alaska Fairbanks, University of Colorado, University of Denver, University of Northern Colorado, University of Wyoming, Utah State University, and Western Colorado University.

ISBN: 978-1-64642-548-8 (hardcover)
ISBN: 978-1-64642-549-5 (paperback)
ISBN: 978-1-64642-550-1 (ebook)
https://doi.org/10.7330/9781646425501

Library of Congress Cataloging-in-Publication Data

Names: LaVecchia, Christina M., editor. | Carr, Allison D., 1983– editor. | Micciche, Laura R., editor. | Rule, Hannah J., 1981– editor. | Stone, Jayne E. O., editor.
Title: Revising moves : writing stories of (re)making / edited by Christina M. LaVecchia, Allison D. Carr, Laura R. Micciche, Hannah J. Rule, and Jayne E. O. Stone.
Description: Logan : Utah State University Press, [2024] | Includes bibliographical references and index.
Identifiers: LCCN 2024002497 (print) | LCCN 2024002498 (ebook) | ISBN 9781646425488 (hardcover) | ISBN 9781646425495 (paperback) | ISBN 9781646425501 (ebook)
Subjects: LCSH: English language—Rhetoric. | Editing. | Academic writing. | Report writing.
Classification: LCC PE1408 .R448 2024 (print) | LCC PE1408 (ebook) | DDC 808/.042—dc23/eng/20240206
LC record available at https://lccn.loc.gov/2024002497
LC ebook record available at https://lccn.loc.gov/2024002498

Cover illustration © Ian Golding

In celebration of first draft readers; active, lingering, or abandoned projects; writing and nonwriting partners; and anyone who has ever stared down a sentence with the hope that it can be made better.

It is deeply satisfying to believe that we are not locked into our original statements, that we might start and stop, erase, use the delete key in life, and be saved from the roughness of our early drafts. Words can be retracted; souls can be reincarnated.
                              Nancy Sommers, "Between the Drafts"

CONTENTS

List of Illustrations xi

Acknowledgments xiii

On the Page and in Our Lives
  Christina M. LaVecchia, Allison D. Carr, Laura R. Micciche, Hannah J. Rule, and Jayne E. O. Stone 3

SET 1: REVISION TAKES A STAND
Hannah J. Rule 19

1. On Choosing Not to Revise
   Joseph Harris 23

2. Consulting Editor to the Rescue: Seeing Storytelling Anew through Veteran Eyes
   Alexandra Hidalgo 29

3. Alejandra Chooses Life: Revising the Resignation Letter toward Counterstory as Epistle
   Aja Y. Martinez 41

SET 2: REVISION MAKES SPACE
Christina M. LaVecchia 49

4. Revising a Cover Letter, Revising a Life: Bridging Professional Identities
   Ellery Sills and Fernando Sánchez 52

5. Re-visioning Letters of Recommendation
   Cameron Becker, Kelly Blewett, and Vanessa Kraemer Sohan 63

6. Creating and Holding Space as Revision in WPA Lives
   Christy I. Wenger 79

SET 3: REVISION APPROACHES FEEDBACK
Laura R. Micciche   91

7. On the Slippages and Swells of Revising Digital Media
   Rich Shivener   94

8. "Another_Draft.docx": The Role of Horizontal Mentoring in Publishing as Graduate Students
   Dana Comi and Alisa Russell   106

9. Revising Scholarly Peer Review: Don't Be a Dick
   Raúl Sánchez   117

10. Revision as Protecting What Is Important
    Cruz Medina   128

SET 4: REVISION MEETS THE WORLD
Allison D. Carr   137

11. Revising an Antiracism Statement for Known and Unknown Audiences
    Mike Garcia   141

12. Feeling Our Way through Collaborative Revision When the World Is on Fire
    Collie Fulford and Stefanie Frigo   151

13. Whose Exigence?: The Social Dynamics of a Writing Across the Curriculum Plan-in-Process
    Christopher Basgier   163

SET 5: REVISION SPIRALS
Jayne E. O. Stone   177

14. Definition as Invention: Turning a Familiar Concept into a Critical Keyword
    William Duffy   181

15. Uncovering the Veil: Revising the Dichotomy between Motherhood and Academic Personas
    Jule Wallis-Thomas   192

16. "That's Where It Sleeps": What I Say When I Point to My Abandoned Project
    Karen R. Tellez-Trujillo   206

17. Drawing a Blank: Illustrating the Revision Process
    Ian Golding   222

    Losses, Leavings, Remakings: An Afterword
    Jessica Restaino   227

    Index   233
    About the Authors   243

ILLUSTRATIONS

FIGURES

4.1.	Excerpt from Ellery's first draft of cover letter	57
4.2.	Excerpt from third draft of Ellery's cover letter	59
4.3.	Excerpt from Ellery's final draft of cover letter	59
7.1.	Author's print article revised for the web	97
15.1.	Screenshot showing revisions and personal notes and reminders	197
15.2.	Pie chart of student enrollment demographics, deleted	199
16.1.	Box of artifacts, asleep in my garage	207
16.2.	Karen and Ivan Klíma in Klíma's home office	212
16.3.	Jiřina Šiklová in her home	214
16.4.	Karen and Vilém Prečan at the ČSDS	216
16.5.	A small samizdat library in the ČSDS	216
17.1.	Early lumpy bird	224
17.2.	One of many sketch pages of awkward birds	225
17.3.	The comic, sped up a bit too fast	226

TABLES

7.1.	A comparison of a print and digital book proposal	96
11.1.	Introduction / statement of beliefs. Revision rule: Name racism and acknowledge its past and present effects; avoid naming whiteness	147
11.2.	Articulating the writing center's place in the discussion. Revision rule: Be direct and uncompromising about how antiracism differs from "nonracism"	148
11.3.	Action items. Revision rule: Focus on tangible actions	149

ACKNOWLEDGMENTS

Thanks, first and foremost, to everyone at Utah State University Press and University Press of Colorado and especially to Rachael Levay, whose support and enthusiasm for this volume from our first conversation gave us the motivation and confidence to see it through. Likewise, we are grateful for the anonymous reviewers, whose careful, detailed readings both assured us we were on the right track and helped us see how the manuscript could be made tighter and more affecting.

We can't say enough good things about our contributors. What a gift it has been to read and work with your stories. Thank you for trusting us.

We'd like to acknowledge, too, that most of the work of this book was completed during a time of personal, national, and global upheaval. On behalf of our contributors, we wish to honor the myriad networks and partners who provided support—material, emotional, collegial—to everyone involved with this book, and we especially want to honor the grief and pain that still contextualizes the lives of so many of us.

Special thanks to Ian Golding, whose revision work on the cover art inspired a shifting visual for the development of this book.

We are grateful to the Charles Phelps Taft Research Center at the University of Cincinnati and the College of Arts and Sciences at the University of South Carolina for supporting this publication. We must also acknowledge the seamless functioning of Google Drive and Google Docs, connecting five editors across four states and two time zones—logging literally thousands of changes to shared texts during two and a half years of production—*almost* as if we were huddled around the same computer.

Much love and gratitude to our families and familiars—Chris, Sammy, Del, Victoria, Inuk, Rumi, Trey, Elwood, Tarzan, two- and four-legged Weissiches, Jonathan, Everett, Waylon, G—for helping to sustain our writing lives and for loving us as unfinished drafts.

REVISING MOVES

ON THE PAGE AND IN OUR LIVES

Christina M. LaVecchia, Allison D. Carr,
Laura R. Micciche, Hannah J. Rule, and Jayne E. O. Stone

Is this really about revision?
  Early in our work on this volume, we had accepted abstracts that looked to be exactly what we asked for: reflections on revision. However, as the chapters began rolling in, they seemed also—in some cases quite prominently—to be reflections on collaboration, or composition, or identity configuration, or professional maneuvering. We loved the stories contributing authors were telling. They took us off the page, showing us children interrupting the scene of revising a grant to ask questions about God's gender (Wallis-Thomas), a faculty of color detailing injurious mistreatment to recast a whitewashed narrative of their resignation (Martinez), a student-teacher collaborative approach to a traditionally top-down practice, drafting a letter of recommendation (Becker, Blewett, and Sohan). But, were these stories really about revision?
  We began to question the assumptions we had brought into this project about how the moves of revision can be made visible. When we wrote the CFP, we thought "bits of or clips from actual text(s) in progress" would capture observable data, trace action in a scene, record activity in and around writing. Yet we began to recognize that the experiences of revising relayed by contributors often didn't "stay put" or cohere around demonstrable examples. Revision wasn't limited to textual change; it became a life activity, immersed in conversation, family life, collaboration, identity formation, years of thinking and rethinking, moments of conflict and resolution, problem-solving, political and social upheaval. Like air, revision seemed to fill all available space.
  As the five of us talked on Zoom about the chapter submissions and emerging book (originally subtitled "Showing and Narrating Revision in Action"), we began to accept that seeing revision in action isn't as simple and transparent a task as showing "bits or clips" would suggest. Just as revision moves, so too did our expectations as we took direction from our contributors, whose work urged us to honor revision's vitality

through stories that immersed us in rooms, life circumstances, and practices where revision comes to life.

ON STORIES

In foregrounding story, we are aware of writing ourselves into existing traditions. Storytelling has long been an accepted mode of knowledge-making in writing studies, owed largely to people of color who, as Victor Villanueva (2010) has written, combine "storytelling mixed with evidence of various other sorts" to demonstrate that "understanding humanity's humanity can best be attained through telling our own stories of ourselves" (131). Indeed, BIPOC scholars have made a convincing case for story as method: story is central to Indigenous epistemologies, rhetorics, and practices and to nondominant cultures and discourses more broadly due in no small part to story's ability to push back on master narratives and emphasize lived experiences and relationality.[1]

In her 2012 CCCC Chair's Address, Malea Powell establishes that stories, always emplaced, "are anything but easy" (384). On the contrary, Powell insists, "When I say story, I mean an event in which I try to hold some of the complex shimmering strands of a constellative, epistemological space long enough to share them with you" (384). Illustrating the difficulty of this work, contributor Madhu writes about not fitting into stories of the discipline: "And when I have tried to articulate my concerns, I have felt subdued, shamed, and disciplined" (390). Over the course of the address, we come to see how "stories produce habitable spaces" (391), as Powell puts it. This powerful idea resonates with the work of Aja Y. Martinez (also a contributor to this volume). She has advanced a counterstory methodology, which "gather[s] and shape[s] data into counterstory contexts and characters" in order to "empower the minoritized through the formation of stories that disrupt the erasures embedded in standardized majoritarian methodologies" (2020, 3). Beyond framing story as a way to document and understand experience, counterstory theorizes racialized experiences, serving an activist function by "exposing stereotypes and injustice and offering additional truths through a narration of the researchers' own experiences" (2020, 17). Turning an analytical eye toward such counternarratives, the recent special issue of *Journal for the History of Rhetoric*, "Americas," functions as a polyvocal revision of "whitestream[ed]" (Cedillo 2021, 18) history and mythology of North American settler colonialism. It features, for example, discussion of the rhetorical nuances and cultural function of "the Talk" in African American households (Erby 2021), racial scripts enabling and endorsing violence at the conclusion of the Mexican-American War (Cedillo 2021), and public performances of "haunting" to challenge public memory of colonial violence in Mexico (Fernandez 2021).

While story can be revisionary and politically potent, it can also be a means for teacher-scholars to narrate the ordinariness of professional work: writing, learning, teaching. For example, Tom Waldrep's edited collection, *Writers on Writing* (1985), features first-person essays by writing scholars that respond to the question, *How do you write?* Contributors narrate their writing practices, often noting that they don't use strategies they teach in their own classes, and generate insights about writing that travel across differing experiences and localities. Fifteen years later, in another edited collection, Richard H. Haswell and Min-Zhan Lu called for "oral narratives from the field, stories that are actually told in the classroom, in the halls, over the tutor's table, in committee rooms, on street corners, over the kitchen table, wherever" (2000, 227). The resulting book, *Comp Tales*, features 108 essayists and eleven chapters that "show how storytelling indeed works in collaboration to define and redefine relations and issues central to the field" (2000, x). More recently, the Digital Archive of Literacy Narratives, established in 2007, continues to collect stories about learning to read, write, and communicate from both the discipline and the public. These collections form a central (and well-traveled) methodological orientation for writing studies that constructs story as located, experiential, and cultural and as a form of situated knowledge-making.[2]

Narrative has also been a familiar tool by which teacher-scholars interrogate and navigate their professional roles. *Kitchen Cooks, Plate Twirlers and Troubadours: Writing Program Administrators Tell Their Stories* (1999), edited by Diana George, includes narratives about administrator life that detail bouts with anxiety, divorce, overwork, and emotional instability. In a similar vein, essays in *What to Expect When You're Expected to Teach: The Anxious Craft of Teaching Composition* (Bramblett and Knoblauch 2002) use humor and empathy to help new teachers in the field gain perspective on the challenging, upsetting, and sometimes gratifying experiences familiar to new teachers. In doing so, the editors hope that new teachers will feel less alone as they encounter bumps along the way. *Women's Ways of Making It in Rhetoric and Composition* (Ballif, Davis, and Mountford 2008) and *Stories of Becoming: Demystifying the Professoriate for Graduate Students in Composition and Rhetoric* (Lutkewitte, Kitchens, Scanlon 2022) likewise use story to illustrate what challenges and advancement look like from different—though not consistently inclusive—professional and personal locations. And beyond the permeable edges of writing studies as a field, narrative or storytelling is a trusted method in sociology, medicine, and interdisciplinary contexts, one that strives to complexify the landscape within which officials, advocates, and communities make decisions.[3] In all, this body of research ties narrative to a range of embodied experiences, a linkage that plays out across this volume.

We embrace story and its multiple, entangled, and often denigrated traditions as important context for this project. Far from new and far from belonging to one single tradition, story allows for multivocal accounts, functions as a tool for describing revision's relationality to everything else, invites embodiment into the conversation, enables theorizing to make larger claims, and brings to light experiences that might be hushed, suppressed, or otherwise privatized. Because they describe being somewhere, stories tell us what something feels like from a location, a body. And stories are forged, never relayed preformed—their telling, a reflective and creative act from which the teller and audience can learn. Story makes room for internal and external factors that come to bear on revising, allowing feelings and storage boxes and years of rethinking to resurface and stick around. Stories intentionally place value on the holistic quality of revising as a lived bodily experience as well as a process of word and image work.

ON REVISION

Because revision is so elusive, narration becomes essential for revealing what happens, particularly off the page. That said, chapters within do contain revision's artifactual presence—marked-up sentences from drafts, excerpts from reader reports, screen grabs, text messages. These instances act as cues that help writers find their way back to revising in situ and forward to revision stories. But though it opens that shimmery, fleeting epistemological space (Powell 2012), narration doesn't guarantee we're getting the whole story. Indeed, while contributors in this volume share some stories—certain and obvious to their tellers—that follow a clear arc, other revision stories struggle to be told at all, never quite coherently answering "what's the story here?" Fittingly, then, embedded in the development of this volume is the failure of a totalizing, stable representation of revision (we think of cover art contributor Ian Golding on this point—revision is pesky, maybe even impossible to visually represent). The fact is that most often writers compose without preserving their process (maybe unless they're being studied) and without retaining or even having access to what they did when they were doing it, in the moment or retrospectively. Revision and its traces often disappear.

But *attempts* to capture revision—through storytelling, through retrospective recreation—prove illuminating. These attempts represent choices authors make to tell their revision stories in one way and not another and to create meaning from experiences that might otherwise have seemed too mundane to recount or too unconnected to be considered relevant. What results in this collection is a wide range of revision stories. We see contributors become nostalgic and grateful when thinking about revision (Medina), and we see them become hyperaware of linearity in order to make sense of revision as a temporal act (Duffy). Others tie revision to morality and ethics (Becker, Blewett, and Sohan; R. Sánchez) and to lifespan or career arc (Harris; Wenger). We see dependencies on others or the desire for others to get involved (Comi and Russell; Hidalgo) and revision as frustratingly other-focused (Golding). We see revision constructed as an act of resistance (Harris; Martinez) and a form of accommodation (Basgier; Garcia). And we see revision as craft, woven into cultural and personal life (Fulford and Frigo; Sills and F. Sánchez; Wallis-Thomas), imbricated in design (Shivener), and re-lived as an act of personal inventory (Tellez-Trujillo; Wallis-Thomas). These dizzying differences consolidate around the idea that revision takes shape on the page and in our lives and in places in between. Given revision's everywhere-and-nowhere quality, this volume explores, among other things, how it can be seen or represented.

We believe that showing the hard-to-represent holistic quality of revising serves academic writers of all varieties. Nancy Sommers (1980, 1992), Wayne Peck (1990), and Alice Horning (2002), among others, have concluded from their research that writers are oftentimes eager to revise but don't know how to do it or can't muster the follow-through. The chapters in this book, which illustrate how professional writers in writing studies revise (or don't!) in all of their situated messiness, serve as mentor-texts. They carry the potential to illuminate strategies of persistence (or resistance) that advance writing and thinking, whether advancement results in radical, discrete changes or no change at all in one's texts. Contributors narrate revision from various locations: writers across the life cycle, writers of color, writers with disabilities, novice and veteran scholars, collaborative teams, writing program administrators, advanced graduate students, and faculty across rank and institution type.

As editors, we too come to this project with stances defined by our positionalities and professional locations. Between the lot of us, we connect with multiple identity descriptors, some of which include cisgender, white, mixed-race, middle-class with family roots in the working-class, woman, heterosexual, pansexual, Midwesterner, single mother, mother, spouse, and disabled. As well, we occupy various professional locations: full, associate, and assistant professor, qualitative researcher, graduate student, past and current directors of various institutional programs. The seedling for this book was planted in communication between Jayne and Laura, and once it was clear the idea had deep roots, the other three editors—frequent collaborators—agreed to participate. Each of us has different connections to the intellectual work of this volume, but more than anything, we like to work together; we like seeing what ideas bubble up when we put our heads together or, as the case may be, knock heads on our way to (imperfect) agreement.

When it comes to our own revision practices, like our contributors, we refuse to be limited by track changes. In fact some of us are "page-avoidant," working on ideas or noodling on a problem in the Drafts section of our email accounts ("emailing isn't writing"), or away from screens entirely, penciling in the margins, while others need to talk through in-process writing, relying on the company of writing groups, running pals, or even just jabber-jawing it out on a voice memo. Others can't or won't talk at all about what we're working on. We revise while our kids nap, or in notes tapped out in the parking lot during weekend errands. Some of us are deadline-oriented, while at least one of us feels most capable of revision while the deadline for something entirely unrelated is bearing down. Like most writers, we have highly particular and maybe even somewhat neurotic rituals for what we do with our excised leftovers and who gets the first look and when. We revise on long walks or, frustratingly, while staring at the ceiling at 4:15 a.m. We have Big Feelings about revising. Maybe something we agree on: writing is only revision. We are revising before the cursor even blinks on a new document, and we are revising even when the project is in the rearview mirror.

In other words, there's nothing systematic about how we revise. Writing researchers would likely feel affirmed reading this, as most work on revision finds it to be plenty inscrutable or elusive. In 1981, Ann E. Berthoff advanced what she called a "tendentious" claim: "revision is poorly taught, or is not taught at all, because composition teachers and composition textbook authors often do not know how writing gets written" (1981, 20). Just a few years later, accomplished scholar David Bartholomae, who clearly knows how to get writing done, characterizes revision as an opaque process that involves "pushing at the first sentence" and then finding that ten pages later he is "following a line of thought that was repressed in the first writing" (1985, 24). Naming it "one of the great secrets of our profession," Nancy Sommers says of her own approach to revision: "I take lots of showers, hot showers, talking to myself as I watch the water play against the gestures of my hands" (1992, 28). More recently, in Christine Tulley's *How Writing Faculty Write*, Thomas Rickert speaks of revision as the most central experience of academic writing: "The most inventive material you will ever come up with comes from working with revising a draft. Typically, my greatest insights will come from that and forcing myself to go back and do various forms of revision, but it always comes from working out a problem that I wasn't aware was a problem yet" (Tulley 2018, 26). We're provoked by academics' cagey ways of describing revision over the years and see this volume as an attempt to *say more*.

While the role of revision in writing classrooms has long been a preoccupation of teacher-scholars, no single book in the field features academic writers' discussions of their own revision processes and experiences, as this volume does.[4] Books on scholarly writing praxis, written for a wide audience in the discipline, focus on rhetorical moves (Harris 2017) or physicality and behaviors during writing (Perl 2004). Others feature self-reflective first-person essays that interrogate instructional practices of response (Lunsford and Straub 1995) or narrativize academics' own writing processes (Waldrep 1985). Revision is also addressed, to some extent, by a growing body of professionalization scholarship that attempts to demystify membership in the academy, though in tantalizingly brief terms (Gallagher and DeVoss 2019; Tulley 2018). For example, Tulley overviews the perspectives of her interviewees—academic writers whose work is well known in the field today—summarizing that, overall, they find enjoyment and pleasure and discovery and deep engagement in revising a text, though by no means ease (26). Like ours, these books invite writing studies professionals to draw insights from detailed descriptions of writers' processes and experiences. We also acknowledge two landmark texts on revision. Donald M. Murray's *The Craft of Revision* (2012), now in its fifth edition, features short, digestible sections and exercises to aid writers at different levels. And Alice Horning and Anne Becker's *Revision: History, Theory, and Practice* (2006), is part handbook, part history, and part pedagogical guide. These texts, like ours, show revision through both observation of textual changes and narration of writers' experiences while doing it.

As Charles Bazerman notes in his preface to Horning and Becker's edited collection, *Revision: History, Theory, and Practice*, teachers have developed "many tricks" to help students revise, and still students revise "shallowly" (2006, xii). Acknowledging the limits of pedagogical methods, Bazerman concludes that teachers need more than "tricks"; we also need "to teach our students something beyond the writing process itself, to develop the underlying knowledge and awareness that need to be brought to bear on revision" (xiii). Developing awareness that includes and goes beyond laboring over a text is one of our goals in this book, though we do so by focusing on the revising experiences of writing studies professionals, rather than that of students. We want to know what revision feels like to accomplished writers. Do we understand just how much identity is entwined with revision acts? Do we know what kind of mindset helps writers face protracted timelines typical when revising academic work? As these questions suggest, we have more to learn about revision as a holistic practice and set of labors, and we can't access all of that through artifactual evidence alone. In this sense, revision stories are essential forms by which writers can tell us about revision as a radically contextualized, distributed practice.

HOW THIS VOLUME MOVES

When we say revision *moves*, we mean this in its full grammatical multiplicity: kinetically, existentially, emotionally. Revision moves in the sense that it means differently to each contributor; revision moves writers, draws something out of them. Revision self-propagates, almost with a life of its own, within and beyond a writer's control: a new perspective on this idea over here reverberates all around, nudging adjustments both small and large. It involves moves that are not always discrete but that accumulate to create change or difference. Revision moves, too, can be acts of refusal or of negotiation, prompting one to reconsider, stall, stand one's ground, flip the script, abandon an idea, go back to the original phrase or draft or stance, chuck it and start over. Considering all of this, perhaps we should have anticipated the problem that greeted us in the middle stages of compiling this volume: we couldn't figure out how we wanted it to be organized.

As a group, we were hyperaware of what particular organizational choices or structures would convey about our subject, and we were likewise sensitive to how individual chapters might resonate differently based on where they were positioned. We spent hours on Zoom talking through various organizational structures, even plotting on a shared Padlet so that we could physically move chapters around in order to identify connections or provocations. We talked ourselves into and out of half a dozen different schemas, each of them bringing distinct themes and connective threads into view. Our original organizational structure (from the CFP and prospectus for the publisher) categorized revision stories based on textual genres under revision (scholarly, institutional, and self-advocacy), but in the course of our conversations we balked at the staid nature of these categories and, moreover, found them increasingly permeable with some chapters making sense in multiple places. At one point, feeling defeated, we resolved to roll with the original proposed structure and to exert destabilizing pressure with interchapters (yep, revision is often surrender, sometimes taking us right back to where we began). Finally, though, recalling our own delighted surprise at the manner in which contributors' narratives shouldered the energy and drama of processes that are so often obscured from view, we realized the structure, too, ought to mimic the drama of revising, at turns absorbing, alienating, thrilling, frustrating, and tedious. With this goal guiding us, we found a progression that felt more intuitive, one that created a sense of movement throughout. Revision, as our contributors remind us, isn't tidy or a separate, discernible stage. Why should a collection of revision stories attempt to be otherwise?

In lieu of conventionally organized and demarcated sections, we arrived at five loose, porous sets of chapters that build on and talk to one another. Headnotes—each written by one of the editors—form connective tissue between the sets, making our associative logic explicit and inviting readers to look for other connections. The volume begins with writers who express (relative) certainty about the work of revision; they approach revision with surety, knowing what they will and will not abide. Joseph Harris describes his decision not to revise an early version of what became *Rewriting: How to Do Things with Texts* (2006; second edition 2017); Alexandra Hidalgo details collaborative revision as the only way to find her film project's premise, hone her narrative voice, and ultimately move the documentary forward; and Aja Y. Martinez's counterstory shows the determination of her composite character, Alejandra Prieto, to use revision as a way to unmask the racism, harassment, and institutional apathy that leads so many BIPOC scholars to resign their positions or leave academia altogether.

Martinez's chapter interlaces personal and political stories, urging revision of institutional norms, while making clear that identity is on the line even in the most mundane of texts: a resignation letter that would ordinarily only be seen by a few administrators. In this way, her chapter serves as a complementary segue to those in the second set, which use revision to explore author identities in the context of often obscured professional discourses. For example, Ellery Sills and Fernando Sánchez describe the process of revising job market materials as akin to shifting and revising one's professional identity. Likewise, Kelly Blewett and Vanessa Sohan, along with one of Kelly's former students, Cameron Becker, take as their focus an occluded genre—letter of recommendation drafts—accessible to internal university committees but not to a wider field of readers. The authors contend that collaboration between writer and candidate can empower candidates to co-construct their scholarly and professional identities and thereby attain a degree of control over how they are represented. Another institutional high-stakes genre, the annual review, is Christy I. Wenger's focus. She details her efforts to make space in her review for documenting writing program administration, which involved revising her university's boilerplate form to foreground and validate a central aspect of her career.

As Wenger illustrates, making space for ourselves in academic cultures is years-long painstaking and deliberative work. Similarly, the writers in the third set narrate ways of making space via scholarly publication; they pull back the curtain to show us the collaborative, emotion-rich experiences of writers in the midst. We begin with Rich Shivener, who narrates what he calls the "affective swells" of revising print articles into chapters of a digital book, a process that is populated by the voices and perspectives of designers, editors, and reviewers. Forming a horizontal mentoring relationship, Dana Comi and Alisa Russell describe how they came to rely on one another's feedback as they transformed seminar papers into first publications. Addressing feedback offered during the manuscript review process, Raúl Sánchez describes the importance of reviewer feedback geared toward revision, cautioning against "dickish" behavior characterized by critique that values toxic judgment over writer-centered feedback. As if providing an example of the fruits of R. Sánchez's call for generous, revision-minded feedback, Cruz Medina discusses how productive editorial intervention enabled him to revise a piece on the decolonial potential for multilingual writers into an award-winning article.

As Medina's essay illustrates, some revision experiences resonate well beyond the text at hand. The chapters in the fourth set similarly show scholars struggling to protect their vision for their work while accounting for countervailing pressures in revision. Mike Garcia describes the work of drafting an antiracism statement with his writing center staff against the backdrop of attempts to chill or censor such speech by state governments. Garcia's narrative shows how he and his team must compose with the knowledge that infelicitous readers will be looking for nefariousness where it doesn't exist. How can they create a statement, knowing some readers' responses pose a real risk? While such responses might be politically motivated, uninformed, and easy to dismiss, the material dangers accompanying them can't be. Also measuring the weight of the outside world on their collaboration, Collie Fulford and Stefanie Frigo describe a writing project completed in the midst of cascading external traumas, warped by review, and finally revised under the auspices of "radical adaptability." Set against the first year of the COVID-19 pandemic and the ongoing brutal murders of people of color by police officers, the narrative foregrounds the well of trust at the foundation of their relationship, which allows for a writing process that can withstand the strain of personal, professional, and societal turbulence. Rounding out the set, Christopher Basgier's description of the drafting and revision of an institutional curricular document recalls the surprising tension of personal investment and labor involved with the creation of a text which, on one level, serves as a vehicle for the values and priorities of a discipline (specifically its emissary WPA) while at another level must account for competing institutional stakeholders and which will ultimately exist as an "authorless" text.

The stakes remain high for authors in the fifth set, and the resolutions to their stories uncertain. The long-term pathways described by Will Duffy, who focuses on changing definitions of "collaboration" across his writing, demonstrate how publications and ideas (like definitions) often evolve over years and are shaped by collaborators, circumstances, emotion, and the contributions of reviewers and editors. Hard-fought paths forward also characterize the story told by Jule Wallis-Thomas, who, like Garcia and Fulford and Frigo, keenly feels the encroachment of the exterior world as she revises, but in her case it is the (at times welcome) interruptions of family that tie into the rhythms of revision as her writing moves and stalls. Indeed, for Wallis-Thomas the interruptions of life threaten to overtake and stymie revision entirely; as a result, the resolution of her revision story remains elusive. Frustrated revision, and the (inability) to tell stories about revision in the first place, also characterizes the chapter by Karen R. Tellez-Trujillo, who is still discovering what she has to say as she ponders her inability to finish a project she began as an undergraduate. Some things, she learns, cannot be revised. Finally, in his artist's statement, Ian Golding considers how revision and its perpetual motion is difficult to visually depict. He recounts how his revisions to the collection's cover illustration unfolded alongside exchanges with the editors, in some ways echoing the resistance to revision outlined by Harris in the opening chapter. After his revisions veer the cover image away from where we (the editors) wanted it, he doubles back to an earlier, less "finished" (to his eye) version that to us captured the affective spirit of the collection.

Finally, Jessica Restaino offers an afterword that meditates on revising alone after the death of her collaborator and on the challenges in a current project of revising with someone who is present and pushing back. She further considers how revision is oftentimes messy or nonproductive and does not always lead to tidy conclusions—observing, in the words of her mentor, that sometimes the work of revising is to find a door where there once was a wall. This is a fitting ending for the volume, for it illustrates the ongoingness of writing and revising and the new learning experiences we are presented with as we move through life and career stages.

CODA

What you are reading is best understood as a revision in progress. A late-stage, heavily revised draft, to be sure, one passed around so many times (tallying over 1,400 large and small changes, in fact[5]) that we have lost the ability to see individual fingerprints. Yet, there remain other ways it could have been written, other ideas we could have explored, other details to which we could have drawn your attention. This is where we have landed, for now. Not stasis, not the final word, rather, a temporary calming of the tides or tremors activating revising's moves, just enough to scan the horizon for the next wave.

NOTES

1. For just a few recent exemplars, see Hillery Glasby, Sherrie Gradin, and Rachael Ryerson (2020) on the use of storytelling in queer Appalachia; Alexandra Hidalgo, Catheryn Jennings, and Ana Milena Ribero (2021) on the "constellative" pull of stories for making meaning in cultural rhetorics; Stephanie L. Kerschbaum (2015) on the need for "critically recasting [compositionists'] anecdotal relations" about disability; Lisa King, Rose Gubele, and Joyce Rain Anderson (2015) for a recent discussion of the centrality of story to Indigenous rhetorics; Carmen Kynard (2014) for a narrative inquiry of African American literacies, rhetorics, and resistance; Ruth Osorio (2021) for storying as method and as a form of activism for motherhood in the field; and Jacqueline Rhodes and Jonathan Alexander (2015) for a multimodal, rhizomatic approach to scholarly memoir.
2. Narrative-based research that foregrounds voice, experience, and perspective in writing studies includes works by Mike Rose (1989), Keith Gilyard (1991), Mary Rose O'Reilley (1993), Victor Villanueva (1993), Linda Brodkey (1996), Joseph Trimmer (1997), Duane H. Roen, Stuart C. Brown, and Theresa Enos (1998), Thomas Newkirk (2002), and Donald Murray (2003), among many others.
3. For example, in medicine, Rita Charon has advanced narrative medicine as "infused with respect for the narrative dimensions of illness and caregiving" that

"bridg[es] the divides that separate the physician from the patient, the self, colleagues, and society" (2001). Projects like the Patient Revolution (n.d.) and the RELATE Lab (n.d.) have taken this call further, harnessing the ability of story to empower individuals and transform care practices and systems. And empowerment is central to Carla Rice and Ingrid Mündel's work at the University of Guelph's ReVision Centre for Art and Social Justice. The Centre collaborates with "urban Indigenous, Inuit, Queer, nonbinary, trans, and disability-identified artists and communities" to enable "story-making methods to (re)author identities and selves," which have the power to "create systemic change" (2018, 212). As Rice and Mündel assert, "the stories produced through this methodology may be pedagogical and impactful, not in teaching people the correct or right way to think, feel, or act but rather in expanding possibilities for living in/with difference" (213). Taking a cue from this rich activist research, we believe revision stories can expand possibilities for writers by showing the diversity of revision behaviors and experiences and by making visible real practices rather than idealized ones.

4. From Peter Elbow and Pat Belanoff's three levels of revising and collage approach (2002), to the promotion of peer review feedback groups, to the role of teacher feedback in student revising, teacher-scholars in the field have been studying, assigning, and guiding revision for quite a while now. Some conduct qualitative research to explore how writers do it (Ballenger and Myers 2019; Lindenman, Camper, Jacoby, and Enoch 2018; N. Sommers 1980; Witte 2013) and others have suggested pedagogical strategies to coach it (Feltham and Sharen 2015; Harris 2003; Lunsford and Straub 1995; J. Sommers 2014). In a recent essay, Bob Mayberry describes revision's presence in the discipline as "pervasive" and "built into the composition curriculum" (2022, 159). It's true. In composition curricula across the nation—or in textbooks published during the past four decades (e.g., Axelrod, Cooper, Carillo, and Cleaves 2022; Giles 2010; Graff and Birkenstein 2021; Harris 2017)—revision is an accepted part of what we say we teach as a discipline.

5. The unseen revision paths toward the "final: introduction" you read here include two different Google Docs, 1,492 tracked "edits" (as of 1:43 p.m. on August 23, 2022), and many dozens of (often dialogic) comments, quips, jokes, tangents, compliments, questions, and disagreements shared amongst our team.

REFERENCES

Axelrod, Rise B., Charles R. Cooper, Ellen Carillo, and Wallace Cleaves. 2022. *The St. Martin's Guide to Writing*. 13th ed. New York: Macmillan Learning.

Ballenger, Bruce, and Kelly Myers. 2019. "The Emotional Work of Revision." *College Composition and Communication* 70 (4): 590–614.

Ballif, Michelle, Diane Davis, and Roxanne Mountford. 2008. *Women's Ways of Making It in Rhetoric and Composition*. New York: Routledge.

Bartholomae, David. 1985. "Against the Grain." In *Writers on Writing*, edited by Thomas Waldrep, 18–29. New York: Random House.

Bazerman, Charles. 2006. "Preface." In *Revision: History, Theory, and Practice*, edited by Alice Horning and Cynthia Becker, xi–xiii. Anderson, SC: Parlor Press; Fort Collins, CO: WAC Clearinghouse.

Berthoff, Ann E. 1981. "Recognition, Representation, and Revision." *Journal of Basic Writing*, no. 3, 19–32.

Bramblett, Anne, and Alison Knoblauch, eds. 2002. *What to Expect When You're Expected to Teach: The Anxious Craft of Teaching Composition*. Portsmouth, NH: Heinemann.

Brodkey, Linda. 1996. *Writing Permitted in Designated Areas Only*. Minneapolis: University of Minnesota Press.

Cedillo, Christina. 2021. "Unruly Borders, Bodies, and Blood: Mexican 'Mongrels' and the Eugenics of Empire." *Journal for the History of Rhetoric* 24 (1): 7–23.

Charon, Rita. 2001. "Narrative Medicine: A Model for Empathy, Reflection, Profession, and Trust." *JAMA* 286 (15): 1897–1902. https://doi.org/10.1001/jama.286.15.1897.

Digital Archive of Literacy Narratives (DALN). n.d. The Ohio State University / Georgia State University. Accessed August 28, 2023. https://www.thedaln.org/#/home.

Elbow, Peter, and Pat Belanoff. 2002. *Being a Writer: A Community of Writers Revisited*. McGraw-Hill Education.

Erby, Brandon M. 2021. "Surviving the Jim Crow South: 'The Talk' as an African American Rhetorical Form." *Journal for the History of Rhetoric* 24 (1): 24–38.

Feltham, Mark, and Colleen Sharen. 2015. "'What Do You Mean I Wrote a C Paper?': Writing, Revision, and Self-Regulation." *Collected Essays on Learning and Teaching*, no. 8, 111–138.

Fernandez, Miriam L. 2021. "La Llorona and Rhetorical Haunting in Mexico's Public Sphere." *Journal for the History of Rhetoric* 24 (1): 54–68.

Gallagher, John R., and Dànielle Nicole DeVoss, eds. 2019. *Explanation Points: Publishing in Rhetoric and Composition*. Logan: Utah State University Press.

George, Diana, ed. 1999. *Kitchen Cooks, Plate Twirlers and Troubadours: Writing Program Administrators Tell Their Stories*. Portsmouth, NH: Heinemann-Boynton/Cook.

Giles, Sandra L. 2010. "Reflective Writing and the Revision Process: What Were You Thinking?" In *Writing Spaces: Readings on Writing*, vol. 1, 191–204. Anderson, SC: Parlor Press; Fort Collins, CO: WAC Clearinghouse.

Gilyard, Keith. 1991 *Voices of the Self: A Study of Language Competence*. Detroit, MI: Wayne State University Press.

Glasby, Hillery, Sherrie Gradin, and Rachael Ryerson, eds. 2020. *Storytelling in Queer Appalachia: Imagining and Writing the Unspeakable Other*. Morgantown: West Virginia University Press.

Graff, Gerald, and Cathy Birkenstein. 2021. *"They Say / I Say": The Moves That Matter in Academic Writing*. 5th ed. New York: W. W. Norton and Company.

Harris, Joseph. 2003. "Opinion: Revision as a Critical Practice." *College English* 65 (6): 577–92.

Harris, Joseph. 2017. *Rewriting: How to Do Things with Texts*. 2nd ed. Logan: Utah State University Press.

Haswell, Richard H., and Min-Zhan Lu, eds. 2000. *Comp Tales: An Introduction to College Composition through Its Stories*. New York: Longman.

Hidalgo, Alexandra, Cateryn Jennings, and Ana Milena Ribero. "Constellating Stories and Counterstories: Cultural Rhetorics Scholarship Principles." Moderated by Kimberly Wieser. *Constellations: A Cultural Rhetorics Publishing Space*, no. 4 (May 2021). https://constell8cr.com/conversations/cultural-rhetorics-scholarship/.

Horning, Alice S. 2002. *Revision Revisited*. New York: Hampton Press.

Horning, Alice, and Anne Becker, eds. 2006. *Revision: History, Theory, and Practice*. Anderson, SC: Parlor Press; Fort Collins, CO: WAC Clearinghouse.

Kerschbaum, Stephanie L. "Anecdotal Relations: On Orienting to Disability in the Composition Classroom." *Composition Forum*, no. 32 (Fall 2015). https://compositionforum.com/issue/32/anecdotal-relations.php.

King, Lisa, Rose Gubele, and Joyce Rain Anderson, eds. 2015. *Survivance, Sovereignty, and Story: Teaching American Indian Rhetorics*. Logan: Utah State University Press.

Kynard, Carmen. 2014. *Vernacular Insurrections: Race, Black Protest, and the New Century in Composition-Literacies Studies*. Albany: State University of New York Press.

Lindenman, Heather, Martin Camper, Lindsay Dunne Jacoby, and Jessica Enoch. 2018. "Revision and Reflection: A Study of (Dis)connections between Writing Knowledge and Writing Practice." *College Composition and Communication* 69 (4): 581–611.

Lunsford, Ronald F., and Richard Straub. 1995. *Twelve Readers Reading: Responding to College Student Writing.* New York: Hampton Press.

Lutkewitte, Claire, Juliette C. Kitchens, and Molly J. Scanlon. 2022. *Stories of Becoming: Demystifying the Professoriate for Graduate Students in Composition and Rhetoric.* Logan: Utah State University Press.

Martinez, Aja Y. 2020. *Counterstory: The Rhetoric and Writing of Critical Race Theory.* Urbana, IL: National Council of Teachers of English.

Mayberry, Bob. 2022. "Where We've Been and Where We Might Go." *Composition Studies* 50 (1): 158–62.

Murray, Donald. 2003. *A Writer Teaches Writing.* 2nd ed. Boston, MA: Cengage Learning.

Murray, Donald. 2012. *The Craft of Revision.* 5th ed. Boston, MA: Cengage Learning.

Newkirk, Thomas. 2002. *Misreading Masculinity: Boys, Literacy, and Popular Culture.* Boston, MA: Heinemann.

O'Reilley, Mary Rose. 1993. *The Peaceable Classroom.* Portsmouth, NH: Heinemann.

Osorio, Ruth. 2021. "Constellating with Our Foremothers: Stories of Mothers Making Space in Rhetoric and Composition." *Constellations: A Cultural Rhetorics Publishing Space* no. 4 (August 2021). https://constell8cr.com/articles/mothers-making-space-rhet-comp/.

Patient Revolution. n.d. Accessed August 29, 2023. https://patientrevolution.org/.

Peck, Wayne C. 1990. "The Effects of Prompts on Revision: A Glimpse of the Gap between Planning and Performance." In *Reading to Write: Exploring a Cognitive and Social Process*, edited by Linda Flower, Victoria Stein, John Ackerman, Margaret J. Kantz, Kathleen McCormick, and Wayne C. Peck, 156–69. New York: Oxford University Press.

Perl, Sondra. 2004. *Felt Sense: Writing with the Body.* Portsmouth, NH: Heinemann.

Powell, Malea. 2012. "2012 CCCC Chair's Address: Stories Take Place: A Performance in One Act." *College Composition and Communication* 64 (2): 383–406.

RELATE Lab. n.d. Accessed August 28, 2023. https://www.relatelab.org/.

Rhodes, Jacqueline, and Jonathan Alexander. 2015. *Techne: Queer Meditations on Writing the Self.* Logan: Utah State University Press.

Rice, Carla, and Ingrid Mündel. 2018. "Story-Making as Methodology: Disrupting Dominant Stories through Multimedia Storytelling." *Canadian Review of Sociology / Revue canadienne de sociologie* 55 (2): 211–31.

Roen, Duane H., Stuart Cameron Brown, and Theresa Enos. 1998. *Living Rhetoric and Composition: Stories of the Discipline.* New York: Routledge.

Rose, Mike. 1989. *Lives on the Boundary.* New York: Free Press.

Sommers, Jeff. 2014. "Revisiting Radical Revision." In *Critical Expressivism: Theory and Practice in the Composition Classroom*, edited by Tara Roeder and Roseanne Gatto, 289–304. Anderson, SC: Parlor Press; Fort Collins, CO: WAC Clearinghouse.

Sommers, Nancy. 1980. "Revision Strategies of Student Writers and Experienced Adult Writers." *College Composition and Communication* 31 (4): 378–88.

Sommers, Nancy. 1992. "Between the Drafts." *College Composition and Communication* 43 (1): 23–31.

Trimmer, Joseph. 1997. *Narration as Knowledge: Tales of the Teaching Life.* Portsmouth, NH: Heinemann.

Tulley, Christine E. 2018. *How Writing Faculty Write: Strategies for Process, Product, and Productivity.* Logan: Utah State University Press.

Villanueva, Victor. 1993. *Bootstraps: From an American Academic of Color.* Urbana, IL: National Council of Teachers of English.

Villanueva, Victor. 2010. "Rhetoric, Racism, and the Remaking of Knowledge in Composition." In *Changing of Knowledge in Composition: Contemporary Perspectives*, edited by Lance Massey and Richard C. Gebhardt, 121–34. Logan: Utah State University Press.

Waldrep, Thomas, ed. 1985. *Writers on Writing.* New York: Random House.

Witte, Chelbie. 2013. "Preaching What We Practice: A Study of Revision." *Journal of Curriculum and Instruction* 6 (2): 33–59.

SET 1

Revision Takes a Stand

Hannah J. Rule

One placement that remained stable throughout our many attempts to organize this book was putting Joseph Harris's "On Choosing Not to Revise" first. We relish our cheeky choice to commence this collection by destabilizing its project from the outset: begin a book on revision with *refusal* to revise. Contributors opening this volume get us thinking about revision as refusals of various kinds: not absence of progress or movement but often proactive defiance, a theme which weaves itself through the volume in different ways. Like Bartleby the Scrivener, sometimes we writers and revisers *prefer not to*, for reasons known and unknown, articulated, left unsaid, or metaphorically shouted. Whatever the motivations, refusal as part of revision's repertoire is performative and creational.

In some ways, revision as resistance is familiar. In processes of feedback and revision, as Andrea Muldoon has observed, professional writers can exhibit a "scholarly defensiveness" that makes us refuse, deny, oppose, or dismiss others' perspectives on our writing (2009, 68–69) (even as, when we teach writing, we prod students to always dutifully receive and act on our feedback). While playing defense can be a posture of revising, across this volume, we often see writers' efforts to avoid this dynamic: Raúl Sánchez aims to diffuse critique dynamics in anonymous peer review processes; early-career scholars Comi and Russel seek more voices, including one another's, for the task of interpreting feedback; collaborators Fulford and Frigo deploy a tactic of intentional emotional distancing, or what they call orphan text, in order to make revisions manageable.

Harris does seem to exemplify revision as refusal; it is almost a classic case: the author maintains one vision for a book and the press editor another, a scene which resolves, in this case, with the author standing firm. But Harris is far from locked in a dyadic "dialectic" (Muldoon 2009, 70) showdown with this editor. He says he refuses revision in order "to keep control over [his] project as a writer" (28), an admission we can read as a writer taking a stand *and*, simultaneously perhaps, as the writer defending *what the text wants*. As Chris Mays has written, more than writers or editors or any other human (or nonhuman) actor alone, texts too "exert something resembling a will of their own" (2017, 61).[1] Mays's complex-systems view of revision, as at once a "deeply personal process that inspires intense feelings of ownership as well as an impersonal function of a complex system neither owned nor created by any one person or agency" (65), reflects back to us the what in the introduction we identify as revision's "vitality": the "hard-to-represent holistic quality" of revising in all of its "situated messiness." Revision is populated, crowded, sprawling, circuitous, and decentered—dynamics which make change possible, though ultimately unpredictable and shared.

If we read Harris's refusal as advocacy for himself and for the will of his text, we see refusal's opposite in Alexandra Hidalgo's story of working with consulting editors and test audiences on revisions to her documentary film. In a driving desire for, not protection against, feedback, Hidalgo's film seems like it too is exerting something—maybe it is the competing narratives that she can't sort because of her closeness to the story. More than a writer going it alone, Hidalgo shows us the fruits of strategically assembling outside forces and voices to help realize our compositional visions. For Aja Y. Martinez, revision exceeds the shepherding of a book, film, or project, sidestepping smaller-scale matters of textual change and showing us that refusal as revision also is nothing less than political, life-affirming action aimed at upending the harms of the status quo.

Stories collected in this first set also hang together for us in that they have maintained (since their first draft, even their proposal) a clear narrative structure—setup, conflict, resolution—that basically has remained unchanged through rounds of revision. It was this observation that had us pursuing one of the logics ordering contributors' stories across this collection: volume. By volume, we invoke audio volume (which equally might become a visual trope in terms of brightness or a tactile one in terms of defined, sharp edges) as a metaphor for a sure or certain quality, an obvious story of sorts, basically begging to be voiced. Stories in this opening set are *loud* (bright, sharp); contributors are sure of the revision story they have to tell (and what will and will not be abided).

Though the stories here are realized, the elements of the narrative arcs differ: conflict is far from equal in these stories, and what resolution looks like differs too. For Martinez, "Alejandra" finds powerful resolution in confronting The Institution's whitely habitus and abusive veneer of politeness through a public resignation letter: the letter as counterstory is a brave act of advocacy for self and for others, at the same time that it aims to crack apart structures of erasure and harm. For Hidalgo, resolution arrives by ceding some control to others. Harris's resolution comes in the form of a perhaps idealized agreement between Harris and his text, along with a resolving of differences with an editor. In different ways, from different social and embodied locations, contributors in this set each assert their narrative control.

If stories that start this book are sure of themselves and "loud," they incrementally (though not consistently) become quieter as the collection moves on. They become messier or multiple (in arc and in details); they struggle or even fail ultimately to find their center; they lack resolution (or find resolution in no resolution); they emphasize ongoingness and possibility, including those opportunities for revision lost or unrealized (for now or for good). We're thinking here especially of Tellez-Trujillo's box of ephemera from her research trips to Prague, which still "sleeps" in her garage as a kind of Schrödinger's Text(s), perpetually somewhere between being and not being realized into the products and projects she originally proposed. We're thinking of Wallis-Thomas's story of revision as nothing less than a story of living, of her whole self (is her story, or any in this book, really about revision alone?). And we're thinking of Ian Golding's artist statement, which accompanies his illustrations appearing on this book's cover. Golding's art and statement provide an interesting mirror of Harris's beginning. While Golding finds similar disagreement with the views of his editors, he ultimately does what they ask (thanks, Ian!). While Harris maintains steady commitment to what his text should be(come), Golding remains committed to not being sure—that is, sure only of the unpredictable and significant consequences any one little adjustment or revision move will set off. What we love about Golding's contributions is how he helps us convey the unsure perpetuities of revision that often end up standing in for the resolution. Maybe we can't get it right, we just . . . ~~get it there~~—we are just the imperfect perfect bird perpetually erasing in the frames of composition that precede and proceed (from) us.

NOTE

1. We thank contributors Sills and F. Sánchez for introducing us to Mays's work in their early draft. They make contact with Mays mainly on the will (for coherence) that drafts or other texts exert, to help them make sense of how hard it is to perpetually revise cover letters for different institutions.

REFERENCES

Mays, Chris. 2017. "Revision as Heresy: Posthuman Writing Systems and Kenneth Burke's 'Piety'." *Kenneth Burke + the Posthuman*, edited by Chris Mays, Nathaniel A. Rivers, and Kellie Sharp-Hoskins, 61–79. University Park: Penn State University Press.

Muldoon, Andrea. 2009. "A Case for Critical Revision: Debunking the Myth of the Enlightened Teacher versus the Resistant Student Writer." *College Teaching* 57 (2): 67–71.

1
ON CHOOSING NOT TO REVISE

Joseph Harris

Like most writers, I am a cheerleader for revision. I love taking a piece through a series of drafts until it feels and sounds like something I want to say. This doesn't always mean articulating an idea that I began with—what I want*ed* to say—more clearly. On the contrary, I'm often surprised by where the work of revision leads me. New lines of thought emerge, new examples come to hand, and the piece I end up with can turn out to be quite different from the one I imagined at the start. But that's pretty much the point. Revision lets you play with a text until you've come up with a version of it that you're happy with.

So how do you know when you've reached that moment, when the draft or version of a piece you've now got in hand is the one you really want to move ahead with? I ask this question because, while I am committed to teaching revising, I'm also aware that several of the turning moments in my own writing career have come when, despite pressure from editors and reviewers, I chose *not* to revise, to stick instead with a version of a piece that felt right to me, if not to them. I'd like to tell the story here of one of those moments. It's a story, I think, that raises questions of who should hold authority over a piece as it is being developed. What happens when an editor and writer (or a teacher and writer) disagree over the direction a text needs to take?

Ironically enough, my story centers on a book I wrote several years ago *about* revising, *Rewriting: How to Do Things with Texts*, published by Utah State University Press in 2006, with a second edition in 2017. Before I launch into my narrative, though, I need to stress how much I admire Michael Spooner, who as the director of the Press during those years oversaw the production of both editions of *Rewriting* with grace and restraint. He's the best editor I've had the chance to work with. The story I want to tell here has to do with some problems I faced in developing the book *before* I ended up taking it to Michael and Utah State.

As has often enough been the case, many of these problems were ones I brought upon myself. In the late 1990s, I had just finished a book on the recent history of composition and was trying to imagine what my next project might be. I had a number of conflicting impulses. While I was pleased with my first book, I now hoped to write something that would speak to students as well as teachers of composition. But I wasn't much interested in writing a conventional handbook or rhetoric, since I almost never used either sort of book in my own courses. So I felt unsure about genre. I was also, frankly, having a hard time formulating what I wanted to say. I knew I wanted it to be something about the interplay of critical reading and writing, but exactly what, I wasn't sure.

Somehow I managed to draft a proposal for a book I called *Op. Cit.* As arcane as that title now seems to me, I liked it at the time for how it suggested that the writing of a critic or intellectual always builds on and refers to other texts. I proposed a series of chapters in which I would first analyze how one writer (or filmmaker) revised or adapted the work of another: Anne Sexton retelling the *Tales* of the Brothers Grimm, Aimé Césaire repurposing Shakespeare's *Tempest*, Ridley Scott reimagining Philip K. Dick's *Androids*, and so on. Drawing on those case studies, I would then guide students in reusing other texts in their own writing. The editor for a leading trade press in our field liked the idea and offered me a contract and advance. I agreed to deliver a full draft in three years.

Which proved a mistake. In proposing such a timeline, I had failed to account for something I should have known very well by then about myself as a writer, which is that I often require a long time to mull over a project before starting work on it. It's not so much that I write slowly but that I can be very slow in sitting down to write. And the longer the project, the longer I am likely to dawdle. Some of this can no doubt be put down to a general lack of discipline and focus, but I also think it has something to do with how my mind works, with a need to let my thoughts on a subject percolate for some length of time before trying to write them out. And the more I thought about what I had proposed for *Op. Cit.*, the more I began to realize that while I had come up with some interesting ideas for chapters, I didn't have much of a sense of how to actually develop them.

I was, in short, stuck. I also switched jobs around this time, moving to a new position at a different university that was demanding and exciting but tended to take me away from writing. And so years passed, and I made little to no progress on the manuscript.

I was, however, working all the time in the classroom with the ideas that had animated my proposal—and particularly with the notion that a creative reuse of other texts lies at the heart of intellectual writing. In trying to explain that idea in ways that students could use in their own work as writers, I began to formulate the brief series of "moves" that became the conceptual spine of *Rewriting*, the book that eventually grew out of the proposal for *Op. Cit*. I also grew less attached to the set of readings I had centered my original proposal around. I thus ended up imagining a very different sort of book than I had first planned, even if it was still one that responded to the questions about "how to do things with texts" I had started with years before.

All this was revision at a pretty deep level, I think. But looking back now, I am struck by how much of that revision took place in an incidental fashion. For several years, I worked to create materials that would clarify my ideas about writing to the students I was teaching, and in doing so I slowly reconceptualized the book I had been stuck on. I didn't move from *Op. Cit.* to *Rewriting* in response to feedback on drafts, because I was never able to produce any drafts of *Op. Cit.* that I felt were worth sharing. It's more like *Rewriting* emerged out of my failure to get anywhere with *Op. Cit.* But once I (finally) realized that I needed to shift approaches—to revise from scratch, as it were—the actual writing of the book went quickly and well. The trick was to recenter the book not on a series of readings but on a set of moves in writing. I abandoned the chapters on Anne Sexton and the Brothers Grimm, *Blade Runner* and *Androids*, and instead drafted ones on how a writer might work with the ideas and phrasings of another author, or against them. I completed a near-complete draft of *Rewriting* during summer and fall 2002, when I was on sabbatical. I remember feeling that, after years of delay and uncertainty, I had at last nailed it, written the sort of book I wanted.

This is not to say that the manuscript had reached its final form. Far from it. There was much fiddling and tweaking left to be done. But most of the essential aspects were in place. I'd found a structure for the book, an arc that took me, chapter by chapter, move by move, from Coming to Terms to Forwarding, Countering, and Taking an Approach. The book cohered. While it didn't map out the work of a course like a textbook, it did describe the values and ideas that drove my teaching. And I didn't speak down to students. The voice on the page felt like my own.

But here I reach the crux of my story. My manuscript was at that point several years overdue. It was, indeed, so late that the editor who had first signed the project had by then left the press, and my draft landed on another editor's desk. In retrospect, I feel for this person. They were stuck with a project that was under contract but that they had not helped to develop and that they clearly didn't think was going to sell very well.

Nonetheless the terms of my contract stated that when I submitted a full draft it would be sent to outside readers for review. So that happened. The ten reviews that came back were glowing, I suspect somewhat to the chagrin of the editor, who continued to press me for revisions. Their complaints piled up. My tone was too intellectual, my title obscure, the organization of my chapters unclear. I suspect that the root problem was that *Rewriting* does not read like a textbook yet is addressed to student writers. But this new editor had not signed on to such a project. They had simply been presented with a book that didn't seem quite one thing or the other.

They also had to deal with an obstinate author. I recall the editor telling me, with some exasperation, that if I were only more willing to rethink what I'd written, I might produce something more than just a "niche book." In a sense, though, a niche book was exactly what I wanted. I liked the quirkiness of the text I had come up with. I knew it wasn't going to sell like *"They Say / I Say"* or *Ways of Reading*, but I was aiming for something different. I have several friends in the field who write poetry or personal essays in addition to the work they do as scholars. I don't. And so for me academic writing has become not only a way of working with texts and ideas but a mode of self-expression.

This was especially the case with *Rewriting*. I had wanted to see if I could write a book that sounded like how I talk in the classroom. The somewhat wonkish and chatty style of my prose was thus not an add-on to my project but an intrinsic part of it. And so, when the editor asked me to rethink my tone and stance, I heard them as pushing me to write a different sort of book altogether. The breaking point came when they asked me to drop my frequent use of *intellectual* to describe the kind of writing I wanted to teach. The editor found the term off-putting. But for me the whole point of the book was to argue for the value of intellectual writing. I didn't want to teach "academic argument" or "writing from sources" or the "analytic essay." I wanted to teach strongly voiced writing about texts and ideas. Intellectual writing. I felt I was not being heard. And so I decided to ask to be released from my contract.

That felt like a real risk. I had spent the advance many years before and was in no position to repay it. And I had no way of guessing if any other press would have the slightest interest in what I'd written. But after several years of living with the project, I didn't want to see just any version of the book in print. I wanted this one.

Some early readers of this piece have asked if I wasn't perhaps in a better position than most to take such a stand. I see their point. I had tenure, and people in the field knew and liked my work. But I also felt that my career had stalled. In 2004, when I asked to be released from my contract, I had been an associate professor for ten years, and I would remain in that rank for nine more. To be considered for promotion, I had been told by my chair and dean, I'd need to show "evidence of an intellectual project" that they felt my work in composition did not offer. In a way, this was freeing. I had a book that my editor didn't care for and that my employer wouldn't count toward promotion. So I figured I might as well try to make it the sort of book that *I* wanted. But I have to say, this decision felt less like an assertion of authority than a sigh of resignation.

Fortunately, the press was very gracious. They released me from my contract with the proviso that, if I ever managed to place the book with another press, any royalties would go first to paying back my advance from them. (Although I do recall an editorial assistant informing me in a rather chippy tone that they didn't really expect to get any of their money back. They did. All of it.) I sent the manuscript and reviews out to acquisitions editors at several other presses, including Michael Spooner at Utah State.

Here I reach the happy-ever-after part of the tale. Michael loved the book and decided to approach his editorial board with the reviews we already had in hand. They approved the project, and I sat down to produce a final version of the book.

Which still involved a good bit of work. While all the reviewers had liked my book as a whole, each of them had also suggested changes I might make to specific sections. And Michael had some useful advice about style. There were points I could clarify and sentences and paragraphs I could reshape. I expanded the intro and added to the framing of the chapters. But at that point, I was less rethinking the tone or gist of the book than refining its form. In *Rewriting* I suggest that one of the things that distinguishes revision from editing is that, in revising, the changes a writer makes are connected. There's a ripple effect. You rethink or revise a piece as a whole. You edit specific parts of it. At that point, I was editing.

I think we often revise to meet the demands of others. What do I need to do to address the concerns of this reviewer or that editor? What changes do I need to make to get this book or article published? I worry, though, that in responding to such external concerns an author can risk losing sight of the piece they had actually wanted to write. I've thus come to prefer talking about revising in terms that are less transactional and more personal. I suspect that if I had stayed with the first press in this story, if I had agreed to restructure my book in the ways the editor asked, I might well have been able to produce something more than a "niche book." But I doubt it would have felt like *my* book in the way that *Rewriting* does. At a key moment, to keep control over my project as a writer, I needed to choose not to revise. As teachers and editors, I think we need to learn how to honor those moments of resistance, of individuality.

2

CONSULTING EDITOR TO THE RESCUE
Seeing Storytelling Anew through Veteran Eyes

Alexandra Hidalgo

Sometimes you live with a story for so long you lose track of where it ends and where you begin. Like in those rare marriages that last numerous decades, the boundaries between two separate entities blur to engender a wondrous hybrid creature. Instead of two people building a life together, however, it's a person and a story. Human and fact. Human and fiction. My story and I met when I was six years old, and we have never spent a day apart since. We love and frustrate each other. We cradle each other's vulnerabilities and face our incapacitating fears together. In this chapter, I share the tale of how feedback from collaborators and audience members helped me revise my story, iteration after iteration, until together we found its heart. But first, let me introduce you to my story so you can feel invested in its transformation.

My story starts with a disappearance, a mystery I've been slowly unraveling since 1983, when my father, Miguel Hidalgo, vanished in the Venezuelan Amazon. As if a disappearing father wasn't intriguing enough, mine was as colorful a paternal character as you could ask for: a writer, mountain climber, philosopher, inventor, genius-IQ MIT graduate, fifth-*dan* karate black belt with a romantic heart and a genuine belief in magic. And that was just the surface of Dad. As decades of my research revealed, underneath it was an even more captivating and baffling person, who'd left a trail of secrets and lies as long as the novel he labored over for a decade—the one they found in a hotel room after he vanished, finally completed.

My story masqueraded as a thriller, a detective novel in which a despondent child grew up assembling clues as she investigated what became of the father she adored. My story lulled me into the relative simplicity of that kind of fact-based search. It tricked me with its straightforward surface into examining something much more daunting. My story forced me to face the fragility of life: not just the fragility of keeping our hearts beating and our brains thinking but of our identities and beliefs about ourselves and our ancestors. My story took me to the abyss of who I thought I was and the family I thought I came from. Once there, it asked me to jump, promising my wings would emerge before we hit the ground, and if they didn't . . . well, at least we'd crash in pursuit of truths that make for a life well lived.

My wings did emerge, but not in the way I thought they would. They did not come from me or my story but from those who helped me tell it. Stories must be told, and I've been telling this one for thirty-nine of the forty-five years I've spent on this Earth. From fiction to memoir to video essay to book chapter to the kind of dinner conversation that makes everyone—spellbound by your words—forget to eat, I have told my story. Yet none of those iterations captured the rich, messy essence of what I wanted to say. My story remained slippery as I retold it in every medium at my disposal. In 2016, I decided to tell it as a feature documentary, but even with three cameras and five mics pointed at her, my story continued to run circles around me.

Exhausted from the chase, I sought help in the form of an editor. Not the kind of editor who works with words, but the kind who works with footage. On December 23, 2017, thirty-four years to the day since my father was last seen, I had a Skype call with Venezuelan editor Cristina Carrasco. Cristina's films have screened at Cannes Semaine de la Critique, Montreal, and Mannheim, but that's not why I decided to work with her. In their cowritten piece in this collection, Dana Comi writes that Alisa Russell's feedback on Comi's work "clicked" and "resonated" and helped her see "how to keep moving forward with the project" (111). Some people get you and what you're trying to do, and those are the ones you want to work with. Within minutes, I could sense that Cristina and I got each other and that she wanted to probe life's brittleness with this film. She was generously willing to probe her own wounds to help me weave a tale around mine.

My father is the rule, not the exception, in a family populated by generations of writers and artists who lead the kinds of passionate lives one *must* write novels and make films about. Cristina and I labored on and off for a year and a half after that call, watching and rewatching over two hundred hours of footage covering a century of my family's fabulously contorted history. Because my dad is missing, in the film we draw from a disparate array of materials woven together through my narration. We have home videos my husband, Nathaniel Bowler (the film's director of photography), shot of our 2004 trip to the Venezuelan Amazon to interview those who last saw him. We filmed present-day conversations with

Dad's family and friends in the US, Venezuela, and Portugal. Finally, Dad is present through photographs, Super 8 footage, and his voice on a tape recorded in 1977.

Cristina and I had intricate conversations about how to turn these knotted strands into a ninety-minute film. From the start, Cristina thought we should tell a personal story, but for practical reasons we went in a different direction. Documentary filmmaking is expensive. In his chapter in this collection, Rich Shivener examines the frustrations that come with creating digital texts. He writes, "Every time I look up tutorials and ideas for creating, my head starts spinning. I simply don't have time or energy to dwell in a code editor" (100). Having to come up with your project's content while also crafting yourself that content's digital home is an exhausting process. My solution to that challenge has been to become a savvy grant writer who gets funding to hire collaborators to contribute by performing the tasks I am not trained in or gifted at doing myself. However, grant writing is its own time-consuming and mysterious world, and sometimes chasing the money can mean sacrificing aspects of your vision so you can (ironically) afford to bring that vision to life.

I'd cobbled together enough grants and research funds to pay for filming and editing, but we needed to cover costly postproduction tasks, like color correction, sound mixing, and composing the score. My plan was to apply for grants to raise the remainder of the financing. However, American granting agencies have a predilection for social justice documentaries, and my US film mentors warned me that, unless I could make my film political, I was unlikely to attract funding. After withstanding a two-decade economic and governmental crisis, my homeland of Venezuela seemed like an ideal social justice topic, but my family comes from the Venezuelan aristocracy and has consequently avoided the cataclysm's most crippling effects. Moreover, Dad vanished long before this particular crisis began.

Cristina and I used every trick in our storytelling bags to intertwine Venezuela with my father, only to be told by focus group audiences and the very granting agencies we aimed to impress that the film's topics were irreconcilably divided. Not all granting agencies provide feedback, but we hung on the words of those who did, revising draft after draft to fix the issues they'd pointed out and getting further and further away from the story's natural strengths. The more we revised to add the political angle to the film, the more the other elements—the compelling, heartfelt ones—hung loosely to the sides with little to unify them. The wing Cristina had helped me grow flapped hopelessly as the ground neared. Frustrated by rejection, I finally heeded Cristina's advice to make a personal film. Maybe no one would want to fund it because it wasn't political enough, but they weren't funding the current version either.

In the spring of 2020, we removed the Venezuelan crisis and used that new rough cut to invite Venezuelan producer extraordinaire Natalia Machado to join the project. Once she did, she suggested we bring in a consulting editor. The latter are common in the film industry, particularly for personal projects like mine. As with any memoir project, it's hard for directors to find enough distance from the memories and events we see through the intimate lens of our experiences to know what will engage those who haven't also lived through them. Not only is it difficult to discern which stories will resonate without the emotional context we bring to them, but the amount of material—our lives, the lives of our family, friends, lovers—is staggering. An editor brings objectivity to the creative team. However, after working on multiple drafts and getting to know the director as closely as Cristina and I have gotten to know each other, they too lose the outsider perspective they had when they joined the project. Consulting editors come in when you have a solid draft, and they have no attachment to scenes, characters, or storylines. They are usually veteran editors, bringing decades of expertise and a sense of impartiality they use to suggest new avenues for reshaping the film.

Natalia suggested a few consulting editors she'd worked with, but I only wanted Chilean editing legend Andrea Chignoli. Andrea's films have screened at Cannes, Venice, Sundance, and Toronto. Her 2012 film *No!* was nominated for an Academy Award. Her characters are passionate, courageous, and irreverent, brimming with heart in worlds where heartlessness prevails. Her characters are what my story and I were hoping to become, onscreen and off-. The question was whether she'd agree to work with us. Natalia sent her our rough cut, and when Andrea told us she wanted to meet, I could feel my second wing beginning to sprout.

Over Zoom, Andrea was as warm and perspicacious as my story and I had imagined she'd be. She asked how willing I was to revise the film, and I explained I'd been telling this story for almost four decades. I wanted to be done, but not until I'd captured its essence. If that was the case, she replied, she'd be happy to work with us. We would have five sessions spread over months. She would watch a draft, provide ideas that she, Cristina, and I would discuss over Zoom, and then Cristina and I would work on implementing those ideas. We'd send her our new draft and restart the process. Between the third and fourth meetings, we'd have focus group screenings to determine which areas needed to be reworked. We'd use the last two meetings to make those revisions.

In this essay, I analyze how Cristina's and my collaboration with Andrea transformed our film and how my desperately needed second wing grew out of it. For the sake of focus, I only discuss a fraction of the revisions we've undertaken with her. I draw from my detailed notes of conversations with Cristina and Andrea (which, with their approval, I translated from Spanish to English), from their written suggestions, and from the film's focus-group screening audience members' feedback, to whom I refer by their first names for privacy reasons.

And now, my story and I invite you to join us in this tale of discovery, revision, and metamorphosis and of how brilliant, thoughtful collaborators can revolutionize our work and our lives.

ENTER THE PREMISE

The question Cristina tried to help me answer from the start was how to articulate the film's theme—the idea pulsating beneath every good story that ties it to shared human experience. It's harder to pin down than the thesis in an academic piece because, unlike a thesis, it isn't directly stated. Here's documentary producer and writer Ronald B. Tobias working toward a definition: "We prefer order to disorder in fiction. We prefer logic to chaos. Most of all, we prefer unity of purpose, which creates a *whole*. Wouldn't life be great if it contained nothing extraneous or coincidental, if everything that happened to us related to a main purpose?" (1993, 17). My film had a sense of purpose—I wanted to figure out what became of my father. However, that quest has to be about something deeper that resonates with viewers (most of our audience) whose fathers haven't vanished.

As film, TV, and fiction writer and script consultant Billy Mernit argues, "pausing to think about what *you* are bringing to this kind of story in terms of a personal, passionate, even provocative point of view becomes a way to enliven and deepen your storytelling choices" (2020, 165). Mernit states that one of the most pervasive definitions of that "point of view" comes from playwright and writer Lajos Egri, whose 1942 treatise on playwriting has been influential in the film industry. Even though Egri's views on women and his staunch predilection for drama over anything lighthearted are woefully outdated, his concept of the "premise" remains useful. He writes, "Every good play must have a well-formulated premise. There may be more than one way to phrase the premise, but, however it is phrased, the thought must be the same" (Egri 2009, 7). Premises should be simple and should make a value statement. Instead of making a film about love, for example, you need to say something about love.

Egri explains that if your story uses a premise like "Great love defies even death" (2009, 15), that belief must be your personal conviction: "You should believe in it, since you are to prove it. You must show conclusively that life is worthless without the loved one" (2009, 15).

I believe many things about my story, but trying to articulate them into a sentence proved onerous. Like a freshman altering margins and font sizes to reach the required word count, I relied on commas and em dashes to fit multiple sentences into one when composing my premise. I fooled no one. At our May 2019 focus group screening, my poor attendees struggled when asked what the film was about. At all my screenings, I ask questions but only listen as attendees talk to each other, letting them linger in the weeds, to determine how tangled those weeds are. The May 2019 attendees agreed that my search for my father was the plot. As Kara pointed out, though, "That's not what it's about." Yet, they couldn't decipher the premise. For John, it was that "everything self-destructs." For Cait, it was how my mother "picked up the pieces and built a life for you." Jessica said we were "looking at Venezuela through the lens of your father's story." Safoi added, "The story is about a child who is looking for closure." In this collection, Karen R. Tellez-Trujillo discusses the "anxiety, stress, panic" that comes with attempting to get our creations into the world. She tells us, "It would take many years before I would figure out a formula for enduring encounters with failure and exhaustion that are inextricably tied to work" (206). The coping formula I've personally developed entails digesting and interpreting feedback with my collaborators. Cristina and my husband, Nate, have been my tireless support systems as we process audience comments and imagine ways to fix what is still not working. Having the right company can take the sting out of learning that our best efforts—*yet again*—fell short.

Our audience had diagnosed a dilemma we needed to address. We tried removing the Venezuelan crisis, then hosted focus group screenings in June 2020. Because of COVID, I collected feedback in writing instead of in person. In response to "What is the film about?" Marian answered, "A whole lot of things!" She mentioned ten topics, ranging from "migration, inclusion, and exclusion," to "a family house with a long history," to "relationships between fascinating women within a family." Tarez summed it up, "I don't mind the dual (or multiple) foci, but if there is intended to be a principal focus, I'm not sure I would guess the correct one." I could picture Egri, so severe in his black-and-white portraits, shaking his head at my story and me. A premise we had not.

At our first official meeting with Andrea in September 2020, she asked me what *I* thought the film was about. I stammered, then delivered a jumble of ideas. She said she couldn't find the film's premise either but that "what stands out the most is the relationship between lies and storytelling." Since explorations of love and its sundry complexities are the undercurrent that runs through my artistic work, I was taken aback. The word *love* was nowhere in what she'd seen. As the meeting unfolded and we discussed possibilities with Cristina, however, a premise began to materialize.

After bouncing ideas around for two hours, Andrea summed up our new direction: "We need to open the curtain and reveal the truths hidden by Alex's childhood infatuation with her father, as well as by his lies, which made it so challenging to really know him." Because this is a family saga, we explored how my father's upbringing caused him to disguise himself from those who loved him. Andrea went on,

> The common denominator is a very creative family that tells stories. Sometimes they go too far and the stories become lies. The film's ideology is that we have to put the lies in the lie box and the truth in the truth box.

I added one vital component: "We reveal the truth in order to heal the wounds that lies have caused. When we unearth the lies, we do it with love, and we digest their aftermath with love."

Yes, we still had several sentences, but they were all, for once, interconnected around one topic. Andrea said she would cut a new draft with these ideas in mind for our next meeting and suggested we read Umberto Eco's *Six Walks in the Fictional Woods* and Adrienne Rich's "Women and Honor: Some Notes on Lying" for inspiration about how to portray the relationship between lying and storytelling. I consumed Eco and Rich's words ravenously. As I digested them over my daily walks in the nonfictional woods near my house, I could feel my story's essence coming closer, its steps mirroring mine over the crinkling fall leaves.

In her new draft, Andrea deleted scenes and moved sequences around, but the real transmutation occurred in the title cards she added throughout the draft, with ideas for narrations I could write. When we met to discuss the new cut, she explained, "You need to give audiences a filter through which to watch the film, a point of view they can follow from the beginning." Her narration suggestions invited me to engage with the film's events to explore the relationship between lying and storytelling. It was seemingly simple—and yet so powerful. It was Egri's premise in all its glory.

One danger we had to skirt was showing me in too positive a light in comparison to Dad. As Cristina explained, "Alex has to be implicated in the lies. We can't have a dichotomy between the lying father and the honest daughter." The problem was that while my father was a consummate liar, I—perhaps in response to his deceit—lead a truthful existence.

But was I always truthful? Over Zoom, I shared these lines from Rich's essay with Cristina and Andrea, "What is the particular fear that possesses the liar? She is afraid that her truths are not good enough" (2001, 191). I felt that my truths were good enough in my actual life, but I couldn't find a premise for my documentary because I was afraid of the wounds the film might expose. Moreover, my story and I had lived together for so long that I was no longer sure how much of what I knew about Dad was mere conjecture I derived from distant memories and from conflicting information I learned from family and friends.

As Eco argues, in childhood we use make-believe to practice our reactions to real situations we may face, then "it is through fiction that we adults train our ability to structure our past and present experience" (2001, 131). While this strategy helps create a semblance of order in a chaotic world, Eco ponders, "if narrative activity is so closely linked to our everyday life, couldn't it be that we interpret life as fiction, and that in interpreting reality we introduce fictional elements?" (2001, 131). As the meeting ended, I knew that my journey in the film was not only discovering what became of my father but accepting that having grown up surrounded by storytellers with a penchant for dishonesty, I had a slippery relationship with truth which we could explore in the documentary.

As the meeting closed, we found our premise: "In order to heal generational traumas we need to uncover our family's lies and mythologies, facing them with love and compassion." Days later, the documentary's title, so elusive until then, came to me: *A Family of Stories*.

OUR NARRATOR FINDS HER VOICE

Now that we had a premise and a title, we needed to tackle the film's other key weakness. My narration, the string that wove the story together, had been a constant source of worry. At the May 2019 focus group, John said my narration "feels very written and not spontaneous and from the heart. I feel like there's a barrier between the narrator and the viewer." Hannah described it as "somewhere between detached and sad." The June 2020 draft was no better. Fiona wrote, "The lowkey, flat voiceover underplays the mystery." I had to fix the prose and the detachment evident in the writing and my performance.

I tackled Andrea's dozen narration suggestions one by one. After the scene where I showed my father's published writing to my children, she wrote, "Develop the idea that you are a family of writers. You have a storytelling gene that gets inherited from generation to generation." When I solve the mystery of what became of my father, "talk about the feeling of getting to the truth after having encountered so many layers of lies." My lightning-speed typing fingers were not quick enough for the words that kept pouring out. My story, my lifelong companion, was finally unveiling her darkness and beauty.

One of the issues I addressed in rewriting the narration was how to present my character as multifaceted and engaging. As the one taking us on the journey, I am the film's protagonist, but we struggled with what to share about me beyond my paternal search. In the draft we originally sent to Andrea, we had inserted a narration that basically shared my bio with viewers:

> I moved to the U.S. at 16 with my mom and my stepfather. When I was in college, they decided to go back and I stayed. I got married. I had two little boys. I got a PhD in English, and I became a professor at Michigan State University in East Lansing, where I still live. I have a happy, satisfying, beautiful life, but I still think about my father every day.

Because we had no clear premise, the bio felt like unnecessary exposition that tried (and failed) to get the audience to care about me as a character. Andrea's suggestion was that events from my past should only be revealed when they helped deepen my relationship to the film's lying and storytelling themes. As a result, I set up my discovery that my father lied about his educational accomplishments this way:

> Since childhood, I tried to live up to Dad's intellectual triumphs. But no matter what I did, I felt like I couldn't match my MIT-graduate father with the prodigious brain for the arts *and* the sciences. His accomplishments pushed me. Not only to keep climbing the academic ladder but to study what would help me understand him. I gravitated toward history and philosophy in college to learn how to research my dad. But then I got an MFA in Creative Writing and a PhD in English because I realized that learning facts about him was not enough. I needed to invent a narrative to make sense of the enigmas he left behind.

Tying my educational choices and achievements to my need to tell my father's story and match his success deepens our exploration of the film's premise. It additionally shows how discovering he lied about his education forced me to question my lifelong drive to excel. It sets me up as a character navigating a major conflict around the core of my identity, which elicits empathy from viewers who have similarly had to rethink the foundations of their lives.

For the first time, performing these words felt easy and natural. They were lyrical yet conversational. When we shared the new draft with audiences in June 2021, they raved about the narration. Chrystel wrote, "The narration is beautiful and poetic." For Jeanetta, "the juxtaposition between the poetic narrator and the raw person searching for understanding was really impactful." Julia added, "The narration was all beautiful and made me feel hopeful." Elle wrote that she loved "Alexandra's poetic narration, the unspooling of truths within lies." My eyes watered as I read their comments. My story, with Cristina and Andrea's help, had given me the voice I'd always longed to have when engaging with the world.

FINE CUTS ARE DELICATE CREATURES

I had a voice now, but did it get the film's premise across? The answer was a resounding yes. When asked what the film was about, Jeanetta wrote, "I think the film is about a daughter demystifying a story that had defined her—and in doing so, achieving some closure/understanding of her father, herself, and her family." For Sophie, "truth is the stories we tell ourselves and others." Elle wrote, "The stories we tell ourselves, family mythologies, a daughter's search for tangible facts, sorting tangible facts from a father's fantasies and lies." For Maren, the film was about "a family coming to terms with its various complicated mythologies and truths and how those stories have, in fact, impacted their lives and identities." Mr. Egri, we have a premise.

Andrea, Cristina, and I celebrated, then brainstormed solutions to the remaining problems. The first act was slow, and the person who revealed my father's fate appeared as a deus ex machina, causing the climax to arrive out of nowhere. Andrea made a new cut, rearranging and deleting scenes. One key problem with the first act was that, while it addressed the storytelling and family sides of our premise, it took too long to introduce the lying side by revealing my father had misrepresented his educational accomplishments. It wasn't until minute 30 that we got to that section. Andrea challenged Cristina and me to instead get to it by minute 20. One key way to make that happen was moving a section that explores my family's long history of blending stories to the third act, where it would now have new resonance because it appeared after my father's fondness for lying had been thoroughly explored. Andrea also suggested we set up the climax through my newly discovered narration powers. She then said, "When I read the audience feedback, I was relieved. We're very close to the end. The new changes have to be very delicate or we'll destabilize the structure we've built. We're looking at one final edit."

My story hugged me as I took these words in, afraid of the separation we always knew would come. I suggested another set of focus group screenings after the new draft to make sure we'd fixed everything, but Andrea said we'd lose ourselves in the endless feedback loop. Instead, we would show it to three people, all of whom had seen it already, and ask if we'd solved the problems. It felt vulnerable not to rely on the plurality of voices that had joined me through this five-year voyage, generously diagnosing *A Family of Stories*'s flaws and celebrating its moments of poignancy. Yet, like the friends we encounter on any quest, they'd given us what we needed. It was time to go on alone to the end of our journey.

TAKING FLIGHT

When you live with a story beginning in childhood, it nests itself in your growing bones, filling your veins with its rhythms. It shapes who you become as an adult, which is why telling it can be so hard. As you reveal its demons and frailties, you're revealing your own. Bringing in collaborators as you manage this strenuous feat will help you unearth your story's secret heart. I think of Eco, Rich, and Egri as collaborators. I think of the dozens of audience members who shared their feedback as collaborators. The collaborators who gave me my wings, however, are Cristina and Andrea. They dug into generations of my family's entanglements and helped me find the core of what my story—and the ancestors from whom I inherited it—can mean to others and to me.

Revision is a painful process. It hurts to hear that the ideas you labored over for hours, if not years, of your life did not come across as you wanted them to. It hurts to be told that you must (yet again!) return to some version of square one if the message you want to deliver is to reach your audience. And yet, if you collaborate with the kinds of editors, coauthors, and feedback providers who help you find the premise—or thesis—of what you're saying and to stay close to it, the pain is only temporary. Once you lick your wounds for a few days or weeks, you get back to work with a renewed sense of purpose and possibility.

Whether you're crafting your dissertation, your first novel, or your tenth theory book, inviting collaborators you trust into your intimate and messy creative process and following their advice as you revise can help you make the kind of work that moves people—to action, to laughter, to tears. As you rely on your collaborators' ideas to leapfrog your own, you realize that you and your story have grown wings. And as your story flies away, you will too—with a renewed sense of who you are and where you want to go, now that you've shared a sliver of your essence with the world.

REFERENCES

Eco, Umberto. 2001. *Six Walks in the Fictional Woods.* 7th ed. Cambridge, MA: Harvard University Press.

Egri, Lajos. 2009. *The Art of Dramatic Writing: Its Basis in the Creative Interpretation of Human Motives.* Hawthorne, CA: BN Publishing.

Mernit, Billy. 2020. *Writing the Romantic Comedy: The Art of Crafting Funny Love Stories for the Screen.* 20th anniv. ed. New York: Harper.

Rich, Adrienne. 2001. *On Lies, Secrets, and Silence: Selected Prose 1966-1978.* 2nd ed. New York: Norton.

Tobias, Ronald B. 1993. *20 Master Plots: And How to Build Them.* Cincinnati, OH: Writer's Digest.

3
ALEJANDRA CHOOSES LIFE
Revising the Resignation Letter toward Counterstory as Epistle

Aja Y. Martinez

This essay presents large-scale revisions made to institutional narratives concerning minoritized faculty resignation. Because I am a writer and teller of critical race counterstories, these resignation letters were written through the method of counterstory as epistle, which, in style, is a longer, more narrative form when compared to other genres of resignation letters (see Bell 1989; Martinez 2020; Solórzano 2013). Due to counterstory's ability to offer strands of the same story from varying perspectives (see Delgado 1989; Martinez 2014), it is the imperative methodological choice for the telling, revising, and retelling of this story (R. Sánchez, chapter 9). At the center of the resignation in question is my chronicled composite counterstory character,[1] Alejandra Prieto.[2] As a contribution, through counterstory as epistle, this revision journey prompts the audience to reflect on and analyze rhetorical decisions made by faculty of color as we navigate and self-advocate within white-dominant and white supremacist institutions. As evidenced in the chair's email, white supremacist administrators attempt to massage, make light of, and diminish realities faced by faculty of color within white-dominant institutions. This form of administrator whitewashing effectively works to obscure the racist and sexist trauma and harassment that culminates in these very resignations. In telling the story (R. Sánchez, chapter 9) of revising a professional practice (Becker, Blewett, and Sohan, chapter 5; Sills and F. Sánchez, chapter 4; Wenger, chapter 6)—a letter of resignation in this case—I offer my audience more than a story of textual change reduced to track changes and a few words rethought, rephrased, or replaced. In narrating, from the perspective of a faculty member of color, what can otherwise be an unremarkable and mundane writing task, this telling, revisioning, and then retelling of a resignation letter puts a foot in the revolving door of white supremacist academic jobs and says, "hold up, I will control the narrative of my own departure."

I put forth this large-scale revision as a contribution in coalition with the radical and risky acts of other marginalized faculty who write and revise institutional narratives toward change. In particular, this contribution builds on and contributes to the work of Carmen Kynard (2019), when she states: "For far too long, the conversations about retaining BIPOC faculty at the college have centered on support for tenure. This logic assumes that tenure and promotion are something difficult for us. I assure you that this has not been the case for me or my peers. My generation of successful Brown and Black professionals are a mobile generation and the most decorated amongst us do one thing when an institution continually devalues us: *we leave.*"

COUNTERSTORY AS EPISTLE

>**From**: Alejandra Prieto <ALEPRIETO@SNOCITYUNI.EDU>
>**Sent**: Friday, March 6, 2020 5:42 PM
>**To**: <WRITGRADSTUDENTS@LISTSERV.SNOCITYUNI.EDU>
>**Subject**: Leaving Snow City University[3]
>
>Dear Grad Students,
>
>It is with a heavy heart that I write to you all this evening to let you know I'll be leaving my employment at Snow City University at the conclusion of this semester. I did not make this decision lightly and wanted you all to know about my decision before it is made public.
>
>This grad program was my initial draw to Snow City University (SCU), and has remained a constant joy for me during the time I've served as faculty. You as students and as a collective program have kept me afloat and given me reason to return to this job year after year. However, if SCU as an institution has taught me anything, it is that my health and safety must be prioritized because I'm no use to anyone if I'm sick or at risk.
>
>For many reasons, that have accumulated over my nearly four years at SCU, this department and institution are not a safe or sustainable space for me to live and to do my work. Please know that I leave in an effort to prioritize and enact critical self-care so I can indeed be available to you all as a mentor, an advocate, a teacher, and a colleague. I may be physically working in a new location, but please know I remain committed to you all as students and that I hold this grad program very dear in my heart. I am so grateful to you all for the incredible learning experiences I've gained from teaching, mentoring, and interacting with you. Know also, that I am open and willing to discuss this decision with any who wish to reach out personally.

Thank you all for the tremendous opportunity to work with you, and remember I am only an email away.

With my love and gratitude,
Alejandra
Alejandra Prieto, PhD
Pronouns: she/her/hers
Department of Writing
Snow City University

From: Official Writing Program List <WPSERV@LISTSERV.SNOCITYUNI.EDU> on behalf The Chair <TheChair@SNOUNI.EDU>
Sent: Saturday, March 7, 2020 8:22 AM
To: <WPSERV@LISTSERV.SNOCITYUNI.EDU>
Subject: Congratulations, Alejandra!

All—

As some of you know, Alejandra Prieto has accepted a position at another university.

I want to thank Alejandra for her contributions to the department and the university more broadly as we continue the hard work of building a more inclusive space.

Please join me in wishing Alejandra the very best in her new position.

—The Chair
Professor of Writing
Department of Writing
Snow City University

Re: Congratulations, Alejandra!
From: Alejandra Prieto <ALEPRIETO@SNOCITYUNI.EDU>
Sent: Saturday, March 7, 2020 11:29 AM
To: Official Writing Program List <WPSERV@LISTSERV.SNOCITYUNI.EDU> on behalf Alejandra Prieto <ALEPRIETO@SNOCITYUNI.EDU>

Dear Colleagues,

I write to indeed confirm I have accepted a position at another university and I will leave my employment at Snow City University. But I also write in an effort to make sure this narrative avoids "any discourse about my departure that deliberately ignores the hostile and inept environments that make [Snow City University] unbearable for faculty of color like me" (Kynard 2019).

Throughout all four years of my employment at Snow City University, I have been serially and increasingly targeted, bullied, and harassed by a member of this department. For all of these four years, I have cooperated with the various administrative institutional apparatuses all of whom requested I answer to complaints filed against me by this department member. As a junior woman of color faculty member, I have continually appealed to departmental and institutional leadership for support and protection from the sustained harassment I have endured for four years in relation to this department member. However, department and institutional leadership have failed to protect me.

The levels of stress and anxiety that I have been navigating for nearly four years of harassment and bullying within this department took a near fatal toll on my health. By March 2019, after experiencing three-days' worth of sustained numbness in my left hand clear up to my left elbow, I drove myself to the ER (after teaching at SCU that day until 8PM). I was admitted with stroke-like symptoms and was eventually referred to a neurologist for additional tests, including an MRI and an electromyography (nerve damage) test. This peak of illness was steadily reached over the course of 3.5 years of increasing and increasingly alarming illnesses, not commensurate with my medical record previous to my employment at Snow City University.

Within my first year at SCU, upon facing the initial harassment from this aforementioned department member, but also in an effort to help lift the immediate and near unbearable emotional and labor-intensive weight of being the sole faculty member of color in my department, I sought support in the form of counseling. I was quickly educated in the colorblindness of the counseling profession upon realizing how difficult it was to find a counselor in the Snow City-area who was a woman of color. Because I am a race and racism theorist, who has spent years studying the dynamics of colorblind racism within professions and institutions, I understood implicitly that it was not in my best interest of time or resources to spend my first free six sessions of counseling explaining to a white (and I'm sure well-meaning) therapist the dynamics of being a sole person of color in a department within a predominantly and historically white institution. There was quite literally ONE woman of color therapist available to me in the Snow City area, and this is who I met with on a weekly basis through the entirety of my first year at SCU in an effort to talk through the stress and anxiety of this job that, as my third-year review file reflects, has placed me in a position of serving on or chairing twelve (and counting!) graduate committees for exams and dissertations, has assigned me thirteen new course preparations in three years, and has allowed a known and unmitigated department bully to target and harass me for the entirety of the time I have served this institution.

It should come as no surprise that despite my best efforts to attend to self-care and self-preservation through counseling, exercise, and nutrition, my health steadily failed. Leading up to my stroke-like symptoms that occurred during my third-year pre-tenure review, I have been diagnosed with shingles, acute bronchitis that began as a cold but progressed to this stage due to stress and lack of rest—and took me a month and a half to recover from, and stress-induced migraines. I am thirty-seven years old and I have no prior medical experiences with chronic illness. Recently, noticing the increased emergency room, urgent care, and specialist visits/expenses through the past few years, my medical insurance company opened an investigation of my work environment in likely pursuit of a workers' compensation claim against Snow City University in relation to my uncharacteristic and increasingly job-related illnesses.

Despite this inhospitable, hostile, and toxic work environment, despite the increasingly alarming physical and emotional toll of this job, I have managed to forge meaningful and productive relationships with students and colleagues within my department and across campus. I have contributed seven original courses to this institution, I have served on multiple departmental, campus-wide, and national committees, I have sustained a steady record of publication with top tier journals, and I have successfully placed my monograph, which will be released in June 2020, with a premier press in my field. In recognition of and demonstration of my success as a faculty member at SCU, I am a Humanities Center Faculty Fellow, I was a finalist for the inaugural Social Justice Center Faculty Fellowship, and I have been nominated by graduate students and faculty in my department for the 2020 Excellence in Graduate Education Faculty Recognition Award—an award I was recently notified I've won. Despite it all, I have been a successful and contributing member of the SCU community.

Thus, I am departing Snow City University because I choose health and life. I did not come to this decision lightly, and I am not leaving to simply seek a better opportunity. Snow City University, upon being hired, was my dream job. But I have been effectively pushed out, as so many other marginalized, minoritized, and precarious faculty, students, and staff have been here at SCU and at other institutions. I have chosen to accept an offer elsewhere in the hopes that I can pursue my career with my health, safety, and quality of life centralized and secured. I do not think it is a coincidence that within this year that I have been on research leave and research fellowship, I have not so much as caught a cold.

Despite it all, I am grateful to the wonderful students and colleagues who I had the extreme pleasure and honor of working with during my time at SCU. I wish you all and even this institution nothing but the best in terms of real healing and transformation. Even though I have to leave, I remain hopeful that this explanation of *why* I left will resonate with some or all of you who read it. I care deeply for the well-being and success at SCU of the undergraduate and graduate students who my departure will separate me from. I care deeply for the well-being and success at SCU of my colleagues, especially my colleagues of color in the department (who have experienced their own share of hostility on this campus), but also the new BIPOC colleagues who are in the process of being hired within the same semester it has become impossible for me to stay. Because I *do* care about recruitment and retention of BIPOC faculty at Snow City University, for the betterment of the SCU community as a whole, I hope my experiences that I have taken the time to document and detail here are taken seriously and that they can serve as a learning experience for my department, but also for Snow City University as a whole. It is my intent that this email provides a representative answer to the question: "Why do faculty of color leave?"

In closing, I leave you all with an important quote, from an important mentor and scholar who also took the time to detail why we, BIPOC faculty, leave:

> For far too long, the conversations about retaining BIPOC faculty at the college have centered on support for tenure. This logic assumes that tenure and promotion are something difficult for us. I assure you that this has not been the case for me or my peers. My generation of successful Brown and Black professionals are a mobile generation and the most decorated amongst us do one thing when an institution continually devalues us: *we leave*. [. . .] Brown and Black faculty are not out here struggling with tenure and promotion requirements; none of us would have made it into and out of PhD programs, racially exclusive and hostile as they are, if we were struggling with research and writing processes. [. . .] I have only ever left a university when I found its racialized exploitation, anti-blackness, organizational incompetence, and misogynoir intolerable. Any discourse about my departure that deliberately ignores the hostile and inept environments that make a place unbearable for faculty of color like me obfuscates the college's failure to develop effective recruitment *and retention* models for BIPOC and promotes the racism that the institution sustains.—Carmen Kynard from "Letter to My Former College President and Provost: Why I Left"

Sincerely,
Alejandra

NOTES

For more on this topic, see Reshmi Dutt-Ballerstadt's "In Our Own Words: Institutional Betrayals" (2020) published in *Inside Higher Ed*: https://www.insidehighered.com/advice/2020/03/06/underrepresented-faculty-members-share-real-reasons-they-have-left-various.

1. In many cases, composite contexts and characters are abstractions representing cultural or political ideologies and could mistakenly be read as stereotyped depictions of certain ideologies and politics. However, in the case of composite counterstories, characters represent more than just a single individual and are intentionally crafted as composites that primarily embody an ideology as informed by a combination of personal experiences, the literatures, and hard data. Composite characters are written into "social, historical, and political situations that allow the dialogue to speak to the research findings and creatively challenge racism and other forms of subordination" (Yosso 2006, 11). For additional reading on composite counterstories and characters, see Martinez's *Counterstory* (2020, 23–25).

2. See Martinez's "A Plea for Critical Race Theory Counterstory: Dialogues Concerning Alejandra's 'Fit' in the Academy" (2014), which introduces the chronicled composite character, Alejandra Prieto. Alejandra is of Indigenous-Mexican heritage and American nationality from the borderland deserts of Arizona. She is a Brown single mother from a teenaged pregnancy, has a doctorate, and is a professor of rhetoric and writing studies. For more on this composite character, see also Martinez, "Prologue: Encomium of a Storyteller" (2020). As is the case with all composite counterstory characters, Alejandra and her interlocutors are fictionalized characters and are not to be identified with any singular individuals.
3. See Gonzalez (2020).

REFERENCES

Bell, Derrick. 1989. "An Epistolary Exploration for a Thurgood Marshall Biography." *Harvard BlackLetter Journal*, no. 6, 51–67.

Delgado, Richard. 1989. "Storytelling for Oppositionists and Others: A Plea for Narrative." *Michigan Law Review* 87 (8): 2411–41.

Dutt-Ballerstadt, Reshmi. 2020. "In Our Own Words: Institutional Betrayals." *Inside Higher Ed*, https://www.insidehighered.com/advice/2020/03/06/underrepresented-faculty-members share-real-reasons-they-have-left-various.

Gonzalez, Martín Alberto. 2020. "'Why You Always so Political?': The Experiences and Resiliencies of Mexican / Mexican American / Xicanx Students at a Predominantly White University." PhD diss., Syracuse University.

Kynard, Carmen. 2019. "Letter to My Former College President and Provost: Why I Left." *Education, Liberation and Black Radical Traditions for the Twenty-First Century: Carmen Kynard's Teaching and Research Site on Race, Writing, and the Classroom*, http://carmenkynard.org/letter-to-former-college-president-and-provost/.

Martinez, Aja Y. 2020. *Counterstory: The Rhetoric and Writing of Critical Race Theory*. Urbana, IL: National Council of Teachers of English.

Martinez, Aja Y. 2014. "A Plea for Critical Race Theory Counterstory: Stock Story versus Counterstory Dialogues Concerning Alejandra's 'Fit' in the Academy." *Composition Studies* 42 (2): 33–55.

Martinez, Aja Y. 2020. "Prologue: Encomium of a Storyteller." *Counterstory: The Rhetoric and Writing of Critical Race Theory*. Urbana-Champagne, IL: National Council of Teachers of English.

Solórzano, Daniel. 2013. "Critical Race Theory's Intellectual Roots: My Email Epistolary with Derrick Bell." In *Handbook of Critical Race Theory in Education*, edited by Marvin Lynn and Adrienne D. Dixson, 48–68. New York: Routledge.

Yosso, Tara J. 2006. *Critical Race Counterstories along the Chicana/Chicano Educational Pipeline*. New York: Routledge.

SET 2

Revision Makes Space

Christina M. LaVecchia

The previous set of the volume ends with Aja Y. Martinez's counterstory, in which her composite character, Alejandra Prieto, revises the whitewashed narrative that university administration has constructed around Prieto's resignation. Prieto's revision, though, is "more than a story of textual change reduced to track changes and a few words rethought, rephrased, or replaced. In narrating, from the perspective of a faculty member of color, what can otherwise be an unremarkable and mundane writing task, this telling, revisioning, and then retelling of a resignation letter puts a foot in the revolving door of white supremacist academic jobs and says, 'hold up, I will control the narrative of my own departure'" (Martinez, this collection, 41–42).

Just as Prieto revises a professional *practice* (resignation), so too do the authors in this second set offer needed insights on oft-occluded practices that heavily feature in our professional lives: applying for jobs (Sills and F. Sánchez) or promotion and tenure (Wenger) and recommending students (Becker, Blewett, and Sohan). In narrating these everyday processes, these writers make space for themselves (and others) within institutional structures: imagining themselves into new roles, holding space for the value of their labor, and imagining futures for recommendees.

Hence, the chapters in this set remind us how revision happens not only on mundane-yet-high-stakes pages but also extratextually, shaping our very lives in the profession. Indeed, many of the professional practices we often approach as transactional (getting a job, keeping and advancing in a position, or supporting the searches of others) also construct, and revise, our *identities*. The revisions of identity narrated in these chapters are processes of (re)discovery, echoing Donald Murray, who writes that "revision is not just clarifying meaning, it is discovering meaning and clarifying it while it is being discovered" (1981, 33). Meaning, like identity, does not simply arrive: it is found, and made, through revision. And so, as these writers narrate journeys of discovering what it is they're really trying to say, their revisions uncover new views of who it is they (or their students or collaborators) are.

For instance, Christy I. Wenger notes that annual reviews are reinscribed each time we approach them, rather than composed anew; indeed, we typically begin with models, thereby revising from the outset even as we compose them for the first time. Wenger writes that these documents are "a palimpsest of academic labor" (81), bearing the unmistakable traces of the iterations that have come before them and the institutional norms that have shaped them. For Wenger, those traces of her institution's annual review structure squeezed out her WPA labor, and thereby her WPA identity; it was only when she grew more confident self-identifying as a WPA (the first such role on her campus) that she found space to represent the work of that role in her annual review.

These "copy/paste" origins (as Becker, Blewett, and Sohan phrase it, 67) are also true for recommendation letters and cover letters. Indeed, Ellery Sills and Fernando Sánchez remind us that cover letters often originate in revision of previous documents, which can lead to a stasis of sorts, our identities getting stuck in well-worn grooves. Sills describes unintentionally representing his identity as a WAC/WID specialist, rather than the multimodal expert with a broad base in English studies that the job ad was looking for, which F. Sánchez attributes to both how Sills's previous professional roles shaped his outlook and the persistence of text on the page from previous cover letters. After his identity as a WAC/WID specialist was destabilized by feedback from F. Sánchez, Sills was subsequently challenged to find a new connecting thread to make sense of his experiences as a newly discovered generalist.

Cameron Becker, Kelly Blewett, and Vanessa Kraemer Sohan call our attention to entrenchments of a different sort: the tacit practices in recommendation letters we have made habit. Through our letter-writing practices (using previous letters as templates, with personalized bits inserted here and there), we may at times construct "fraught" representations of the students for whom we write letters (75). Calling for critical reexaminations of these habits, Becker, Blewett, and Sohan assert we "need to examine carefully our unthinking descriptions of students' bodies in our classrooms" to ensure we are anticipating the perceptions those descriptions will build in others' minds (68).

Looking to the larger volume, reflections on revising professional practices is a through line that not only traces back to Martinez in the first set but also will continue on in the third set. There Raúl Sánchez calls for revised approaches to peer review feedback, noting that all of us are prone to "dickishness" and must work to overcome such proclivities in order to respond to our colleagues in generative, revision-centric ways (119–120). But despite the focus on professional practices, these pieces also always bring their insights back to the personal. In each of these narratives, authors find the confidence and necessity to, as Nancy Sommer describes, speak back to and remake the authoritative "voices"—the chorus of institutional patterns coalescing into local expectations for an annual review, or their words from previous drafts persisting on the pages of cover and recommendation letters—that precede their compositional acts. Sommers writes: "By confronting these authorial voices, I find the power to understand and gain access to my own ideas. Against all the voices I embody—the voices heard, read, whispered to me from off-stage—I must bring a voice of my own. I must enter the dialogue on my own authority, knowing that other voices have enabled mine, but no longer can I subordinate mine to theirs" (1992, 29). By actively revising documents and practices, authors in this set find new paths forward, new visions of themselves and others, new spaces of belonging.

REFERENCES

Murray, Donald. 1981. *Journal of Basic Writing* 3: 33–40.
Sommers, Nancy. 1992. *College Composition and Communication* 43 (1): 23–31.

4

REVISING A COVER LETTER, REVISING A LIFE
Bridging Professional Identities

Ellery Sills and Fernando Sánchez

All writers struggle with incorporating feedback from peers and reviewers. For instance, when reflecting on our manuscript submissions, we may shudder to think of the dreaded Reviewer 2—a trope that has become so infamous for providing "unacceptable, unnecessary, and toxic" feedback on manuscripts (R. Sánchez, this collection, 123) that it has spawned memes, Facebook pages, Twitter profiles, and, yes, even peer-reviewed articles (Watling, Ginsburg, and Lingard 2021) dedicated to it.[1] Reviewer 2 notwithstanding, however, even feedback that is well-intentioned, insightful, and congenial may also create some "revision anxiety" in writers—particularly when our revisions deal with making changes to foundational and structural issues as both require more than exchanging or replacing one idea for another, or one argument for a better one.

Indeed, Chris Mays (2017) has suggested that written documents—even in (or perhaps especially in) draft form—resist changes because they desire to retain their original stability. That is, revision threatens the stability of the existing text by forcing the writer to imagine new possibilities, thus potentially dismantling what had once seemed a coherent and cohesive whole. In essence, a writer's greatest challenge may not necessarily be when facing a blank page but when needing to revise what is already seemingly written and complete.

With this in mind, in this chapter we seek to explore how such destabilization through revision can affect not just the document being revised but the writer as well. If the act of revising academic texts is met with resistance, revising job documents for positions in the academic job market is doubly so given that revising these documents signifies both a threat to their stable textual coherence (Mays 2017, 70) and to a textually "stable" professional identity as well. Such an application of resistance to job documents may be particularly intriguing given that documents conveying one's professional identity are both communicative and formative for the writer as well (see Martinez, this collection).

Thus, we examine how one of the authors of this chapter, Ellery, negotiated this reshaping of his professional identity through an analysis of the revision choices he made as he applied to an academic position. Ellery reflects on his revisions in multiple drafts of his cover letter and, in doing so, demonstrates how revisions of written texts can both reflexively signal and generate revisions to identity (Hall 2002). He also discusses how the feedback from his friend Fernando, the second author of the chapter, helped him to bridge old and new professional identities in his cover letter. In narrative interludes, Fernando recounts how he saw his role as a reviewer whose comments, however inadvertently, led Ellery to revise his identity in the first place. In doing so, we hope to reveal how job document revision "reopens possibilities" of identity construction and professional acculturation in text and writer alike (Mays 2017, 67).

FROM HEDGEHOG TO FOX: PROFESSIONAL IDENTITY REVISION IN ACTION

Individuals on the job market continually face reminders not only that they must build a professional identity but that such an identity should be created in the writing. This is precisely the advice that Karen Kelsky (2015) gives academic job-seekers in *The Professor Is In* when she advises applicants that the cover letters that they submit should transmit information about their identity. She urges readers to avoid emotionally laden language because "this language is painfully overused. It doesn't communicate some original and compelling *truth about you*" (137; emphasis added). Instead, she advises applicants to focus on the facts about themselves and use those as drivers of their cover letters. Such a reminder makes evident that the writing in job documents does not simply convey one's experiences to readers but puts forth claims about identity in ways that can be corroborated through one's experiences. Or, as Kelsky states in her advice on writing teaching philosophies, "we want to know *you are* an innovative teacher. How do you show that? Again, with *evidence*" (143; emphasis added).

As such, if identity is synchronic with argument, the writer has no room to deviate from the way they present themselves and must focus on crafting a professional persona that is not only internally coherent (makes consistent claims about themselves that are backed up) but also externally relevant (makes consistent claims about themselves that are meaningful to the search committee). Yet constructing such an identity can be difficult precisely because who we are is always in flux, and we may rely too much on past iterations of our selves that are difficult to completely abandon.

In what follows, we present Ellery's journey in crafting a letter and Fernando's insights as a commenter on his drafts.

Ellery: Entering the job market for the second time after earning my PhD in rhetoric and composition, I applied to an assistant professor of English position with a focus on first-year writing at Upper Midwest University (UMU), a private liberal arts college.[2] The position called for applicants with experience and research in composition theory as well as developmental writing. Most notably, the ad emphasized that the committee and department were in search of candidates who "demonstrated interest in pedagogies of difference and multimodality." Applicants were also asked to teach a range of advanced composition and theory courses, participate in a college summer bridge program, and show a "commitment to broad liberal arts and interdisciplinary education." The position thus clearly asked for candidates with specialized strengths and interests in composition (e.g., composition theory, basic or developmental writing, multimodality), yet also suggested a desire for a generalist "commitment" to liberal arts writ large.

I was drawn to the position at UMU because I believed that it touched upon my professional strengths in composition theory and pedagogy, multimodality, advanced writing, and interdisciplinary collaboration. Accordingly, in drafting my cover letter, I worked to present a stable professional identity that emphasized these strengths. After a brief introductory paragraph listing my primary qualifications, my second paragraph stressed my extensive and varied experience in rhetoric and composition by describing "twelve years of teaching a wide range of developmental, first-year, and advanced composition courses" and discussing my approach to incorporating students' diverse linguistic and multimodal practices. My third paragraph then highlighted my experience with advanced writing and WAC/WID courses, thereby working to establish my interdisciplinary credentials. My fourth paragraph foregrounded my research expertise in composition theory and multimodality, discussing my dissertation research into writing programs' "construction of learning outcomes, particularly multimodal and digital composing outcomes," and indicating my research's application to "building a 'student-ready' writing program." Finally, my fifth paragraph connected my past administrative experience to my history of prioritizing interdisciplinary collaboration. I worked especially hard on demonstrating that my experience matched the expected qualifications, and I felt confident that the identity I'd presented was what they were looking for.

Nonetheless, since my interest in this position was so strong, I felt it would be a good idea to get some additional feedback. I turned to Fernando, as a long-time friend and colleague from graduate school with whom I had often traded documents for review in the past.

Fernando: Because job documents act as an applicant's first introduction to a search committee, writers obviously experience much pressure in crafting them. From my own experience on the market, I understood why Ellery would want to make sure that he was hitting the right notes for his cover letter, and indeed, looking through the document, I thought that Ellery had adeptly communicated his previous research and the courses he'd taught as a way of showing he fit the job description. Still, I felt that there were opportunities for Ellery to speak more specifically to the implied context of the position. My interpretation of the job ad led me to focus more on the committee's emphasis on multimodality, and I understood their discussions of interdisciplinarity to mean "teaching a breadth of courses within English studies at a small, liberal arts college"—not necessarily teaching or administering WAC/WID courses across the university.

Thus, I was confused why Ellery would wait so long in his cover letter to stress his work in multimodality and choose to instead highlight his experiences with WAC/WID (both in teaching advanced writing in WAC/WID courses as well as in his administrative work in WAC/WID). I was not necessarily convinced that this would speak to the needs of the department, which called for more attention to expanding departmental writing needs across their courses in English. It became evident to me that, as much as Ellery had been tailoring his experiences to meet the needs of the job description, he might also have been allowing his previous professional roles and cover letter drafts from previous job searches to dictate the identity that would come through the most. That is something to be expected given how difficult it can be to disentangle previous contexts embedded within previously used drafts (Swarts 2010, 149; see also Wenger, chapter 6, on how professionalization documents like annual reviews serve as a "palimpsest of academic labor" [81]).

I felt that more time should be spent on Ellery's multimodal work and his commitments to English studies. Therefore, I suggested that Ellery should "position [himself] as a multimodal expert right away" to better align with the job ad, by advising that he move his fourth research-focused paragraph on multimodality to a position earlier in the letter. I also recommended that Ellery elaborate on his experience with multilingual learners by "provid[ing] a quick glimpse of student experience" from different institutions and populations. At the same time, because of the variety of needs stressed in the ad, I urged Ellery to "go for breadth" and present himself as a versatile generalist who could teach a variety of subjects within English and writing studies, such as advanced composition, writing across disciplines, basic writing, and even writing that dovetails within literary genres—all of which I knew Ellery had done in his previous teaching experiences.

In this way, I hoped that Ellery would better prove himself as a good fit for a position that highlighted "a strong commitment to broad liberal arts and interdisciplinary education." While I had given Ellery my suggestions via these written comments, I, of course, also followed up with him during one of our conversations to elaborate on my thoughts and address any questions he might have had.

Ellery: I remember that, on my first read-through of Fernando's comments, I was initially surprised by the feedback he had given me. Even though Fernando had stressed describing the breadth of my teaching, I felt that discussing my experience with teaching professional writing and WAC/WID courses *already* proved my interdisciplinary commitment. Furthermore, I was demonstrating my ability to teach advanced writing courses, something the job position specifically asked for. However, Fernando's feedback made me question my assumptions: why was I interpreting the job posting's call for experience in "interdisciplinary education" and "advanced writing" as professional and technical writing and WAC/WID? Why was I not also attending to its expectation of a "commitment to broad liberal arts . . . education," which was bound to complicate my interpretation (especially given its status as a private liberal arts college)?

I noticed that, in connecting the job posting expectations to a WAC/WID background, I was using written material similar to the cover letters for interdisciplinary writing positions I had applied to previously. For example, I had used my professional writing and WAC/WID experience to apply for Writing Across the Curriculum director positions or positions that called for building STEM-centric writing curricula, positions I sought due to my ongoing research interests in disciplinarity and interdisciplinarity. In applying for these positions, I had conveyed my expertise in writing in the sciences, engineering, and other STEM organization, and visual presentation of scientific reports. Given this experience, I would look forward to developing and teaching courses such as Teaching Writing Theory and Topics in Professional Writing (possibly with an emphasis in research and report writing). In addition, these curricular choices reflect one of my key teaching and research values—that students see themselves as well prepared for their disciplinary and professional futures.

These values closely inform my research into writing programs' structures through their construction of learning outcomes, particularly multimodal and digital composing outcomes. In assessment work at Purdue, I discovered that several first-year composition instructors saw multimodal composition as central to students' future preparedness; at the same time, however, they experienced a persistent anxiety and lack of confidence when teaching and evaluating multimodal projects. This persistent anxiety inspire: my dissertation, *Emerging Genres, Dangerous Classifications: The Kairos of Digital Composing Policy*,

Figure 4.1. Excerpt from Ellery's first draft of cover letter.

disciplines; I had built a professional identity around interdisciplinarity; and I had construed this interdisciplinarity in WAC/WID terms. Similarly, in my cover letter for UMU, I was implicitly presenting my preparation for teaching "advanced courses" and fostering "interdisciplinary education" as future WAC/WID instruction and administration. In presenting my experience in this way (at least prior to Fernando's feedback), I believed that I was establishing myself as a candidate who was well-versed in composition pedagogy and theory and an interdisciplinary expert. Moreover, I saw my interdisciplinary expertise and my work with multimodality as closely related, and my draft cover letter as evidence for this relationship (for example, see the transition between the third and fourth paragraphs, highlighted in figure 4.1). However, for Fernando, this presentation of my professional identity was, in fact, at odds with the job posting's needs. Fernando was raising questions about my identity that, however reluctantly, I needed to confront.

After reflecting on Fernando's feedback, it struck me that, to borrow Isaiah Berlin's famous distinction, I was presenting myself as a hedgehog, an expert in "one big thing"; instead, as Fernando recognized, I should be presenting myself as a fox, knowing many things (Berlin and Ignatieff 2013, 1). I was, frankly, a bit embarrassed that I had not realized this before. Fernando was right: it was breadth, not depth, that was called for.

By making this recommendation, however, Fernando was also inadvertently compelling me to destabilize my professional identity. In retrospect, it appears that, while recognizing and answering UMU's desire for an expert in a breadth of specializations, I was also seeking to preserve a professional identity as a specialist in WAC/WID—an identity that I was not only familiar with constructing but to which I also aspired as a future teacher-researcher. As a result, my draft letter framed the position's call for "a strong commitment to broad liberal arts and interdisciplinary education" in exclusively WAC/WID terms. However, in presenting my experience in this way, I was neglecting an opportunity to present a more flexible, broader interdisciplinary identity that would fulfill a variety of the job posting's needs: for example, participating in summer bridge program-building, developing an undergraduate research program, *and* teaching advanced composition and theory courses that could possibly (but by no means necessarily) include WAC/WID offerings. In revising my cover letter, then, I also had to learn to revise *myself*, opening up to new professional possibilities.

Revising myself turned out to be a struggle—one that eventually took four additional drafts to complete. At first, I just made quick organizational adjustments in the letter; for example, in my second draft, I foregrounded my multimodal expertise, moving my research on multimodal and digital composing outcomes to a more prominent place in the draft's third paragraph. However, when it came to Fernando's suggestion of presenting myself as a generalist "fox," I found myself at a loss. I would string together sentences that simply listed all the different classes I had taught, then delete them in frustration. I couldn't find the thread that tied them together, since I still implicitly wanted to hold onto the WAC/WID identity I had constructed for myself. Finally, to save myself the trouble of building a new identity from scratch and get some relief from my frustration, I started reading through old teaching materials and job documents I had saved: student evaluations, teaching philosophies, curricula vitae, and cover letters. I didn't exactly know what I was looking for; I was just hoping to find different language with which to describe myself.

In the meantime, by drifting into new organizational patterns, I was able to see new ways to link my professional experiences. Having already moved my research paragraph forward in the second draft, I used a foregrounded self-identity as a multimodal expert to bridge the discussion of pedagogy and research in the third and penultimate draft: "I welcome the opportunity to prepare college students to compose in multimodal environments" (figure 4.2). In linking my multimodal pedagogy and research, I abandoned the earlier draft's connections of my multimodal research with my WAC/WID background. It's worth highlighting that it took three drafts to do this, and it was largely a result of writing new transitional sentences to link paragraphs together. This shows how resistant to revision both a draft and an identity can be. Even if it was, ironically, somewhat incidental, this linkage contributed to the desired result: foregrounding my identity as a multimodal expert and sidelining or leaving implicit my identity as a WAC/WID practitioner.

different forms, such as microblogs or public service announcements. By practicing remediation, students receive practice in composing for diverse publics beyond the classroom. I can see a strong potential to bring in these practices in first year courses and courses such as Critical Digital Media Theory, wherein students would **put media theory into practice with multimodal cross-cultural projects, as well as another course?**

I welcome the opportunity to prepare college students to compose in multimodal environments. This goal closely informs my research into writing programs' structures through their construction of learning outcomes, particularly multimodal and digital composing outcomes. In assessment work at Purdue, I discovered' that several first-year composition instructors saw multimodal composition as central to students' future preparedness; at the same time, however, they experienced a persistent anxiety and lack of confidence when teaching and evaluating multimodal projects. This persistent anxiety inspired my dissertation, *Emerging Genres, Dangerous Classifications: The Kairos of Digital Composing Policy*, which examined how national policy statements afford (or impede) writing programs' adoption of new digital genres. In order to examine program components at a national level, I studied the Council of Writing Program Administrators' 2014 revision of the Outcomes Statement for First-Year Composition.

Figure 4.2. Excerpt from third draft of Ellery's cover letter.

As my curriculum vitae indicates, I have extensive experience designing instruction, teaching, and administering in a wide variety of contexts. Some of my most recent instruction, such as teaching Advanced Composition and the Writing Across the Curriculum component of Animal Science 311 at Purdue, makes me particularly well suited to developing professional, technical, and interdisciplinary writing courses. My first-year courses often include a community engagement focus, which I could readily incorporate into FYC courses at ▮▮▮▮▮▮▮▮. In addition, my extensive liberal arts background, including a Master of Arts in Teaching English, prepares me to teach courses in literature, theory, and criticism. Given this breadth of experience, I would be happy to teach [courses such as] Introduction to Professional Writing and Rhetoric; Literary and Cultural Theory; Organizational Writing; Critical Digital Media Theory; Teaching Writing; or any number of other courses. In <u>any and all</u> of these contexts, I would seek to pursue my key teaching and research goals—that students see themselves as well prepared for their disciplinary and professional futures.

Figure 4.3. Excerpt from Ellery's final draft of cover letter.

By revising my (formerly) third paragraph on advanced writing to "go for breadth" and moving it to the end of the final draft, I destabilized my specialist identity as a WAC/WID practitioner even further (figure 4.3). Instead, drawing from my previous teaching materials and job documents, I presented a generalist and "broad liberal arts" identity. I touted my "extensive experience designing instruction, teaching, and administering in a wide variety of contexts": professional, technical, and interdisciplinary writing; service learning and community engagement; and literature, theory, and criticism, demonstrated by my experience teaching literary theory at a previous institution. I underlined my range using Fernando's original words—"breadth of experience"—and listed a wide variety of courses I would be prepared to teach. The final sentence in the paragraph about my teaching and research goals—"that students see themselves as well prepared for their disciplinary and professional futures"—now appears at several removes from its original placement in a WAC/WID–oriented pitch.

By the time I had made these revisions, I no longer felt the frustration, tension, and "dissonance" of having to negotiate between identities (Ballenger and Myers 2019). Gradually, through a series of inventional, organizational, and stylistic changes that grew across four different drafts, I had changed my sense of identity as well. I could see that, while I had certainly had some formative WAC/WID experiences earlier in my career, I also had a breadth of teaching experience that met the job posting's call for a "broad liberal arts and interdisciplinary background." I could indeed be a generalist—a "fox," as it were.

CONCLUSION

Just like texts, writers' professional identities want to remain stable; indeed, texts like job documents play a considerable role in constructing academic and professional identities, and this deliberate, careful identity construction only reinforces the desire for stability in text and writer alike. However, when job hunters tailor their documents to apply for multiple positions, often asking for widely varying qualifications, they may resist identity revision—reimagining and reconceptualizing who they are as researchers and academics. In essence, to revise one's professional identity according to various job opportunities requires writers to conceive of a "surplus [of] possibilities" (Welch 1998, 378) and to commit to one or several versions of themselves that are dictated by outside factors (job requirements, relevant experiences, etc.).

What we have discovered through this re-vision of Ellery's job document is that although one's identity does tend to desire to remain intact when presented in job documents, it is possible to rely on previous experiences to reconceptualize how one thinks of and presents oneself.

Ellery: In a 2017 book-length discussion of "personal branding" on the twenty-first-century job market, Ilana Gershon (2017) questions how a personal brand can express both a "cohesive self" and the flexibility sought in a neoliberal economy. Reflecting on the cover letter that I wrote for UMU that same year, I find myself wrestling with the implications of this question. Initially, as an aspiring WAC/WID teacher-researcher, I was anxious about Fernando's advice to "go for breadth," fearing that I could spread myself so thin that no coherent professional identity would remain. But, in the end, I embraced my revised identity as a generalist. Why? Had I always been a generalist in some way, or did I simply choose to become one, pliantly adapting myself to a new job posting?

Gershon concludes that job seekers find ways of linking their personal brand with an "authentic self." While I am far from believing that everyone possesses a singular authentic self (much less endorsing the neoliberal dictates of "flexibility"), I do believe that the intensely competitive pressures of academia demand a kind of bridge-building among potential professional selves. This is not to say that academic job-seekers should surrender or betray their professional and personal commitments. Instead, they should be prepared to frame these commitments rhetorically, aligning them with the departmental, programmatic, and institutional needs they are being asked to fill. In doing so, they may surface previously submerged experiences, capacities, and identities. When I finally took Fernando's advice to demonstrate my range, I felt a kind of satisfaction: a feeling that my letter held together better, as well as a sense of "fit" between my varied experiences and my claims of breadth. Over time, this feeling helped me to build a bridge between my past professional identity and a new one. The bridge-building was a difficult process, one I resisted at first; however, in the end, finding new ways to revise a cover letter gave me a new appreciation for the "surplus [of] possibilities" I could become (Welch 1998, 378).

Fernando: Ellery drafted these documents on his second time through the market, at which point he had accumulated numerous "versions" of his identity, which were spread throughout his application materials for not only separate jobs but years on the market too, many of which I have had the privilege of looking through and providing constructive feedback on. Of course, many academics would find various "versions" of themselves in their files as we continue to find job opportunities that have the potential of emphasizing certain aspects of our professional identities over others.

It would be worth exploring this connection between drafting and identity in job documents further by comparing the different ways that job applicants revise their presentation of themselves at different points in their careers. That is, is it more difficult to revise previous job documents the further removed one is from them after years at one institution or organization, or when one has fewer versions of oneself to draw on coming out of their graduate studies? As important would be to study how scholars and students whose work is closely connected to their own marginalized subjectivities and communities feel if they must revise their identity (or erase it) with various application letter drafts that they produce for academic jobs or to apply for positions in industry (see Becker, Blewett, and Sohan, chapter 5, for a similar discussion with regard to letters of recommendation). Exploring the affective and stylistic aspects of revising job documents can help us provide better feedback to our students and colleagues about who they are and might want to be as they apply to academic positions, programs, and jobs in industry.

In closing, we note that so much of what lasts in a text remains not because of reluctance or intransigence on the part of the writer. Rather, these enduring elements persist because they are the most fundamental pieces that shape the story a text wants to tell. Highlighted throughout our recounting is how identity is an "ongoing individual project" (Dugas et al. 2020) in which we attempt to integrate our past, present, and future selves across a "learning trajectory" (Wenger 1998, 57). In perpetually striving for integration, identity itself is the ultimate act of revision.

NOTES

1. See also Dana Comi's experience with these types of reviewer comments (111) in her coauthored chapter with Alisa Russell in this collection.
2. Pseudonym.

REFERENCES

Ballenger, Bruce, and Kelly Myers. 2019. "The Emotional Work of Revision." *College Composition and Communication* 70 (4): 590–614.

Berlin, Isaiah, and Michael Ignatieff. 2013. "The Hedgehog and the Fox." In *The Hedgehog and the Fox: An Essay on Tolstoy's View of History*, 2nd rev. ed., edited by Henry Hardy, 1–90. Princeton, NJ: Princeton University Press.

Dugas, Daryl, Amy E. Stich, Lindsay N. Harris, and Kelly H. Summers. 2020. "'I'm Being Pulled in Too Many Different Directions': Academic Identity Tensions at Regional Public Universities in Challenging Economic Times." *Studies in Higher Education* 45 (2): 312–26.

Gershon, Ilana. 2017. *Down and Out in the New Economy: How People Find (or Don't Find) Work Today*. Chicago, IL: University of Chicago Press.

Hall, Donald. 2002. *The Academic Self: An Owner's Manual*. Columbus: Ohio State University Press.

Kelsky, Karen. 2015. *The Professor Is In: The Essential Guide to Turning Your PhD into a Job*. New York: Three Rivers Press.

Mays, Chris. 2017. "Revision as Heresy: Posthuman Writing Systems and Kenneth Burke's 'Piety.'" In *Kenneth Burke + the Posthuman*, edited by Chris Mays, Nathaniel A. Rivers, and Kellie Sharp-Hoskins, 61–79. University Park, PA: Penn State University Press.

Swarts, Jason. 2010. "Recycled Writing: Assembling Actor Networks from Reusable Content." *Journal of Business and Technical Communication* 24 (2): 127–63.

Watling, Chris, Shiphra Ginsburg, and Lorelei Lingard. 2021. "Don't Be Reviewer 2! Reflections on Writing Effective Peer Review Comments." *Perspectives on Medical Education* 10 (5): 299–303.

Welch, Nancy. 1998. "Sideshadowing Teacher Response." *College English* 60 (4): 374–95.

Wenger, Etienne. 1998. *Communities of Practice: Learning, Meaning, and Identity*. Cambridge, UK: Cambridge University Press.

5
RE-VISIONING LETTERS OF RECOMMENDATION

Cameron Becker, Kelly Blewett, and Vanessa Kraemer Sohan

Wherever we find the body rhetorically contested, and wherever we find rhetorical contestation about the body's role in meaning-making, we see intensely fraught negotiations.

—Jay Dolmage

Subject line: Asking about a letter of recommendation

Dear Professor X,

I hope you are well. My name is Student Y, and I was in your writing class. I am applying to graduate school, and I was wondering if it was possible for you to write me a letter of recommendation for my application. I really enjoyed your class and teaching style and learned so much from you.

Thank you in advance,
Student Y

Ubiquitous to the point of parody, the letter of recommendation takes up a great deal of faculty and students' time and labor. Faculty and students email about and meet to discuss recommendations; draft, read, and review personal statements and resumes; draft and revise recommendations; upload recommendations to overly complicated online submission systems; and wait to hear back from the institutions that review the recommendations. And yet, in spite of the time and space these letters take up in faculty's working lives and students' aspirations, academic scholarship has largely ignored this important document as a genre, an oversight which mirrors the devaluing of recommendations as a form of service by the very institutional apparatuses that require recommendations for internships, graduate applications, and career promotions. Existing studies of the recommendation genre rarely unpack writers' choices or how they address differing identities, much less how recommendations have been revised in relation to the time, place, and space of their production. Instead, most studies rely on anonymous corpus analysis (see Bouton 1995; Colarelli, Alampay, and Canali 2002; Greenburg, Doyle, and McClure 1994; Grote, Robiner, and Haut 2001; Precht 1998; Trix and Psenka 2003). Anonymous analyses of recommendations rarely get at the people involved—the identities, linguistic and cultural backgrounds, and the very bodies themselves—that will either enter or not enter spaces, in part as a result of these letters. Because letters ultimately are required to facilitate the movement of bodies into spaces (whether professional or academic), they necessarily participate in Dolmage's (2020) "fraught negotiations" as faculty recommenders try to make possibilities for students more achievable. The prevailing, polite idea that students shouldn't even *see* these letters intended to enhance their ethos as applicants underscores how little agency students are expected to have in this process.

What if faculty and students re-visioned these letters together, framing them not as bureaucratic chores to deal with or yet another gate to let good students in and keep bad students out, but instead as moments of mentorship where faculty and students talk directly about issues of representation? In some cases—especially if students are entering a space where their body will be marked as nonnormative—students will need to be savvy about their self-presentation in ways that may be aided by a thoughtful recommendation at the beginning of the process (see Sills and F. Sánchez, chapter 4, for discussion of how professional documents construct, reflect, and revise personal identity). Students should be a resource that faculty consult to revise their prior recommendation letter templates to compose individualized letters that are distinctive and effective.

One example in the literature of an ineffective approach to letter-writing appears in Amy Vidali's "Rhetorical Hiccups" (2009), which traces the representation of one student, Nara, and her experience of traumatic brain injury (TBI) across a set of five letters of recommendation. Four initial recommenders addressed Nara's TBI, in spite of her email stating, "I hope if you do feel the need to mention my disability that you are able to do so in a favorable way" (194). Though the faculty writers were trying to be supportive by positioning Nara's management of her disability as evidence of resilience, their sporadic and nonuniform approach to the disclosure functioned as awkward, inconsistent, ill-explained "rhetorical hiccups" that exposed her to potential bias, which she tried to counter by requesting a letter from the disability resource center on campus (186). Vidali concluded her study by calling on writers of recommendations to do better, beginning with analyzing how they represent difference across a corpus of their own letters. Vidali argues that scholars who want to discuss students' identities in ethical ways should undertake a critical self-examination of their own recommendations, a process that requires that scholars "print out the recommendations we have written over the years, spread them on the desk, and determine just where our priorities and politics lie" (2009, 201). And so Vanessa and Kelly did just that, eventually asking Cameron, a graduate student for whom Kelly had written a letter, to join us in puzzling over the pitfalls and potentials of the genre.

As the previous paragraph suggests, we write this chapter as three differently situated academics in rhetoric and composition. Vanessa is an associate professor at a public R1 Hispanic-Serving Institution (HSI) in the southeast, where she writes numerous recommendations each year, often for students applying to law school. Kelly is the WPA at a teaching-focused public institution in the Midwest and is newer to the genre. And Cameron, a doctoral student at a public institution in the Midwest, recently navigated asking for recommendations, including from Kelly, and was interested in reflecting on her experience from her vantage point as a disabled student now in the second year of her PhD program. Here's what we learned: rather than a bureaucratic chore, recommendations offer an opportunity for mentorship that may be empowering for students both in the context of the letter and in their ancillary and future performances of self. Below we detail the different phases of our study.

PHASE ONE: SPREADING OUR LETTERS OUT ON THE TABLE (KELLY AND VANESSA)

Initially working in the summer of 2021, Vanessa and Kelly swapped letters that we had written over the years. We realized right away that neither of us started from scratch; instead, we both began by opening the last letter we had written for a similarly situated student and adjusting it for this newest request. Our letters seemed to get longer over time, especially Vanessa's, as the amount of boilerplate language increased with each passing year. Vanessa in particular took space to explain the various certificates and tracks. When discussing, we also realized the length of our letters signaled our support of the students, a particular response to reading recommendation letters while serving on hiring and graduate committees where obvious form letters with short, standardized, generic contents were unhelpful to our assessment of applicants.

We also heard echoes of the people who had written our own recommendations, like eerie ghosts from the past. For instance, one of Kelly's recommenders had said that she could imagine Kelly leading a reading group in a doctoral program. With surprise, Kelly realized this had become a go-to rhetorical move in her recommendations for students trying to get into doctoral programs, even though Kelly was writing more than ten years after receiving this letter. Vanessa noticed that she had unthinkingly employed the same ranking system her professors included in their recommendation letters for her (recommend without reservations, highly recommend, recommend), even though she now found the distinctions between these categories arbitrary and pointless.

In fact, as we discussed the topic more generally, much of the information requested by institutions regarding students seemed arbitrary and pointless, such as the additional forms required alongside the letters asking recommenders to situate applicants in the top percentile of students. Which students? Those who had taken that particular course? All students we had ever taught? We agreed that when trying to support students' applications, we would invariably rate our students favorably on quantitative surveys, whereas a colleague mentioned being much more critical when ranking students' performance. Such anecdotal variance suggests that letter writers approach recommendations with different understandings and expectations of the rhetorical situation. Re-visioning letters of recommendation requires that we call these quantitative forms what they are: BS. Instead, if we rethink who letters of recommendation are for and how they can best serve students, we can perhaps share with students how we approach and respond to these kinds of pseudoevaluative situations. Maybe not in all cases—for instance, if we actually do have reservations about a student's ability to perform in a particular role (which, we think, probably should be communicated to the student *before* the letter-writing process)—but once we've agreed to write a letter, we can help students acclimate to the norms and conventions of the genre by being more open about how these forms function and how we respond to them.

As we looked at the letters more closely—spread them out over the virtual table, so to speak—we realized that while our structures for letters were different (with Vanessa focusing on work a student had completed in her course and Kelly focusing on key adjectives to describe students), our politics and priorities were similar. We wanted to use the letters to create space for our students—especially students who needed a little extra support—to have opportunities that they wouldn't otherwise have (99). We also handled the letters in a similar way, often sharing them with students before submitting them. In doing this, we were already taking a mentoring approach, "holding space" (Wenger, chapter 6) for students to talk through their options and make informed decisions about how they were represented. We wouldn't have a student that had the experience described by Vidali, who was totally surprised by something that appeared in the letter. At the same time, we still saw traces of bias in our letters, which we will discuss below. In Phases Two and Three of our study, we each took a closer look at particular artifacts within our archive of letters, and we asked Cameron, the student who received Kelly's letter, to join the conversation.

PHASE TWO: VANESSA'S EVOLVING APPROACH

When I started my faculty position in fall 2012, I had no idea how much my mentorship of undergraduate and graduate students would center around letters of recommendation or how much time I would spend writing such letters. As I laid my letters on the table with Kelly, I began to see not only how my scholarly disposition toward translingual approaches to writing could positively impact my letter-writing, but also how I need to better account for biased and prejudiced language in my representations of students. In the following brief case study, I explain how I've tried to evolve as a letter writer by reviewing multiple letters I wrote for one student over several years.

Two years into my position, I distinctly remember meeting Ana[1] at a coffee shop. I had written her a letter for her law school applications, but after her first year, she had decided it was not for her. We strategized how I could best position her new trajectory in my recommendation for graduate journalism programs. She told me about her work writing for a feminist law blog and starting a nonprofit, and then, while she worked on her application, I worked on her letter. In her law school recommendation, I had filled in my copy/paste template with examples praising Ana's specific writing projects and more generally explaining the research skills and professionalism she demonstrated in class—key for law school committees. In the new letter, I spent more time describing her "work to start a nonprofit dedicated to promoting educational opportunities and support for young Latinas," which I argued stemmed from her high engagement with and research into "the complex interactions of race, class, privilege, and education that have worked to inhibit many young Latinas' success in high school and college." I commended Ana for being "determined to make a difference and serve as a role model," stating that "I have no doubt she will succeed in attaining both goals, since she has already taken concrete steps to achieve them." Her application was successful, and after journalism school, I continued to serve as a reference for Ana's applications for fellowships, summer internships, and more long-term positions.

The collaborative and dialogic evolution of my letters for Ana mirrors the revisions I've gradually made in my process and approach to such letters over the past ten years. Although I still often begin by opening as a template a letter written previously for a similarly situated recommendation, I have come to spend more (not less) time personalizing my letters—inserting information from our conversations in class, office hours, emails, and discussions of personal statements. Ideally, as in the case of Ana, I can sit down with the student so as to understand how they want their work and identities to be represented in their letter, collaborative work that Burnett and coauthors argue is necessary to "deconstruct[ ] some of the toxic hierarchies inherent to the academic system" (2022). However, in the case of harried students who frantically email at the last minute, I often have to resort to a more generic copy/paste approach.

However, as I write more letters for students, who at my institution overwhelmingly identify, like Ana, as Hispanic and multilingual, I have become increasingly concerned about the ethics of identity representation, given the research on recommendations as a highly problematic site for bias and prejudice against applicants (see Stewart and Valian 2018). This concern was reinforced in a university-sponsored diversity advocate training workshop, which cited Frances Trix and Carolyn Psenka's (2003) study finding that letters written for women and underrepresented minorities were shorter and had fewer "standout" terms (e.g., "driven," "motivated," "intelligent") and more "grindstone" terms (e.g., "responsible" vs. "exceptional"; Stewart and Valian 2018, 222). I was left wondering how my framing of students like Ana affected the success of their applications and potentially exposed them to bias. How were the recommendations I was writing a site of rhetorical contestation of my students' bodies, both in terms of gender and their status as multiply marginalized or underrepresented (MMU) students? My later letters more adeptly described Ana's "determination" and "drive" to start a nonprofit and highlighted her linguistic and cultural identities as resources. However, in my first letter, I described her as a "calming presence" during classroom discussions. Such a description might put off a committee looking for "driven" students. As Kelly will discuss more later, we need to examine carefully our unthinking descriptions of students' bodies in our classrooms—such descriptions can potentially expose them to bias during the application process.

One way to counter such biased language is to consider whether there are embodied strategies by which we can employ *metis*—which is often translated from Greek as "cunning"—to sneak in an approach to difference as the norm in recommendations. Such an approach to "difference as the norm" is foundational to the translingual approach (Lu and Horner 2013), which is at the center of my own research and teaching. Through this study, I've realized that part of my evolution as a letter writer has come from translating what I know about language difference into generic social action via the letters I write. It often comes down to simple practices, such as the one I instituted lately where, regardless of my relationship with the student, I ask them about how I will be describing their linguistic resources. The email I send students looks like this:

> In my letter, I will likely refer to the excellent writing you have done exploring your language, identity, and culture in my courses. Please let me know if you are OK with me referencing your multilingual and multicultural identity as an academic resource/asset in my recommendation letter. If you would prefer me to omit such references, or would prefer me to use particular language in representing your identities and experiences, please let me know!

In the case of Ana and other students, I navigated discussions of identity during meetings or while providing feedback on their drafts of personal or diversity statements, but I didn't explicitly ask how they preferred to be referred to or positioned in their recommendations or whether and how they wanted me to frame their classroom projects, which often built upon our classroom discussions and applications of translingualism and so revealed their linguistic and cultural identities. Thus far, students have responded positively to this practice, and I will continue to revise it in discussions with students, alumni, and colleagues. Like Kelly and Cameron, I have come to realize that my relationship with students in the classroom has shaped the writing of recommendations, which circulate beyond the classroom.

PHASE THREE: TALKING ABOUT A PAST LETTER WITH THE STUDENT RECIPIENT (KELLY AND CAMERON)

In December 2019, Cameron asked me (Kelly) to write her a recommendation for an application to Ball State's PhD program in rhetoric and composition. I already knew Cameron was concerned about her ability to navigate a PhD program with a chronic illness, since we'd talked about it a few times over the phone that fall while Cameron was working on an independent study with me. I was excited to write her the letter and, more generally, enthusiastic about her interest in graduate school. Cameron's reception of the letter, which I shared with her after I wrote the first draft over winter break, was gracious. She got into the program. But after reading Vidali's scholarship, what stood out to me about the letter was that it didn't hint at Cameron's illness. For the purposes of this chapter, Cameron and I want to share our divergent reactions to the letter (to read this letter in its entirety, see appendix 5.A). We came to these reactions through several conversations, which first took place asynchronously on the edge of a copy of the letter and then continued by phone and Zoom.

Kelly's Reaction: Selective Representations and Concealments Embarrass Me

One of the first things I noticed was that the language of the letter blurred physical and digital spaces. The letter talks about Cameron as "a good colleague to everyone in the room," not mentioning that the room was on Canvas. And many of the "rooms" in our praxis-focused MA program were online, a fact that was very appealing to Cameron as a chronically ill person. Looking at the recommendation again, I wondered, "Why was the wording so slippery?" The slipperiness of the language seemed heightened by other choices in the letter where I overtly mentioned the physical campus, such as offering an example about running into a colleague in the hallway. The letter concealed fundamental facts about Cameron (her disability) and our relationship (that we'd never met in person) and the MA program itself (which served a disproportionately high percentage of high-school teachers who needed additional credit hours to teach upper-level courses, and very few applicants to PhD programs).

When I asked Cameron what she thought of these concealments, Cameron responded over email:

> Hindsight is 20/20, of course, but I think we would have benefitted from a conversation about how to represent my disability in my recommendation. I do wonder what that conversation might have looked like, how the examples in [the] letter might have changed (to focus on my online writing pedagogy scholarship, for example), and whether we would have made different choices about representing my scholarly identity if I had identified my interest in disability studies at the time—I think it's easier to talk about identity when we can very directly tie it to our scholarly work.

These comments intrigued me. I wondered how the language I could have used to describe Cameron's teaching could have changed. For instance, in the letter I talk about her interactions with students over the discussion board by commenting, "Cameron's ability to positively impact students in the classroom is already strong, and . . . it will only get stronger with additional reading, training, and reflection." Again, the word "classroom" here suggests a physical space, rather than a digital one. What is lost and gained by this elision? What does it mean that I didn't realize it was there? By acknowledging Cameron's illness, could I have positioned this feedback as even more of a strength? Or talked about the way she could uniquely connect with online students as a student who had taken the majority of her graduate courses online? What insights had I missed because I hadn't talked with Cameron directly, hadn't made space for a collaborative conversation that could reveal rhetorical potentials (see Duffy, chapter 14, for more on collaboration)? Like Vanessa's realization that "grindstone terms" may have been showing up in her recommendations, my experience of carefully rereading the recommendation I wrote for Cameron helped me see the way that normative representations of able-bodiedness were sneaking into my recommendation. It was unintentional, of course, but it was also definitely there.

On the other hand, it also emerged that Cameron received the letter in productive ways. After I sent it to her for an initial review in December 2019, Cameron immediately wrote back that the letter "perfectly conveys" what she wanted it to. While Cameron thinks that direct conversations about representation in recommendations would have been helpful, she also perceived some of the language choices of which I was most critical as moments that gave her agency and power, which she describes below.

Cameron's Reaction: Recommendations Reveal Underlying Politics and Priorities

When Kelly shared her concerns that her language choices unintentionally obscured or obfuscated my disability and my "cripped" participation in academic spaces (Price 2011, 72), I was surprised and a little resistant, and it took me several conversations with Kelly and Vanessa to understand why. I wholeheartedly agree that students should have agency in how their identities are constructed and discussed in recommendations, but I also think that a single conversation about identity is an insufficient approach to true advocacy, mentorship, and inclusion. It's true that Kelly and I had not had that single conversation, and that we might have benefited from it; however, I felt that Kelly had shown me over the course of our work together that she was someone I could trust to advocate for my inclusion and participation in academic life, and I do feel positively represented in her letter. By deconstructing and reflecting on Kelly's rhetorical choices alongside Kelly, I realized that a meaningful and productive discussion of representation or disclosure cannot be a singular event on a recommendation prewriting checklist but, rather, must be a collaborative and ongoing conversation between an instructor and a student, built on a foundation of inclusivity, respect, and trust.

In rereading the letter and thinking through how Kelly's representation of my strengths and experiences shaped my own scholarly identity, I realized that the foundation for my interpretation of Kelly's letter was laid when Kelly proved herself to be an ally in other ways, by making her course curriculum, policies, and feedback practices accessible and inclusive. In *Mad at School: Rhetorics of Mental Disability and Academic Life*, Margaret Price (2011) offers an analysis of online learning as having the potential to "crip" some academic spaces by incorporating principles of Universal Design for Learning (UDL) to offer flexible and multiple modes of presence, participation, feedback, and communication for increased accessibility (76). Kelly demonstrated a commitment to inclusive and accessible teaching and mentoring practices in the way she structured her classes, and it enabled me to understand my "cripped" participation in academic spaces as valid and valuable (Price 2011, 72). She also invited me to provide feedback on how I was represented in the letter, which demonstrated to me an "attempt to construct conditions that invite—but don't coerce—revelation of disability" and difference (Wood 2017, 90). I am confident that if I had asked Kelly to more overtly represent my disability in the context of our work together, she would have done so respectfully and thoughtfully. I see similar connections from the classroom to the letter in Vanessa's case: Vanessa's ability to advocate for her students from diverse linguistic backgrounds was possible because she had already addressed linguistic diversity in her classes with them and positioned these qualities as unique and important strengths. Burnett and coauthors (2022) recommend "an intervention on this individual level . . . [where] letter writers can resist institutions' expectations and collaborate with applicants in the letter-writing process to grant the applicant greater agency." By opening the door to conversations about identity and inclusion, Kelly and Vanessa invite collaboration and promote student agency.

Rather than interpreting Kelly's rhetorical choices as "concealing" or "eliding" my disability and the virtual nature of my work, I interpreted Kelly's focus on my collegiality and scholarly collaboration as a *microrebellious* challenge to the normalizing and restricting conceptions of what it means to be an academic. Price defines microrebellions as acts of resistance which "get beyond the inside/outside notions of systems and houses to recognize that academic discourse is always already composed through and by the deviant" (2011, 72). Recommendations have historically been used for gatekeeping and have excluded disenfranchised students, and it can be a difficult balancing act to understand recommendations as both opportunities to protest exclusionary academic practices and to advocate for marginalized students in a potentially hostile system, all while still adhering to genre conventions and expectations. Price's microrebellions offer a way to accomplish those goals by allowing letter writers to construct a reality in which students' differences are naturally included and positioned as strengths in the academy rather than othered, overcompensated for, or ignored.

Like a lot of graduate students, I had major imposter syndrome applying to a PhD program, and like a lot of disabled academics, I had real concerns about how to disclose my disability and how that disclosure would be received in a new institution. Every disabled academic has a different approach to disability disclosure and for myriad reasons may choose not to disclose. Reading Kelly's letter was an intensely validating and fortifying experience for me, because Kelly insisted on the value of my work by not qualifying it as different or setting me apart from nondisabled, face-to-face candidates. For example, while Kelly worries over the possible erasure of my cripped participation and presence as a teacher because she did not note that I learned and worked online, I felt affirmed by her insistence that "Cameron will be—and already is—an excellent teacher," not just because it's positive feedback, but because her emphasis that I am a teacher, despite my never having met a student in person, helped quell doubts that my online experience could be accepted or valued in a face-to-face program. I had a similar feeling when I read her comment that I was "a careful, conscientious, and thorough colleague to everyone in the room"; the fact that the "room" was on Canvas didn't need an asterisk, because care and collegiality are valuable traits in a student and teacher regardless of the vehicle through which they are expressed. Kelly didn't other me in the space of the recommendation, which helped me navigate feeling othered and rhetorically contested in the academy at large. I also still laugh at Kelly's comment that "one book led to three more," because while she positions it as a positive attribute in her recommendation, it reminds me of all the times she guided me out of a rabbit-hole after my research took an unnecessary detour. Kelly resisted institutional expectations about the value of disabled students' participation by giving me the opportunity to see myself as someone who could belong, without reservation, equivocation, or stipulation.

To engage in these radical practices of inclusion and revision, we must first put in the work to make academic life accessible to marginalized students. Asking a student how they'd like their identity to be addressed and constructed in a recommendation is meaningless at best when coming from an authority figure who has not demonstrated a commitment to inclusive classroom and mentoring practices. Allyship, like collaboration, is a set of attitudes, as opposed to a set of procedures (see Duffy, chapter 14). Conversations about representation and identity construction cannot be items on a checklist, but must be informed by participatory design (Oswal and Meloncon 2021).

CONCLUSION

While a review committee will likely read a recommendation quickly once, a student may reflect on it more deeply. Especially within the context of a mentoring relationship, a recommendation may become a resource to facilitate the student's enculturation into a new space. In this way, a recommendation can be an empowering re-visioning of the candidate that projects parts of the past into a new future. Before engaging in this study, Kelly and Vanessa perceived writing recommendations as a largely invisible form of administrative labor with little positive impact on students (or on us). Now, after reflecting and collaborating, especially with Cameron's insights, we are more aware of our politics and our priorities, and we hope our three-phase study may prove useful to others. We have already suggested that letters should be shared with their recipients at an individual level. We offer suggestions below for revising our approaches to letters of recommendation at the institutional level.

Drawing on the concept of *metis*, we can artfully use the language of the university to ascribe value to labor the university doesn't often acknowledge, either as labor or as valuable. The Social Sciences Feminist Network Research Interest Group (2017) classifies letters of recommendation as a form of "care work" engaged in by faculty (231). The group's data suggests that such labor disproportionately affects marginalized faculty, including "faculty of color, sexual minorities, and individuals from disadvantaged backgrounds" (240). The research group suggests "making the visible invisible" through the development of "systems that link such labor with its economic value," including institutional student success and retention initiatives (241). Given the prominence of such initiatives at both Kelly's and Vanessa's institutions, we call on faculty to make such labor more visible by documenting the letters they're writing in their annual reviews and for their tenure files, noting in particular how such work professionalizes students and functions as a key aspect of teaching, advising, and mentoring students. If we collectively act to document and archive letters of recommendation, we can begin to foster conversations around this "occluded genre" (LaVecchia et al., introduction, 12).

We also call for recommenders to analyze, revise, and reflect on their letters periodically, with care and with students' input, so as to better understand the impact of the revising moves we make. Recommenders should undertake this work regularly, because approaches to recommendations can become entrenched, and recommenders can unconsciously fall into the trap of biased language, misrepresentation, or inattention. While individual letters could and should be reviewed with students, as is recommended by Burnett and coauthors (2022), we also suggest recommenders review a selection from their archive of letters with each other as an institutional intervention. Such work could be part of a professional development session focused specifically on student mentoring, becoming aware of implicit bias, and promoting inclusion. Such work could contribute to a better understanding of our individual and collective revisions of the genre across time.

The recommendation is an artifact that, while received by an outside reader we may never meet, is an output of a relational space that could mean a lot both to the writer and receiver, the recommender and the applicant. Advocating for students and navigating the "fraught negotiations" of "the body's role in meaning-making" alongside them—especially if their bodies and cultural or linguistic identities have not traditionally been welcomed in the academy—helps us re-vision who we are in the academy and may help students see themselves there too.

APPENDIX 5.A: KELLY'S LETTER OF RECOMMENDATION FOR CAMERON

December 22, 2019

To the Ball State University Admissions Committee:

I'm writing to express my enthusiastic support for Cameron Becker's application to Ball State's PhD program in Rhetoric and Composition. Cameron earned her MA from Indiana University East, where she took two of my graduate classes. Additionally, I was her faculty mentor on her capstone project, "Honoring the Legacy of Latin American Testimonio: Applying Decolonized Methodologies to Narratives of the Northern Triangle," a version of which appears in this application as her writing sample. Finally, I had the opportunity to see Cameron's teaching presence in one of the undergraduate classes she assisted with this fall. Based on these varied experiences over the course of a year, I can say without reservation: Cameron is a talented teacher-scholar who will be an asset to

Ball State's PhD program. In this letter, I want to briefly describe three of Cameron's standout strengths: her research, her teaching, and her collegiality.

Cameron has a strong and identifiable research trajectory. Many of her projects at IUE explore the intersections of multiculturalism, rhetoric, social justice, and pedagogy. Her capstone project foregrounds her interest in, as she puts it, "sourcing, amplifying, and analyzing" *testimonio* narratives to serve marginalized actors at the US southern border. As Cameron's mentor for this project, I was impressed that Cameron never stopped reading as she was researching; one book led to three more. As she researched, she consistently asked me for recommendations, wondering, for example, how to shape her literature review so that it was as pointed and argumentative as possible. Following our conference, she read several short advice pieces on the topic and analyzed two recently published articles. In addition to pursuing her interests through vigorous inquiry, Cameron has demonstrated an interest in participating in a research conversation that extends beyond her institution. As Cameron was working on her capstone project, for example, she found herself relying heavily on recent scholarship from Patricia DeRocher and Cruz Medina, both of whom have made the case that polyvocal, digital *testimonios* are necessary to revitalize the genre. Cameron took initiative in wanting to share her work with these scholars, and I reached out to them on her behalf in November. Medina and DeRocher will be sending Cameron feedback on her capstone project in January. I mention this because Cameron is not a student who works in isolation; even at the MA level, she is seeing research as a community-based activity in which one engages conversation with others to move projects forward. Finally, Cameron is a talented writer with genuine skill in revision, which can be a difficult process for graduate student writers. Cameron impressed me with her ability to receive feedback and thoughtfully respond with much-improved work. Her persistence in refining her work leads me to believe that she will have much success in pursuing publication. Moreover, the topics she wants to pursue matter; they matter to her personally and they matter to the field. When I shared her capstone project with two other faculty members in our program for their review, both came back with compliments on Cameron's ability to focus on significant questions. Her testimonio project had so many promising elements to it; clearly, it is the seed of much work that is to come.

Next, Cameron will be—and already is—an excellent teacher. While in graduate courses at IUE, she's put together two complete course plans, one of which focuses on teaching multiculturalism in a writing-course context. In my own classes, I've read through two smaller pedagogy assignments, and both impressed me. In each case, Cameron moved from theories about teaching that we'd read for the course to practical applications that were highly relevant for student writers. She has creative ideas for incorporating analyses of students' social media into writing classes, and an awareness of how to design writing assignments to foreground the interests that students bring to the class. Based on her thoughtful and systematic approach to designing teaching materials, I was unsurprised to see how effective Cameron is in the classroom. This fall, she began serving as a Course Assistant (CA) in several writing courses, including a section of first-year writing class taught by a friend of mine. Three weeks into the term, my friend caught me in the hallway. "Cameron Becker is amazing!" she enthused. "I love her feedback to students!" Later, when I observed this class in my capacity as the Writing Director, I could see what my friend meant: Cameron has an ability to connect with students over feedback, personalizing her comments to them in a way that fosters care while also communicating high expectations. My sense, based on reading Cameron's teaching materials and seeing her interactions with students, is that Cameron's ability to positively impact students in the classroom is already strong, and that it will only get stronger with additional reading, training, and reflection.

Finally, Cameron is a generous and insightful colleague, and she is particularly gifted in fostering community among students and faculty. One especially wonderful story about this unfolded in our recent class on style. Students' final projects involved sourcing three scholarly articles on a topic of their interest and creating a multimodal presentation directed to classmates. Unsurprisingly, Cameron chose to explore how style and multiculturalism intersect. What took this presentation to the next level, however, was that she began the presentation by foregrounding questions her colleagues had posed on the discussion board over the course of the semester. As this story suggests, Cameron demonstrates deep listening to her classmates. Her presence encourages the best participation of the others in the class. She is a careful, conscientious, and thorough colleague to everyone in the room. The effect of these efforts is that the classroom community is stronger than it would be without her, and the discussions go further. In response to Cameron's presentation quoted above, for example, several students responded in uniquely personal and specific ways. One wrote: "I thought the way that you incorporated questions that had come from our earlier discussions was a fascinating way to tackle this project."

In all, Cameron's fundamental intellectual curiosity, skillful written communication, and ability to foster community make her a very good fit for doctoral-level work in the field of rhetoric and composition. Please let me know if I can elaborate on any of the above. I can be reached at 765-973-8637.

Best,
Kelly Blewett
Dr. Kelly Blewett
Writing Program Director
Assistant Professor of English
Indiana University East

NOTE

1. Name changed to protect student's anonymity.

REFERENCES

Bouton, Lawrence. 1995. "A Cross-Cultural Analysis of the Structure and Content of Letters of Reference." *Studies in Second Language Acquisition* 17 (2): 211–44.

Burnett, Rebecca E., Rebekah Fitzsimmons, Courtney A. Hoffman, and Patricia R. Taylor. 2022. "Fixing the Broken Letter-of-Recommendation Process." *Inside Higher Education*, June 14, 2022. https://www.insidehighered.com/advice/2022/06/14/writers-and-students-should-collaborate-recommendation-letters-opinion.

Colarelli, Stephen, Regina Hechanova Alampay, and Kristopher G. Canali. 2002. "Letters of Recommendation: An Evolutionary Psychological Perspective." *Human Relations* 55 (3): 315–44.

Dolmage, Jay. 2020. "What Is Metis?" *Disability Studies Quarterly* 40 (1). https://doi.org/10.18061/dsq.v40i1.7224.

Greenburg, A. Gerson, Jennifer Doyle, and D. K. McClure. 1994. "Letters of Recommendation for Surgical Residences: What They Say and What They Mean." *Journal of Surgical Research*, no. 56, 192–98.

Grote, Christopher L., William N. Robiner, and Allyson Haut. 2001. "Disclosure of Negative Information in Letters of Recommendation: Writers' Intentions and Readers' Experiences." *Professional Psychology: Research and Practice* 32 (6): 655–61.

Lu, Min-Zhan, and Bruce Horner. 2013. "Translingual Literacy, Language Difference, and Matters of Agency." *College English* 75 (6): 582–607.

Oswal, Sushil K., and Lisa Meloncon. 2017. "Saying No to the Checklist: Shifting from an Ideology of Normalcy to an Ideology of Inclusion in Online Writing Instruction." *Writing Program Administration* 40 (3): 61–77.

Precht, Kristen. 1998. "A Cross-Cultural Comparison of Letters of Recommendation." *English for Specific Purposes* 17 (3): 241–65.

Price, Margaret. 2011. *Mad at School: Rhetorics of Mental Disability and Academic Life*. Ann Arbor: University of Michigan Press.

Sohan, Vanessa Kraemer. 2020. *Lives, Letters, and Quilts: Women and Everyday Rhetorics of Resistance*. Tuscaloosa: University of Alabama Press.

Social Sciences Feminist Network Research Interest Group. "The Burden of Invisible Work in Academia: Social Inequalities and Time Use in Five University Departments." *Humboldt Journal of Social Relations* 39 (2017): 228–45. http://www.jstor.org/stable/90007882.

Stewart, Abigail J., and Virginia Valian. 2018. *An Inclusive Academy: Achieving Diversity and Excellence*. Cambridge, MA: MIT Press.

Trix, Frances, and Carolyn Psenka. 2003. "Exploring the Color of Glass: Letters of Recommendation for Female and Male Medical Faculty." *Discourse and Society* 14 (2): 191–220.

Vidali, Amy. 2009. "Rhetorical Hiccups: Disability Disclosure in Letters of Recommendation." *Rhetoric Review* 28 (2): 185–204.

Wood, Tara. 2017. "Rhetorical Disclosures: The Stakes of Disability Identity in Higher Education." In *Negotiating Disability: Disclosure and Higher Education*, edited by Stephanie L. Kerschbaum, Laura T. Eisenman, and James M. Jones: 75–93. Ann Arbor: University of Michigan Press.

6
CREATING AND HOLDING SPACE AS REVISION IN WPA LIVES

Christy I. Wenger

I have learned as much about hopeful revision on my yoga mat as I have at my computer. Revision occurs in the space between what is and what can be. As Bruce Ballenger and Kelly Myers learn from studying student writers, what our *writing* can be is as intimately personal as what *we* can be: revision is fueled by "a tension between who we are and who [we] want to be" (2019, 592). What WPA cannot relate to this insight? In my eleven years on the job, I actively revised my identity many times based on who I wanted to be. When I began my first WPA job, I began revising my identity from graduate student to writing expert and professional—a hopeful and forward-looking revision at that time. I manifested these identity revisions through my actions as a WPA: in big ways, like sitting on the university core curriculum committee to lend my expertise across campus; and in smaller ways, like encouraging my students to take food leftovers after a workshop, like I had done so many times myself as a student. I also wrote my way through these identity revisions—in professional articles and in less widely public genres like my university's annual review.

I revise to take advantage of the potential between what is and what can be. I revise as a means to create myself anew on the page and, therefore, in real life. In this chapter, I examine how revision, when motivated by mindfulness, makes transformative growth possible. My annual review over the past ten years at my current institution has both engaged me in mindful revision and enabled me to relate, and to create my professional identity, as a WPA. Revising my annual review has allowed me to mindfully construct my WPA identity by purposefully documenting my labor and creating a space for my work in a genre that at first felt silencing. Revising my annual review has taught me how to pause judgment about my WPA labor to create and hold a space for my agency and self-expression.

HOLDING SPACE AS MINDFUL REVISION

The first three annual reviews I submitted as a pre-tenure writing professor and WPA were quite literally defined by a lack of space for my burgeoning identity as WPA. As a yogi, I recognize that everything changes and that my desperate clinging to stability is the cause of my suffering. Yoga, through the physical movement practice of *asana* and the mental training of meditation, literally teaches us to "go with the flow" through the cultivation of mindfulness. The annual review doesn't seem like a document permitted to "flow," given its rigid structures and high-stakes nature; however, approaching this document with mindfulness can help to change our orientation to what spaces are allowable and what spaces can be created in such professional work genres. While practices of mindfulness have a long history and stem from Eastern traditions and from Buddhism, John Kabat-Zinn introduced contemporary mindfulness study to the Western world. John Kabat-Zinn defines mindfulness as "paying attention in a particular way: on purpose, in the present moment, and nonjudgmentally" (1994, 4). Kabat-Zinn's secular mindfulness is what I apply here.

Mindfulness is a process of confronting dissonance, like the dissonance encountered in revision, but its successful end is the *pausing* of judgment not the anticipation of it. In this way, we can both hold space for who we are in that moment and see the potential of who we might become. Holding space is the conscious act of being present in the moment and allowing for what we or others need in that moment; it is creating a safe, nonjudgmental space to process feelings, ascertain identifications, recognize emotion, and attend to your own or another's needs. This heuristic of paused judgment to create space for hopeful transformation through revision is what I want to explore and expand upon as a strategy of mindful revision when applied to the annual review.

My university's annual review is a seemingly straightforward but ultimately vague genre divided into four sections: teaching, research, public service, and plans for next year. Genres like the annual review "are not merely passive backdrops for our actions or simply familiar tools we use to convey or categorize information; rather, [these] genres function more like rhetorical ecosystems" (Bawarshi 2003, 82), and we can both reproduce and disrupt these systems through revision. When I complete my annual review each year to note the service, teaching, and research I have accomplished, I enter a rhetorical ecosystem meant to create my professional identity. And that identity can be reactive to an audience, but it can also be responsive to the self's own needs when approached mindfully.

The annual review is itself a palimpsest of academic labor, an artifact of revision, typically inscribed over each year rather than created anew. This reinscription itself creates a hopefulness of revision that opens a space for mindfulness. How I revise can be inspired by a mindfulness of what is *and* what can be, as I have learned slowly over the years. Each year, I make a copy of last year's document and revise over it, like so many of my colleagues. Mike Garcia calls these "zero drafts," these patch-written documents whose inception is cutting and pasting, a process of drafting that supports the writer to compose in unknown genres and as shows solidarity to the work that has come before (chapter 11, 142). As an inexperienced writer of the annual review fearing the judgment of my chair, dean, and review committee, I did little to disrupt the genre at first and instead focused on changes "made in compliance with abstract rules about the product, rules that quite often do not apply to the specific problems in the text" (Sommers 1980, 383). Indeed, my first annual review contains no explicit mention of my WPA work at all. Here is an excerpt of the service section, where I would later begin to document my WPA labor:

Year 1 Annual Review:
III. Professional and Public Service

Service:
    University:
        N/A

    Department:
        Chair of General Studies Composition Committee

That first year, I did not include my title as Director of Writing and Rhetoric anywhere on my review. The only representation of my labor as WPA was the single line detailing my department service as chair of the General Studies Composition Committee. This representation doesn't distinctly mark my work as WPA, because the committee existed before my hire and was dedicated to writing in general studies courses across the university. As the first WPA position on my campus, I inherited the committee and a specific representation of what it meant to "do" writing on campus.

My first review was essentially a revision, and not a mindful one at that. I did what many new hires do: I asked a colleague for a copy of her review and revised it to create my own. The colleague I asked was hired exactly one year before me and hadn't taken on any university committee work in her first year either, so I kept her description after university service, using her very sterile "N/A," even though my work as WPA engaged me in university service from my first moment on campus—and chairing general studies writing ensured that I was really doing that university-level work, even if I didn't represent it on the annual review because I was told by my department chair that my service was department-level. I also kept my review to 5.5 pages, since her model was just about as long.

In this review, I was motivated by the judgment of readers who expected rule-following above all else. As a new faculty member coming straight from graduate school to this WPA position, the desire to fit into preexisting categories of identity and labor, to follow the prior models of the academic review, was compelling: "following" was indeed my primary motivation for revision. I knew my department chair, my dean, and the review committee of tenured professors would be reading my review. I therefore was more reactive to others than responsive to the spaces I needed in this review, the latter of which is required for mindful revision. Indeed, my first year on the job wasn't dictated much by mindfulness; I felt invisible on campus as a WPA and reactive to a writing culture I inherited. While I identified as WPA foremost, my colleagues didn't recognize this identification since I was my campus's first WPA. Instead, I was identified as a member of the English Department, where the writing program was housed and where the general studies composition committee lived. The ignorance surrounding my position frustrated me, but I didn't know yet how to intervene.

I was an inexperienced writer approaching a new genre for the first time and was unable to see my revision process as a techne. My review was a tangible illustration of this writing process. I saw my writing of the annual review as translating standing conventions and expectations. I therefore lacked the ability in those beginning annual reviews "to review [my] work again, as it were, with different eyes, and to start over" (Sommers 1980, 382). What I have since learned and what I document here is how revising professional documents like annual reviews can reveal the productive knowledge of the revision process, which allows us to intervene and invent the rhetorical ecosystem of the university—a gesture of mindfulness that inspires agency. I have learned, as Ellery Sills and Fernando Sánchez in this collection note, "documents conveying one's professional identity are not only communicative but formative as well" (53). Indeed, with each annual review completed, my allegiance to mindfulness grew stronger.

By year two, my confidence as a WPA had grown, and I began to tackle serious revision projects both in the writing program through curricular revision and in the core curriculum through committee efforts in writing across the curriculum. With more campus influence and more revision experience, I began to experiment with a more detailed description of my labor as WPA, even if I didn't identify it yet under such a title. I was now practicing revision as a techne, an act of productive knowledge that both invents and intervenes in the world, simultaneously creating and amending what is possible (Atwill 1998, 2)—in order to intervene if not yet invent an identity for myself as WPA. This was a mindful practice of using revision to create a space for my work where none before existed:

Year Two Annual Review:
III. Professional and Public Service

Service:
   University:
      Member of Assessment Task Force Committee

   Department:
      Chair of General Studies Composition Committee
      Revised ENGL 101, 102, 103, 104 common syllabi
      Worked to establish writing across the curriculum pathways
      Established faculty writing groups

I still didn't include my director title in year two, but I did provide more detail about the projects I did as a WPA, even if I couldn't nest them under tidy committees like my colleagues could do on their reviews. Nevertheless, this was a beginning attempt at mindful revision that created space on the review for my burgeoning identity as a WPA, an intervention in the genre that began to insert my labor into this space to make it legible to others and to myself.

By year three, I had, if not a better understanding of the annual review genre, a clearer understanding of the work involved in being the first-ever WPA and the first pre-tenure administrator on my campus. In three years on the job, I had revised the 101 and 102 curricula based on the WPA Outcomes Statement and the Framework for Success in Postsecondary Writing, created assessment plans for our first- and second-semester writing classes, established monthly professional development opportunities for teachers, created collaborative leadership opportunities through committees and regular meetings with my teachers, met monthly for writing and reading groups, and reduced our dependence on adjunct labor by successfully advocating for the creation of the first-ever non-tenure-track (NTT) teaching lines at the university. And my work was just starting.

I began to feel frustrated by the structure of the annual review, which didn't seem well suited to represent my labor. As my identification as a WPA grew, I began to question the ways my review silenced my administrative labor. For instance, teaching was an action directed only toward students; teaching teachers through professional development—a common and persistent task of WPAs—was actively erased. How did I represent this work on my review when there was no space for it, no allowance for administrative labor that transgressed the boundaries of the traditional categories? I compromised. This was the first year I listed my work as WPA explicitly and under the university service heading. I had begun that year to talk intentionally and purposefully to higher administration about the writing program as a *university* program. And so, my descriptions of the labor became longer on the review, and my labor was categorized as a department and university benefit:

Year Three Annual Review:
III. Professional and Public Service

Service:
    University:
        Director of Rhetoric and Composition
        Wrote proposals for ENGL 101, 102 for adoption to Core curriculum
        Established learning communities within the university
        Coordinated faculty writing groups
        Member of Women's Studies Committee
        Member of Faculty Awards Committee
        Member of Assessment Task Force Committee
        Member of Common Reading Committee and Special Projects

    Department:
        Chair of General Studies Composition Committee
        AP Committee
        Ad Hoc: Wrote proposals for ENGL 101 and 102 (updates to Core curriculum)
        Coordinator and Chair of Faculty Writing Groups
        Chair of General Studies Composition Committee
        Created a "monthly writing challenge" for the department

    Special Projects:
        Worked with the office of Institutional Research to compile data about the first-year writing program and to conduct assessment of the program
        Worked with Academic Support Center to increase connection between first-year writing and the Center
        Developed and implemented an assessment plan for first-year writing program
        Advocated for separate writing program budget

This revision was an act of mindfulness and creation of space for my emerging and developing sense as a career WPA. Even so, I remember how much it bothered me to write my title under service. I was hesitant to pigeonhole directing a writing program as simply "service" after internalizing lessons from Susan Miller's "Sad Woman in the Basement" (1991) and hearing tragic stories from colleagues at other universities. Plus, WPA work wasn't a committee, which is how service was classified on the annual review template. But meaningfully accounting for all the work I had accomplished would entail a large-scale revision, the consequences of which felt scary and unknown as a pre-tenure WPA. As Laura Micciche points out in *Doing Emotion: Rhetoric, Writing, Teaching*, "the WPA must navigate the murky waters of institutional hierarchy where decisions to create any sort of change are seriously constrained; where daily existence requires pragmatic, sometimes morally problematic decisions, and where one's ability to act on one's conscience or political ideas is seriously compromised" (2007, 84). Claiming my WPA status was an act of writing myself into the space, of holding space for my WPA identity in an ecosystem that didn't yet recognize it. To further intervene, I added a "special projects" category to list my WPA labor and make it visible even though it didn't fit in the preexisting categories. This was just the beginning of my intervention. I waited to be told that I could not add categories of my own, to be reprimanded for my mindful revisions as they challenged accepted conventions of this genre. Interestingly, I received no comment about my revisions, which emboldened me to make more changes in my next report.

Going into the fourth year on the job, I was determined to hold even more space for myself as WPA within the pages of my annual report even if that meant dramatic revisions without a sense of how they might be received. While I didn't hear any feedback about my revisions from the year prior, I was still concerned that the bolder my revisions, the more I might jeopardize the work I was doing to build a writing culture on campus. My work was to build a writing program that was less reactive to current academic labor conditions and presumptions about my WPA labor and, as a result, more responsive, more mindful, to my ambitions and goals. Ironically, I worried that the very act of writing my work into the annual report, of refusing to be erased by the genre, would bring negative attention to that work. Even so, I wanted to better recognize and reward my labor—if only for myself. For example, I was tired of not being able to represent my teaching *of teachers* through continuous professional development as teaching or my creation of hundreds of university-level proposals, accreditation documents, and program handbooks as a significant portion of my scholarship. The annual review, by design, only recognized teaching aimed at a student audience, not an audience of faculty and staff, unless this teaching was codified as "service," an inscription of labor that again felt reactive to existing categories and not responsive to the writing culture I was striving to bring about through my writing as much as my actions.

I realized that creating space for myself as WPA meant that I had to create recognized textual spaces to document my WPA work, where at first none were evident. My prior revisions proved that to me. It's not that I faced critique from my first three annual reports; indeed, my departmental reviews were glowing and my path toward tenure looked secure. My revision work was motivated by my need to see what space the review might hold for my desired WPA identity, a way to both recognize my labor and write myself into being. Revision of annual reviews allows us to "start over," to transform "what is" into "what is possible" (Atwill 1998, 70), creating agency for WPAs to change how they represent their professional identities, which can lend itself to eventual curriculum and program change. For example, I was able to successfully argue for my university's first NTT faculty lines because of the visibility I created for the writing program as distinct from the English Department. This was in part due to the efforts of my annual reviews claiming a space for my work as WPA. My then provost, who approved those NTT faculty hires, mentioned to me that he was beginning to see how adding those lines was not in service to the English Department (since faculty lines are typically claimed as such) but rather a benefit to the entire university. This recognition was a huge step forward. Our WPA textual artifacts have the power to incite major change (Graben and Ryan 2005, 91) over our programs and ourselves.

Who could I be in my annual review if I revised it to reflect what I did and who I wanted to be as WPA instead of following its templates so closely? Using mindfulness as a lens has helped me answer this question. Mindfulness can help WPAs to resee revision as a self-generative process of creating productive knowledge that is less concerned with the judgment of others and more invested in creating our own presence through the act of holding space. As Kabat-Zinn notes, "Mindfulness provides a simple but powerful route for getting ourselves unstuck . . . it is a way to take charge of the direction and quality of our own lives, including our relationships . . . [and] our relationship with ourself as a person" (1994, 5). Mindfulness certainly did help me get "unstuck" as a writer, by providing a means for me to hold space and establish presence in my reviews.

Holding space became a mindful revision strategy that led me to rewrite the university-sanctioned annual review to add my own "WPA Philosophy and Addendum" section, which I have now included for seven years, during which time it has changed to both represent and produce my administrative leadership. The section serves to listen to, acknowledge, and establish my presence as a WPA. Listening to myself mindfully as I revised the review meant that I had to meaningfully represent what I had accomplished as WPA over the past year and from the moment I set foot on campus. For instance, in my section on curricular design, before I could discuss my more recent revisions to incorporate multimodality into our courses, I needed to first discuss how there was no curriculum per se when I arrived, just a loose assemblage of courses. So, I provided enough detail to fully explain my scaffolded labor. In creating this narrative of my work, I was holding space for complicated labor, such as building relationships across campus, establishing a consistent curriculum, and supporting contingent faculty, all of which came before more current changes to modernize our program. But I was also revising the very nature of the annual review itself.

Acknowledging my work in the review wasn't simply a matter of listing the tasks I completed, as my first three reviews illustrate. Instead, for me it meant calling out the silence of WPA work in order to call attention to the first three years of my WPA career, which were defined by a lack of space for my identity and therefore a lack of documentation of my work. To begin to acknowledge this work and the persistent challenges in documenting it within our professional genres, I modeled the Addendum after the position statement by the Council for Writing Program Administrators, "Evaluating the Intellectual Work of Writing Administration." I began the Addendum with an explanation:

> The work of a writing program administrator is often invisible within university structures, especially when they are situated as I am within a department and without formal reporting structures to the Provost and/ or Dean. Because they are traditional measures of review within the university, teaching and research are generally accepted and understood as intellectual and professional activities of merit, worthy of tenure and promotion. Administration should be viewed in similar terms, according to the national Council for Writing Program Administrators (CWPA) position statement on "Evaluating the Intellectual Work of Writing Administration."[1]
>
> The goal of this document is to argue for the intellectual and professional merit of WPA work that produces new knowledge and requires and demonstrates scholarly expertise and disciplinary knowledge.

The WPA position statement helped me to create an official, recognized space for my labor and set a context for my description of it in the document. It also provided an exigence for my revisions to the review, which is just one of the many university structures that keep this labor invisible. After acknowledging my labor and setting the stage for its context, I finished my framing of the addendum by articulating my intention to establish presence for myself as a WPA in the annual review document:

> I have created this addendum to my annual review in order to create space for the work I do as a writing program administrator as Director of Writing on campus. I am guided by the CWPA's statement in the structure and purpose of this addendum. I also use their suggested guidelines for evaluating writing administrators, what they call the "five categories of intellectual work" (2019, 11) to organize the kinds of duties I regularly perform as an administrator. The five categories are:
>
> 1. Program Creation and Maintenance
> 2. Curricular Design and Implementation
> 3. Faculty Development
> 4. Program Assessment and Evaluation
> 5. Program-Related Textual and Knowledge Production
>
> I take each category in turn below.

I organized the Addendum using these five categories and offered a narrative in each section to help explain not only new changes that occurred that year to help support actions in program creation and maintenance but also the revisions that I had previously undertaken to support the new changes. The Addendum itself became a testament through rich historical narrative of the revisions of the writing program throughout the years I have led it. This major revision to my annual report has created my administrative identity as a WPA, because it has helped establish a narrative of my administrative labor on campus, sanctioning it and making it visible. I have now been a WPA at my university for ten years; my last annual review was forty-six pages long, and thirty of these pages are my WPA Addendum. I have worked under several provosts and deans during this time, and each has commented on how they better understand my administrative work based on my review; not one person has critiqued my revisions or told me to shorten the review. The acceptance of my revisions reaffirms to me how important it is for WPAs to take charge of textual spaces like the annual review as a means of detailing the work we are doing and of creating the narrative of that work in ways that we control and in an effort to help craft our programs mindfully based on our goals.

My practice of mindful revision and holding space has helped create a narrative of my administrative labor on campus that is now better recognized by other stakeholders, but it has also, and more importantly, helped me to establish my presence as a WPA and to grow my understanding of that work. It has, in other words, allowed me to see where I can take my ideas and where they can take me. And that has provided me significant autonomy. For instance, when several faculty administrative positions were recently scrutinized and found to not have updated job descriptions, upper administration took it upon themselves to craft these without input from the faculty holding those positions. I was not among those faculty, because I was told that my annual review essentially updates my job description each year. Each year, as I revise my review, I am able to see threads of connection in my work that tie my efforts together. I have seen proof of my experiments in collaborative leadership with my NTT writing faculty and my attempts to create inclusive, online pedagogy that have spurred new research interests and helped to shape how I understand myself as a WPA. My mindful revision efforts have helped me to actualize "the art of rhetoric as a valued mode of intervention into existing conditions and a means for the invention of new possibilities" (189). What has been invented, in turn, is me-as-WPA.

The revision process is complex, as any writer knows. As my annual reviews illustrate, writers often visualize and (re)write ourselves into being through revision. Approaching mindful revision as a means of holding space for oneself can reveal additional motivations for the revision process, which can reveal new ways to talk about and teach revision in and beyond our classes. Writers, both student and professional, benefit from a learned practice of mindfully holding space for themselves on the page to test the limits of where we can go when we start from a place of mindful revision.

NOTE

1. Please see the following for the full CWPA statement: http://wpacouncil.org/positions/intellectualwork.html.

REFERENCES

Atwill, Janet M. 1998. *Rhetoric Reclaimed: Aristotle and the Liberal Arts Tradition.* Ithaca, NY: Cornell University Press.

Ballenger, Bruce, and Kelly Myers. 2019. "The Emotional Work of Revision." *CCC* 70 (4): 590–614.

Bawarshi, Anis S. 2003. "Genre and the Invention of the Writer: Reconsidering the Place of Invention in Composition." Logan: Utah State University Press.

Council of Writing Program Administrators. 2019. *Evaluating the Intellectual Work of Writing Administration*. First published 1998. WPA. https://wpacouncil.org/aws/CWPA/pt/sd/news_article/242849/_PARENT/layout_details/false.

Elbow, Peter. 1994. "Ranking, Evaluating, Liking: Sorting Out Three Forms of Judgment." *College English* 55 (2): 187–206. https://scholarworks.umass.edu/eng_faculty_pubs/12.

Graben, Tarez Samra, and Kathleen Ryan. 2005. "From 'What Is' to 'What Is Possible': Theorizing Curricular Document Revision as In(ter)vention and Reform." *WPA* 28 (3): 89–112.

Kabat-Zinn, Jon. 1994. *Wherever You Go, There You Are: Mindfulness Meditation in Everyday Life*. New York: Hyperion.

Micciche, Laura R. 2007. *Doing Emotion: Rhetoric, Writing, Teaching*. Portsmouth, NH: Heinemann.

Miller, Susan. "The Sad Women in the Basement." Textual Carnivals: The Politics of Composition. Southern Illinois UP. 1991. 121–41.

Sommers, Nancy. 1980. "Revision Strategies of Student Writers and Experienced Adult Writers." *CCC* 31 (4): 378–88.

SET 3

Revision Approaches Feedback

Laura R. Micciche

Writing in communities of practice is something of a theme throughout this book. In the last set, revising cover letters, letters of recommendation, and annual reviews are acts inflected by membership in or on the edges of specific communities. How do we revise our way into academic spaces? How do we create or assert belonging through writing? These questions permeate the previous chapters and function as background in this set, which deals with publication as a path toward belonging but also lingers on the idiosyncrasies of each author's labor. Among other things, we are privy to external factors that influenced the paths writers in this set ended up following.

Authors attempt to show revision in progress, marking a deep contrast between what revising looks like at certain moments and its tendency, as Joseph Harris says, "to be hidden from view" (2017, 100). Because of the way labor is concealed by finished texts, Harris notes that "it can often seem as though other writers work, as it were, without ever blotting a line, confidently progressing through their texts from start to finish, paragraph to paragraph, chapter to chapter, as if they were speaking them aloud" (2017, 100). Writers in this set resist that image of the writer by inserting us in the messy, time-hungry, circuitous fits and starts of writing marked by productive and unproductive external interventions: technical problems that stopped Rich Shivener in his tracks, a negative review leading to heightened imposter syndrome for Dana Comi, a too-quick dismissal by an editor for Cruz Medina. There are no shiny surfaces in the following chapters by Shivener, Comi and Alisa Russell, and Medina—all of whom narrate how revising intersects with feedback, time, reflection, feeling, and professional status.

Revision, for these writers, is not a chance to get something right the second time around. It's a dialectical process that has no clear beginning or ending points, calling to mind Ann Berthoff's "allatonceness" (read as "all at onceness") as the reality of revising, which she frames as "a resource, not the mother of dilemmas" (1981, 21). During composing, which is not separate from revising for Berthoff, "everything has to happen at once or it does not happen at all" (21). This might be why revision is hard to see or show, relenting to the appearance of ease and sure-footedness in finished texts that Harris describes. Through re-creation of back-and-forth dialogue with others or with one another in the case of Comi and Russell, authors in the third set offer a glimpse of the dullness beneath the shine of finished texts. By showing us that revising is happening as new ideas form, as tangents are pursued and abandoned, as disappointments mount, these writers help us embrace the allatonceness of revising as a resource for getting real about what it takes to produce intellectual work.

From the other side of the desk, Raúl Sánchez too shows us that learning how to give feedback toward revision is a fits-and-starts process that requires practice, deliberate care, and an ability to grasp the allatonceness of the task, which is about more than writing or reviewing. The reviewer's job "is to recognize that the author is consciously situating their work in certain epistemological contexts, contexts that they are inviting readers to learn about, if they don't already know them, because doing so deepens and widens the discipline's knowledge base. And, having recognized this attempt, my job is to help the author succeed at it." To that end, Sánchez urges reviewers, especially senior faculty, to not be "Reviewer 2," or, as he puts it, to not be a dick. Framed as an "ethical, professional, and moral obligation," not being a dick asks reviewers to combat the critique imperative and instead train themselves to read openly before forming judgments that would forestall helpful feedback.

Together, these chapters are about a search for words and framing and organization. But, they are also about an *assisted* search for researcher identity, meaning that others—collaborators, mentors, editors, and peers—aid the search. As writers articulate the relationship between revision and identity, they get personal. Medina describes the early drafts of his article, which he had submitted to NCTE journals, as requiring him to "contort [his] writing to something it wasn't," prolonging the revision process by years. Shivener describes months of "mulling over and crying a lot about a book proposal . . . caught between mixed reviews from prospective editors and my indecision about the book's approach and delivery." Russell looks back at what she now views as thoughtful and clear feedback on a twice-rejected article and muses that "perhaps I didn't understand enough about how articles work in the field to grasp what this feedback was suggesting." Comi characterizes her revision story as one about "waiting, and waiting, to have the confidence to actually make revisions and move forward." And R. Sánchez calls out the peer review process as "no place (in fact, is one of the worst places) for competition, egoism, animosity, pettiness, and other forms of aggression that we dignify as 'rigor.'"

In their various ways, these chapters link revision, and feedback leading to revision, to stages of professional identity and the different forms of labor associated with those stages. These themes are further illuminated in and expanded by the fourth set of readings, which address high stakes revision, collaborative revising, and the presence of the outside world in the life of texts.

REFERENCES

Berthoff, Ann E. 1981. "Recognition, Representation, and Revision." *Basic Writing* 3 (3): 19–32.

Harris, Joseph. 2017. *Rewriting: How to Do Things with Texts*. 2nd ed. Logan: Utah State University Press.

7
ON THE SLIPPAGES AND SWELLS OF REVISING DIGITAL MEDIA

Rich Shivener

INTRODUCTION

In *Cruel Auteurism: Affective Digital Mediations toward Film-Composition*, bonnie kyburz argues that "with the generous range of compositional options open to us for scholarship, teaching, and learning, we are more fully able to act on our capacities for engaging our vibratory affects in ways that delight, provoke, and at the same time articulate rhetorical dispositions and creative vision" (kyburz 2019, 15). In response to kyburz and new initiatives to make visible the editorial workflows of digital scholarship (Ball 2021), this chapter foregrounds revisions I made while transforming a print article into chapters for a digital book. I focus on revisions that were ripe with feelings, from uncertainty to joy. To shed light on these revisions and the feelings entwined with them, I also refer in this chapter to a companion video (see this book's website) that features segments in which I revise text, web pages, and audio.

Preparing a text for the web is not a matter of copy-pasting the text of an article into HTML web pages. Rather, revising a print article for a digital book demands significant changes to text and media unavailable in print-centric composing processes; it demands using available means and media to layer argumentation with the feelings of and between an author, her writing tools, and source materials. To demonstrate such an idea, this chapter is organized by a series of time-stamped "slippages and swells," what Lauren Berlant and Kathleen Stewart call felt experiences and sensations of pain and pleasure encountered during composing and revising (Berlant and Stewart 2019, 58). Behind-the-scenes stories of pain and pleasure that shape digital media scholarship are few in number when we look at the field's recent publications (see Tulley 2018). In the journal *Kairos: A Journal of Rhetoric, Technology, and Pedagogy*, the "Inventio" section has eighteen entries over its twenty-five-year-plus history, the fewest in number among its sections. Those of us in academic

https://doi.org/10.7330/9781646425501.c007

positions, with digital tools and resources available to us, ought to make our revision processes public for fellow creators. Discussing our slippages and swells better aligns our field with the long, rich history of public "postmortem" documents that game developers write. In postmortems, developers detail and reflect on the many moving parts of a game (Brown 2015; Politowski et al. 2018; Shahbazi 2018). Public documentation is a means for sharing what Tim Lockridge and Derek Van Ittersum call workflow thinking, "a lens through which [writers] can look at their broader writing process and begin to analyze the connections, intersections, and fissures within the component parts of their work" (Lockridge and Van Ittersum 2020, "Chapter 1"). In the spirit of postmortems and workflow thinking, this chapter and its companion video center on my process and the feelings that encompassed several parts of a digital book project.

This chapter's sections are narrated in present tense in order to make feelings of revision more immediate and immersive. In addition to narrating moments of revision, I close with two practical suggestions for documenting revisions with digital tools Open Broadcaster Software (OBS) and GitHub. Finally, I encourage readers to check out the companion video of this chapter for multimodal renderings of the slippages and swells discussed here. In-text references in the chapter direct readers to corresponding segments in the video.

DECEMBER 4, 2020: REVISING A PROPOSAL IN DEVELOPMENT HELL

For the past few months, I have been mulling over and crying a lot about a book proposal. The proposal has been in development hell, caught between mixed reviews from prospective editors and my indecision about the book's approach and delivery. Should it be print or digital? For sale or open-access? What the hell do I do with all of this multimodal qualitative data—audio interviews, screen recordings—that I've gathered over the last two years? Should I filter it into textual paragraphs or transform that data into audio and video segments? These questions are commonplace for prospective authors of digital media scholarship. For me, print seemed easier and more streamlined, while digital seemed overwhelming and time-consuming—mainly because I would have to work as writer, designer, and temporary publisher while drafting the project (see companion video section "Moving from Print to Book" at 1:15).

However, today my lingering questions and affective orientation toward the book proposal have changed. I enter a Zoom call with

Table 7.1. A comparison of a print and digital book proposal.

Excerpt from book proposal for print publisher	Excerpt from proposal for digital publisher
"For the purposes of visualizing the work of scholars and digital content creators and their practices, I anticipate including illustrations in each chapter, amounting to 10 total (two per chapter). A benefit of studying scholars of webtexts and independent creators is that they often own all of their content, making permissions theoretically easier to secure and/or cite under Fair Use guidelines."	"I envision *Feeling Digital Media* reflecting audio and video approaches in recent digital books such as Hidalgo's (2017) *Cámara Retórica: A Feminist Filmmaking Methodology for Rhetoric and Composition* and VanKooten's (2020) *Transfer across Media: Using Digital Video in the Teaching of Writing*. How might I help readers feel what creators have felt? To answer that question, I present podcast-style segments for each section of each chapter. Music, narration, and interviews, plus some help from colleagues, added layers to my argument. My thought is that the body text would serve as the transcript for the sound installments. The sound installments could double as a podcast series upon publication."

editors of a digital press, and I leave excited, smiling, ready to write. They liked my book proposal and text-only sample chapter, an adaptation of my *College English* article, "Theorizing Rhetorical-Affective Workflows: Behind the Scenes with Webtext Authors" (Shivener 2020). Previously, my book proposal suggested digital media companions to a print book, while this version was more assertive about digital media (see table 7.1).

Reading the proposal, the editors asked good questions: "How do you plan to design the book with multimedia?" "Can you send us a prototype by late January?" I'm excited, because the editors have positioned themselves as mentors, the kind who ask formative questions and want to help get a digital project in rhetorical shape before it goes to reviewers. I tell myself that all of that crying and self-questioning was necessary affective work, a gift because it helped me realize that I wanted to do a digital book. (For more on the affective value of editorial relationships that stem from media-rich projects, see Alexandra Hidalgo's chapter, "Consulting Editor to the Rescue," chapter 2)

FEBRUARY 5, 2021: REVISING TEXTUAL PASSAGES FOR CODE AND AUDIO NARRATION

From the initial editors' meeting until now, I have been working on two items: moving the print text to HTML code and revising a web design template that I pulled from the website HTML5UP.net. The site has

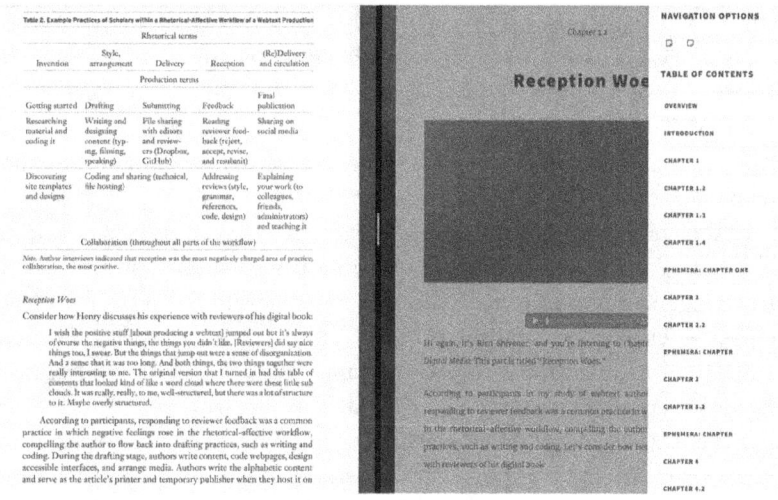

Figure 7.1. The author's print article (left) revised for the web (right). Article subheads such as "Reception Woes" and "Collaboration: Embodied Intensities" are displayed as separate web pages.

templates available under a Creative Commons license, meaning they are free to use for noncommercial purposes (see companion video sections "Converting Article to HTML" at 3:25 and "Revising a Web Design Template" at 4:07). These items require a kind of production loop. I begin copy-pasting passages from the article into Ulysses, a writing application that rather seamlessly turns words into clean HTML code through a language called Markdown. When a passage is ready, I move the code into web pages that serve as sections of the chapter. As figure 7.1 indicates, each section of the chapter is a web page on its own, because I'm concerned about a web page's readability—that it shouldn't be more than 2,000 words and loaded with myriad media lest it require too much scrolling. These print-to-digital revisions are about pace, and they're informed by my time writing as a music blogger and editing for *Kairos*. I've come to appreciate clear links and tabs that make a webtext easy to experience.

Revising for pace does create a tension, though. By keeping these passages short, I run the risk of losing readers every time they have to click on a new section.

Later, another idea about pacing hits me. I decide to experiment with audio recording, thinking that perhaps narrating each chapter will set the pace for readers—and to boot, the book could be read online or listened to on the move, just like podcasts. I record voice-overs for each section, using a Zoom H5 mic and capturing takes with Adobe Audition.

FEBRUARY 12, 2021: SUBMITTING THE PROTOTYPE

It's a few days before my agreed-upon deadline to submit a prototype of a chapter based on the *College English* article. I listen to my voice again, thinking, *Gah! It doesn't have any life to it! And is that my son I hear somewhere in the background?* I decide to rerecord two sections again rather than finish voice-overs for the entire chapter. In a way, my voice causes me to revise the voice-overs before anyone hears them. It reminds me of proofreading a written text aloud before submitting to it a journal—except this time, I'm revising the text *and* the voice-overs layered with it. For help, I watch National Public Radio's (2017) "Three Tips for Training Your Voice" with vocal coach Jessica Hansen. One takeaway is that revising audio requires revising how I prepare my lungs, my voice, and stance for a recording session. When layered with text, voice-overs foreground more of the full-body experience of composing (see companion video section "Re-recording Voiceovers for Ch. 1" at 6:03).

When I finish the revisions a few days later, I submit the chapter and some development notes to the editors, writing the following to them:

> In December and January, some thoughts occurred to me: How might I help readers feel what creators have felt? To answer that question, I decided to do podcast-style segments for this prototype. Music, narration, and interviews, plus some help from colleagues, added layers to my argument. My thought is that the body text would serve as the transcript for the sound installments. The sound installments could double as podcast series upon publication.
>
> The current prototype has sonic versions in the first two sections of Chapter One:
>
> - http://richshivener.com/prototypebook/chapterone.html
> - http://richshivener.com/prototypebook/chapterone_parttwo.html
>
> The index page has a book trailer. I'm considering doing one short video per chapter to set the tone of it. This test version layers interview sound with Creative Commons footage. Future iterations will integrate screen recordings from interviews and other original footage—I just wanted to test the concept before I ask my participants once again to use their work (I have the permissions; just being safe).

MARCH 8, 2021: A DISCUSSION WITH EDITORS ABOUT WEB DESIGN TEMPLATES AND ACCESSIBILITY

The editors and I meet a few weeks later to discuss the chapter and prototype design for the book. The editors enjoyed the overall approach to the book and have one critical suggestion for revising it. They invite me to experiment more with the template that gave rise to it. "We've seen this template elsewhere," they essentially tell me, kindly. "I think you can do something truly remarkable with this book," one editor offers. It's a helpful note for revising the chapter and expanding on it before the full submission for reviewers. Yet there is a tension here. I'm not exactly interested in flexing my coding muscles, something already done by many dudes who code (see Easter 2020). For me, the HTML5 template was just a starting point, a shell, a set of boundaries in which to innovate. As you'll see in the companion video of this chapter (9:41), I eliminated the responsive navigation bar, added "Navigation Options" in the navigation menu on the right, and added my own multimedia configurations. While I have changed the template somewhat significantly, it's still rather easy to navigate, just as the template was intended to be. To me, the biggest challenge was to make the template my own. Channeling Gallagher's argument, I acknowledge that "templates"—including those on HTML5UP.net—"may erase many choices of design, [but] I have argued that possible design choices still remain through creative subversion and innovation" (2015, 9). Gallagher suggests that the subversion of a template parlays into an original design, or at least one that looks and feels more unique to the designer. Because they are delivered with a Creative Commons license, the HTML5 templates are quite open to subversion and innovation.

Furthermore, the editors reminded me that all audio narrations should be accompanied by transcripts for accessibility—and not just the textual scripts I used for my audio files (see companion video section "Revising for Accessibility" at 8:15). Musical selections, names of speakers, and visual descriptions are required for each transcript. One editor writes me with some helpful tools for creating transcripts that are baked into the text rather than linked as PDFs:

I used this script [for making transcript tables]:
    https://van11y.net/accessible-hide-show/
And then made a "show/hide" button that expands the table when clicked. If you're interested, I can send you the link to a github repo where you can see a sample chapter & look at the code. Just let me know.
For the toggles, I would use the jQuery toggle function, because your template is already loading jQuery: https://api.jquery.com/toggle/ If you scroll down to the bottom 50% of that page, you can see examples of the toggle at work. If you need help trying this out, just let me know!

Digital book production can be a massive time-sink, so presubmission feedback is crucial for effective revision. This kind of feedback from a group of editors is similar to how *Kairos* does tiers of reviews for prospective authors (see the journal's "Editorial Board and Review Process").

JUNE 1, 2021: A PRODUCTIVE INTERMISSION. KIND OF.

Ugh. . . . This sucks. Coding sucks. My voice sucks. The world sucks. Between working from home amid the pandemic while ensuring our kiddo attends remote kindergarten on Google Classroom, I haven't done a thing with the technical ends of the book. Every time I look up tutorials and ideas for creating, my head starts spinning. I simply don't have time or energy to dwell in a code editor such as Brackets or Atom, so I continue writing and revising the textual elements of the book in the writing program Scrivener. It's a productive intermission between heavy periods of preparing and revising the book's prototype and revised submission for reviewers. Traditional writing practices like reading articles, combing through interview transcripts, and writing paragraphs have been most welcome, a way of staying out of the weeds of coding and media production. I'm having an utter block about how to make the design and code more interesting. Ideas for revising digital media simply take time to appear in the foreground and writing textually is a way of passing that time. (For more scenes of emotional pain in relation to time, see Jule Wallis-Thomas's chapter "The Messy, Painful, Personal, and Transformative Journey of Revision," chapter 15.)

In fact, I once again start exploring web design templates by third parties such as Webflow and Squarespace. A turn to these would make the design revisions of this project so much easier, but at the same time, it would compromise the expectation of doing scholarly webtext work all on your own. The trick, I guess, is finding an ethical way to revise the design in a such a way that it becomes your own. Maybe digital media scholarship is more about remixing than inventing something entirely original. These speculations give me pause for months on end. So I keep writing until I can make a decision.

AUGUST 11, 2021: REVISING AUDIO AGAIN, BUT LESS PAINSTAKINGLY

This evening is an intense period of recording and revising audio passages. For months, I've just been writing. Tonight is the first time I come back to listening to my narration. To help with revisions before my deadline in October, I decide to record very short passages—a paragraph at a time—of chapter 1 and 2, listen back to them, then edit them on the spot.

I also play music in the background the entire time, as if I'm narrating a podcast live (see companion video section "Revising Voiceovers [Again!]" at 12:41). The sonic vibe I've surrounded myself with makes for a smooth recording and revising process. I feel comfortable with recording two takes and picking the best one. The experience reminds me of why I play music whenever I'm writing a passage; it distracts me from that internal voice telling me that every line is terrible and should be revised immediately. If anything, I leave this session more mindful of revising my recording practices rather than the prose and audio itself.

SEPTEMBER 20, 2021: REVISING CODE

Something transformative has happened. Sifting through coding tutorials and community forums on Stack Exchange, CodeCanyon, CodePen, and W3Schools, I finally discover useful lines of HTML, CSS, and JavaScript that help me revise my navigation bar and the placement of my audio narration (e.g., W3Schools' page "How to Create a Sticky Element"). My navigator bar can now switch between the main chapters and behind-the-scenes chapters for making the book, feeling less static and a bit more interactive for readers and listeners (see companion video section "Revising the Web Design [Again!]," 9:44). Out of its HTML context, the new navigation bar is coded like this:

```
<nav id="nav">
<buttonnav onclick="myFunction()"><i class="fas fa-toggle-on"></i>
   Navigation Options</buttonnav>
<p>Welcome! Click on the above box to switch between the whole book
   and the "Ephemera" chapters, which discuss the behind-the-scenes
   work of the book. </p>
<div id="myDIV">
<ul class="links">
<h3>Table of Contents</h3>
<li><a href="#">Overview of the Book</a></li>
<li><a href="introduction.html">Introduction: Rhetorical Practices in
   the Now</a></li>
. . .
</ul>
</div>
<div id="myDIV2" style="display:none;">
<h3>Ephemera Table of Contents</h3>
<ul class="links">
```

```html
<li><a href="index.html">Overview</a></li>
<li><a href="chapterone_ephemera.html">Ephemera: Chapter One</a></li>
```

A few lines of code can make for an aesthetically pleasing revision. In addition, a tutorial helps me create audio tracks that are "sticky" at the bottom of each web page, meaning that they will always be in view during the reading and listening experience (see my companion video "Revising Web Design to Better Integrate Audio" at 13:24). Ultimately, the revisions I was stuck on for so many months were about the user experience—or the reviewer experience that I'm anticipating ahead of my official submission to the editors and subsequent reviewers. User experience, in the design sense, is something that just doesn't come up in print-based scholarly contexts, as the presentation of articles is similar across many publications. Unless you're presenting something like Mark Z. Danielewski's nonlinear book *House of Leaves* (2000), you have little to worry about in terms of design when writing for print.

OCTOBER 5, 2021: SUBMISSION DAY

It's submission day, the day I'm submitting the project to the editors. In the afternoon, I'm still revising. I'm doing all of the necessary checks, making sure all of the hyperlinks work, the pages are usable, etcetera. This is an unnerving task—beyond wondering about the overall argument of the book, I'm wondering about the usability of the table of contents, the pop-out windows for images, the embedded audio. On this afternoon, it hits me once again that digital book production holds you accountable for revising several elements, and those elements often depend on each other. Change a line of code, and it can fuck up an entire web page. I'm living the experience that Beverly Kolosseus, Dan Bauer, and Stephen A. Bernhardt wrote about in 1995: "We learned the hard way that small, early decisions have large consequences on later revising. Planning assumes major importance in designing hypertext. A lack of planning leads to tedious, time-consuming revision" (85). I take screenshots of all my changes, upload a new zip file of a server, and send it off.

OCTOBER 25, 2021: AND NOW, THE WAIT . . .

The editors have been preparing my submission for reviewers. As one wrote:

> We are preparing your sample chapters for external review, and we think it might be helpful to simplify the navigation for reviewers. Before doing that, I want to verify with you. So: The Introduction, Chapter 1, and

Chapter 2 are the chapters currently ready for review. Am I correct on that? If so, is it ok with you if I hide the navigation links for Chapters 3, 4, 5, and the Conclusion?

A day later, I get another message from an editor: "Rich—I'm writing to let you know that your book is out for review. We'll be hearing from the reviewers by the end of January, so you'll likely be hearing from us again in February."

I sigh with relief, awaiting helpful feedback. I'm convinced this waiting period will put some distance between me and the project's technical side, where many of the slippages and swells have lingered.

ON YOUR OWN TIME: DOCUMENTING YOUR SLIPPAGES AND SWELLS

Working on a digital book has been a transformative experience for understanding some key differences between revising for print and revising for digital publication. While working on my digital book, I've been documenting my own process by recording my screen and livestreaming work sessions on the digital platform Twitch. I close, then, by suggesting two tools for doing such documentation. Documentation can be useful for sharing insights with fellow writers and producing evidence of productivity for a tenure and promotion committee. What might audiences learn from our slippages and swells?

Open Broadcaster Software

In the world of livestreaming on Twitch, creators often use third-party software to broadcast game sessions, writing sprints, and more. For this book project, I have been using Open Broadcaster Software (OBS Project, n.d.), which is free, open-source (meaning community members can contribute to it), and available on major platforms. OBS can record a screen, webcam, and microphone of your choice simultaneously. This recording can be saved offline and streamed to a digital platform like Twitch. In addition, the recording can be set up in such a way that it doesn't yield a massive file when saved. For a brief comparison, I'll note that the Mac application QuickTime has similar features but requires a bit more work to set up (Kinney 2018). Also, Screencastify is a cross-platform web application for Google Chrome browsers, but the free version permits just a few minutes of recording (Screencastify, n.d.). Ultimately, OBS is an efficient way to capture work sessions and perhaps sessions of authors who are revising their work for a research study.

GitHub

Beyond streaming software, another way to document revisions to digital media scholarship is to use a digital repository and development platform like GitHub. Unlike Google Docs and Microsoft Word, coding programs have lacked internal version histories of projects. Tracking changes is usually done by cloning projects. At *Kairos*, for example, we download and clone a webtext for each stage of copyediting before publication. Similarly, GitHub offers a history of "commits" that show changes to code and file uploads (GitHub, n.d.). For a field-specific reference, check out Tim Lockridge's GitHub repository for rhetorlist.net, which has more than a hundred commits (Lockridge 2022).

These suggestions for documentation might help you move through the "hard way" to finishing a webtext. At the very least, documentation is a means to understanding and demonstrating the myriad feelings and revisions behind a project.

REFERENCES

Ball, Cheryl. 2021. "Outreach and Mentoring Goals." *Kairos: A Journal of Rhetoric, Technology, and Pedagogy* 25. https://kairos.technorhetoric.net/25.2/loggingon/mentoring-outreach.html.

Berlant, Lauren, and Kathleen Stewart. 2019. *The Hundreds*. Durham, NC: Duke University Press.

Brown, Lisa. 2015. "An Indie-Style Experiment at a AAA Studio: Insomniac's Slow Down, Bull." *Gamasutra*, April 12, 2015. https://www.gamasutra.com/view/news/259163/An_indiestyle_experiment_at_a_AAA_studio_Insomniacs_Slow_Down_Bull.php.

Danielewski, Mark Z. 2000. *House of Leaves*. New York: Pantheon.

Easter, Brandee. 2020. "Fully Human, Fully Machine: Rhetorics of Digital Disembodiment in Programming." *Rhetoric Review* 39 (2): 202–15.

Gallagher, John R. 2015. "The Rhetorical Template." *Computers and Composition*, no. 35, 1–11.

GitHub. n.d. "Git Commit." Accessed November 30, 2021. https://github.com/git-guides/git-commit.

Hidalgo, Alexandra. 2017. *Cámara Retórica: A Feminist Filmmaking Methodology for Rhetoric and Composition*. Louisville: University Press of Colorado; Logan: Utah State University Press. https://ccdigitalpress.org/book/camara.

Kairos: A Journal of Rhetoric, Technology, and Pedagogy. n.d. "Editorial Board and Review Process." Accessed November 30, 2021. https://kairos.technorhetoric.net/board.html.

Kinney, Michael. 2018. "QuickTime Player Tutorial: How to Record Computer Screen AND Webcam (Mac)," *YouTube*, September 5, 2018, 12:43. https://youtu.be/mLyPrblmPp4.

Kolosseus, Beverly, Dan Bauer, and Stephen A. Bernhardt. 1995. "From Writer to Designer: Modeling Composing Processes in a Hypertext Environment." *Technical Communication Quarterly* 4 (1): 79–93.

kyburz, bonnie lenore. 2019. *Cruel Auteurism: Affective Digital Mediations toward Film-Composition*. Louisville: WAC Clearinghouse / University Press of Colorado.

Lockridge, Tim, and Derek Van Ittersum. 2020. *Writing Workflows: Beyond Word Processing*. Ann Arbor: Sweetland Digital Rhetoric Collaborative / University of Michigan Press.

Lockridge, Tim. n.d. "Rhetorlist." Accessed 4 July 4, 2022. https://github.com/timlockridge/rhetorlist.

National Public Radio. 2017. "Three Tips for Training Your Voice." *YouTube*, June 19, 2017, 9:12. https://youtu.be/cSTqKi7Wuq4.

OBS Project. n.d. "Open Broadcaster Software." Accessed November 30, 2021. https://obsproject.com.

Politowski, Cristiano, Fabio Petrillo, Gabriel Cavalheiro Ullmann, and Yann-Gaël Guéhéneuc. 2018. "Learning from the Past: A Process Recommendation System for Video Game Projects using Postmortems Experiences." *Information and Software Technology*, no. 100, 103–18.

Screencastify. n.d. "Screencastify Pricing." Accessed November 30, 2021. https://www.screencastify.com/buy.

Shahbazi, Sina. 2018. "Postmortem: Amazia, a CCG for Mobile." *Gamasutra*, April 1, 2018. https://www.gamasutra.com/blogs/SinaShahbazi/20180401/315886/Postmortem_Amazia_a_CCG_for_mobile.php.

Shivener, Rich. 2020. "Theorizing Rhetorical-Affective Workflows: Behind the Scenes with Webtext Authors." *College English* 83 (1): 42–65.

Tulley, Christine E. 2018. *How Writing Faculty Write: Strategies for Process, Product, and Productivity*. Logan: Utah State University Press.

VanKooten, Crystal. 2020. *Transfer across Media: Using Digital Video in the Teaching of Writing*. Louisville: University Press of Colorado; Logan: Utah State University Press. https://ccdigitalpress.org/book/transfer-across-media/index.html.

W3Schools. n.d. "How To Create a Sticky Element." Accessed November 30, 2021. https://www.w3schools.com/howto/howto_css_sticky_element.asp.

8
"ANOTHER_DRAFT.DOCX"
The Role of Horizontal Mentoring in Publishing as Graduate Students

Dana Comi and Alisa Russell

The graduate seminar was over, but our projects were just starting. At the end of our first year as PhD students, we had an idealistic (and rather panicked) sense of urgency to publish, as well as a sincere commitment to the ideas we'd generated in this seminar about public rhetorics. Although we were asked to write a traditional seminar paper, the two of us were adamant about drafting all our papers as potential articles. We were both committed to landing tenure-track jobs out of graduate school, and we knew the only way to do so was to publish as soon as possible (see Ellery Sills and Fernando Sánchez, this collection, for more on creating one's professional identity through writing). One of our mentors and the teacher of this particular graduate seminar, Mary Jo Reiff, encouraged us to continue our projects through to publication. We knew revision was necessary to prepare an article but didn't yet know the extent to which revising alongside one another—giving and responding to feedback—would fundamentally shape our long revision journeys towards publication.

Our revisions emerged through our horizontal mentoring practices: the suggestions, advice, critical questioning, emotional support, and insights we shared with one another as we developed our articles. We are borrowing Pamela VanHaitsma and Steph Ceraso's formulation of horizontal mentoring: "the offering of help, guidance, support, and training . . . that is carried out within a horizontal rather than hierarchical relationship (between peers, as opposed to a more and less experienced mentor and mentee)" (VanHaitsma and Ceraso 2017, 211). Also referred to as "peer mentoring" in our field, horizontal mentoring is distinct from expert-novice mentoring with its "power-laden, vertical mentoring dynamics" (for more on mentoring practices in rhetoric and composition, see Anderson and Romano 2006; Belcher 1994; Bloom

2007; Bommarito 2015; Eble and Gaillet 2008; Lu et al. 2008; Lunsford 2018; Ribero and Arellano 2019; Simpson and Matsuda 2008).

Our horizontal mentoring practices, then, didn't extend from expert knowledge or experience; on the contrary, our mentoring extended from our shared status as graduate students (i.e., academics in training) and our shared awareness that we were new and inexperienced and needed to "figure out" how to publish as quickly as possible (for more on graduate publishing, see Adams et al. 2020; Aitchison, Kamler, and Lee 2010; Lee and Norton 2003; Wells and Söderlund 2018). This awareness shaped our feedback to each other, the revisions we made to our articles, and our encouragement of one another to keep writing. Through this horizontal mentoring, we not only learned from each other how to better articulate our ideas, justify our methodologies, and acknowledge where our projects were situated in the field, we learned how to think and write as academics.

"THIS PUBLISHING BUSINESS IS HARD!": ALISA

Two desk rejections later, I finally accepted that I needed to go back to the drawing board on this article. And that meant turning back to Dana for feedback and support.

Fresh off the public rhetorics seminar, I sought to argue (using about ten different theoretical frameworks) that publics could be created through seemingly nonpublic genres, and I demonstrated this theory with a small qualitative study of a graduate student group who used their own internal genres to contribute to a larger public conversation about health insurance. Today, in rereading the feedback that accompanied my two desk rejections, I am surprised at how thoughtful and clear it was. For example, the editor of *College English (CE)* took the time to kindly identify key issues with the article:

> What is the reader benefit here? How will the pursuit of this essay improve the understanding of the readers of your target venue? If I needed to revise this for a highly selective venue, I would consider starting with part of the example and show how current theories do not adequately account for the action/exigency. I would also foreground my own voice and essay structure, particularly in the first third. In fact, to show how my argument addressed a real need, I might consider organizing my lit review around current theories vis-à-vis my theory (in this way the lit review is, I think, its own kind of argument).

Perhaps I didn't understand enough about how articles work in the field to grasp what this feedback was suggesting. Or maybe I was simply desperate for validation. But out of all that great feedback, I only clamped onto the editor's idea that "this reads like a *Rhetoric Society Quarterly* submission."

The *Rhetoric Society Quarterly* (*RSQ*) editor wrote much less than the *CE* editor in her rejection but still clearly pointed out issues in scope, contribution, development, and methodology:

> I admire the boldness of this effort. Given the daring of the project, the case study seems a bit parochial—a graduate student group[. . .]. If you pursue [revision], I suggest that you spend more time acknowledging the dramatically different theoretical grounds of the frameworks [*sic*] you seek to combine, and that you select a more consequential discourse site for your case study.

I remember showing the *RSQ* rejection email to Dana the next time I saw her in class, and she shared one of her own harsh rejections as a consolation. We ended up laughing quite a bit. As Collie Fulford and Stefanie Frigo (this collection) likewise describe, witnessing someone else's (humorous) response to your own reviewers' comments lessens some of their power. Sharing those emotions with Dana—and knowing I wasn't alone—relieved the sting of the two desk rejections and some of the prideful pressure that had mounted.

With Dana's validation, I began looking at this article draft not as a publishable piece in itself but as the groundwork that could lead to an article with clearer scope, a defined contribution, and appropriate methodology. I reflected in an email to Mary Jo about a line I had written in the conclusion: "I actually think I could move this finding up to the main claim and re-tool the whole introduction and lit review to set up this finding instead. I would be able to keep everything I have about genre and uptake, but I'd locate it in existing theories of rhetorical ecologies instead of introducing activity systems and assemblage theory into the mix." The actual work of resituating my argument so as to have this clear contribution took *over a year*, during which I also finished coursework, passed my comprehensive exams, and proposed my dissertation. When I finally emailed this evolved draft to Dana, I wrote, "Yeah, I don't even know what kind of feedback I want on this. I've been looking at it for too long. So any direction would be helpful!"

We met to discuss our drafts at our trusty local coffee shop, J&S Coffee, which offered bottomless cups for $2.10 and worn-out booths you could lounge in for hours. We had both prepared marginal comments, but we knew from our years of collaboration in and outside of coursework that we got to our best ideas when we could talk it out. One of Dana's marginal comments focused on some quick pedagogical implications I had thrown out in this draft's conclusion:

> I think this needs more elaboration? Some examples could be helpful if you've encouraged this in your classroom, or potential assignments or activities? . . . Further explanation here seems important.

In our discussion, I started describing some pedagogical examples from my classes, and, in real time, I could see Dana suddenly *get* my article. She began recasting the rest of her marginal comments in light of this discovery. I recall hand-sketching a fresh outline right there, with Dana confirming each point of how I needed to progress through this argument. In other words, I had to have her insightful question—and her reaction to its answer—to finally see what my most significant contribution was and how I needed to present it.

Energized from our conversational breakthrough, I sent Dana a new draft only two weeks later. Dana's response:

> I just did two read-throughs of your draft. So, so good. I think its ready! I stopped adding marginal comments after the introduction because it was just me saying "Cool, so good, wow!" The introduction is much clearer and engaging, the gap is much easier to understand.

To which I replied, "Ah! Thank you, Dana! Your feedback was obviously the key that unlocked this whole piece."

In an email of the same draft to Mary Jo, notice how much of the *CE* and *RSQ* rejection language I'm using to describe scope, contribution, and methodology:

> I do have a new draft now (attached) based on talking through the previous draft with Dana. I originally wanted this study to simply expand our understanding of how publics work, as you suggest, but I really struggled with situating that argument. The claims seemed a little too big for my small study . . . ? And it was very interdisciplinary, which is part of why previous versions received desk rejections (although there were other reasons for those desk rejections, too!). Oh, and the identity/agency piece added this whole other layer that turned the framing into a theoretical palooza that I just could not smooth over. So I ended up leaning further into the pedagogical angle by reframing the study and adding classroom examples. I think the piece still expands our understanding of how publics work even as it focuses that understanding on how it can expand our public pedagogies.

Over many drafts, then, I did develop the understanding and values of the expert editors that attempted to give me feedback. But I was only able to process, engage, believe, and address that expert feedback by collaborating with Dana.

When I received a revise-and-resubmit for this article from *College Composition and Communication* (*CCC*) in September 2019, I went straight to Dana with the reviewers' comments. My email to her shows increased maturity in accepting the reviewers' feedback this time, but it also shows the need for Dana's collaboration to engage that feedback:

> Reviewer #2 is really confused by the concept of uptake in general, so I'm not sure how to address that. And I think Reviewer #1 makes really good points about clarifying my spectrum of narrowly-dispersed to widely-dispersed genres. I'm just interested in your general thoughts of how to best address their comments.

And of course, the email ends with an invitation to meet back at J&S Coffee.

"I'M NOT SURE HOW TO MOVE FORWARD WITH THIS": DANA

The revision story of this article is primarily a story of waiting, and waiting, to have the confidence to actually make revisions and move forward. Throughout this waiting, Alisa's mentoring, especially her understanding of how my article needed to develop and her encouragement to keep writing, kept the project alive and lent me enough confidence to submit the project to a journal. By the end of Mary Jo's spring 2017 public rhetorics seminar course, I had a kernel of an idea I loved: a way to name when lived, embodied experience is co-opted to claim space for political gain. I (very overambitiously) termed this rhetorical concept an *ideobody* and fleshed out this idea in the last two pages of the seminar paper, as it related to the public testimonies I had qualitatively analyzed. At the end of the semester, we shared our projects in class by giving short conference-style presentations. I wrote down each classmate's feedback, knowing I could return to these notes later as I continued to prepare this project for publication. Following my presentation, Alisa said: "This is really interesting! It does sound like you have two articles in one seminar paper right now—one about rhetorical appeals to democracy, and another about the role of the ideobody in the testimonies."

Alisa's feedback was reinforced by the comments I later received from Mary Jo on the final draft of the seminar paper, and I was left with what felt like a daunting (and unappealing) task—abandoning the first fifteen pages of the paper, preserving the section on ideobodies, and building the rest of the article from the ground up again, all the while figuring out how to correctly target a journal, find an exemplar, and gear the literature review towards the focus of the journal. By the summer, I felt foolish for trying to create a brand-new rhetorical concept from one small-scale study and second-guessed myself about whether any of the paper was publication-worthy. I ended up doing nothing. Instead, I submitted a seminar paper-to-article attempt from another class. Although that article progressed to peer review, I was met with a brutal assessment of the article by one reviewer (so bad that the editor sent an apology letter to me because they knew I was a graduate student). The reviewer included condescending comments like, "Are you sure you understand this theory?" and "Yes, [this idea] is obvious, I don't see how this would be of interest to the field," and while the editor tried to frame this feedback, it confirmed my fears of inadequacy as a new graduate student. This experience set me back, and I ended up pausing my work on the ideobody project for several months. I contemplated scrapping the project entirely to avoid another demoralizing review process.

However, over the next year, I slowly returned to the project. I joined a writing accountability group that had started in my department, which included Alisa, who was also working on her article from the public rhetorics class. Throughout the class, and into the writing group, I'd found that Alisa's feedback "clicked"—her marginal comments and overall perception of where a given draft was "at" resonated and helped me understand how to keep moving forward with the project. Alisa's feedback helped me cut sections that no longer served the article, develop sections that hadn't existed before, and hang onto the notion of the ideobody with increasing confidence that it actually was worth writing about:

> You might consider cutting this section entirely, now that you have pgs. 7–8.
>
> Yes, this section helps SO much. I am starting to get what you mean here.
>
> Okay, I'm understanding how the ideobody functions, fascinating.

In addition to this feedback, Alisa's work on her own article was a model for me as I decided what journal to target (and how to even understand how to make that decision). We spent hours at J&S, a local coffee shop, often not revising or writing at all, but talking about how to write and revise towards publication.

As my draft developed, I decided to target *Present Tense* for publication and began formally structuring the article based off of an exemplar. I waited to submit, however, until I presented the project at the Rhetoric Society of America (RSA) conference in Minneapolis in the summer of 2018. I wanted to know how the project would be received by people outside of my department. The panel I was on was sparsely attended, but afterwards, someone approached me and encouraged me to submit the project as a book chapter for an edited collection. That was all I needed to hear: second-year graduate student me decided that I should give *Present Tense* a go and see what happened next. I found an exemplar *Present Tense* article, annotated the "moves" I saw the author make, and tried to structure my article the same way. I finally let go of the first fifteen pages of the original seminar paper and, through Alisa's encouragement, focused on the ideas I had introduced in the paper's conclusion.

I submitted the article on February 7, 2019, and waited. I heard back from the editor over five months later, on October 22, with a revise and resubmit (R&R). While this was exciting news, the R&R had no deadline because of the journal's online format. I read both reviewers' comments, the editor's overview, panicked, and waited. I felt like I was back at square one, not understanding how to move forward.

My mentors, including Mary Jo, were supportive ("It's a big deal to get a revise and resubmit, congratulations!"), but I ultimately needed to return to Alisa's feedback and suggestions for revision to figure out what to do next. Alisa suggested I sort the reviewers' comments into areas of consensus and dissensus, which helped me understand what I needed to revise and where I had decisions to make about which revision suggestions to take up and which to reject. The reviewers suggested I change the introduction to a narrative opening, include more examples of participant testimonies to showcase the differences between both sides, and provide a more in-depth explanation of ideobodies in relation to McGee's ideograph, but each suggested organization and sentence-level changes that contradicted one another. For example, Reviewer 1 suggested I move a description of the committee hearing to the beginning of the article, while another suggested I further develop this description in the middle of the article.

I wrote out a detailed timeline to make these changes, then another, and then another. I created a checklist for revision, then assigned tasks to particular days, then reassigned tasks, until I had done no revision work for four months. Then, finally, a week before winter break in mid-December, I locked myself in my GTA office with a carafe of coffee and a frozen dinner and made all the revisions in a day-long revision spree. The pent-up nerves I'd accumulated over months of stalling slowly subsided as I returned to the consensus/dissensus chart I had made in response to Alisa's advice, and I found that I was able to systematically resolve the necessary revisions with far less difficulty than I had imagined. Because I was acutely aware of my novice status as a graduate student, I read through both reviewers' feedback initially as edicts instead of feedback that I could address in a variety of ways. Alisa's suggestion to systematically sort their feedback, then decide how to negotiate it, extended from our shared awareness of the power imbalance inherent in academic peer review for graduate student work. The process of sorting and negotiating reviewers' feedback enabled me to build the confidence to make necessary changes, while also explaining and justifying my revision choices in my resubmission cover letter. I sent the updated draft and letter to the writing accountability group and waited for our next meetup. In our last meeting of the semester, I received a printed copy of the draft with Alisa's written comments—at the top of the page, she wrote, "This is ready!"

Even then, I delayed resubmitting the article until March 3, 2020. After rereading the draft again and again, trying to see if there was anything else that needed to be fixed, I finally sent the draft to the editors. In late April, I heard back from the editors that the article would be accepted with minor revisions, and in October 2020 the article went live after over three years of horizontal mentoring, waiting, and revising.

CONCLUSION

Our graduate program provided a host of resources to assist us in breaking our way into publication: we took an "article-writing" course our very first semester; we attended multiple professional development workshops; we were in a variety of writing groups with other graduate students and faculty; we had some of the most attentive and caring mentors, who looked at draft after draft after draft. All of these pieces played a role in our acculturation into the discipline and into publishing, by offering accountability, motivation, and instruction. Our horizontal mentorship, though, provided a consistent shared space to *make sense* of these resources. In our many revision conversations, we constantly referenced these other activities, and in those references we could work together to better figure them out and operationalize them. In other words, our horizontal mentorship is where we put our learning into action.

For both of us, revision was not just an individual journey of polishing, nor was it a natural extension of simply fixing up a piece that originated in a graduate seminar. Our collaborative mentorship may have started as peer review partners in the graduate seminar, but it had to continue over three years of both drafts fundamentally evolving. We would not have had the confidence or know-how to make those kinds of radical revisions if we had not seen the other's draft go through a similar process. For example, even in our "article-writing" class, we didn't talk about how *long* revision toward publication can take, nor how those revisions could change fundamental aspects of the piece, such as the intended journal and thesis.

Furthermore, because we both had similar objectives (publish ASAP) and similar challenges (little clue as to how to publish ASAP), there was a sense of reciprocity to our draft-sharing and feedback that we could not quite get anywhere else. We felt comfortable giving each other dozens of drafts, because the other also had dozens of drafts to share. Mentors and journal editors often provided feedback that imagined projects twenty steps ahead of where they were, whereas our feedback for each other was much more incremental and focused on the ultimate objective of getting published. Our feedback to each other, then, had a sense of urgency and pragmatism. (See Cruz Medina, this collection, to explore how this kind of sustained, generative back-and-forth might be taken up between journal editors and prospective authors.)

Importantly, our horizontal mentorship became an exercise in translation that improved over time. Because we were involved with each other's projects through the full life span of each article, we developed a shared language and shorthand tailored for one another. For example, Dana knew that Alisa tends to overtheorize, and Alisa knew that Dana tends to write her way to topic sentences by the end of paragraphs. While expert feedback tended toward the descriptive, our feedback to one another tended toward the prescriptive because we knew where to find each other's ideas. There were no implicit expectations or ideals, because neither of us had yet internalized or fully acclimated to this genre and the discipline. Our status as beginners meant we, in our heightened meta-awareness, could give each other more workable feedback than experts could.

And finally, perhaps the only thing that tops publication in terms of emotional distress is the academic job market—and in the case of these articles, those were two sides of the same coin. We were unprepared for the range of emotions that accompany these long revision processes: disappointment, embarrassment, fear, doubt, frustration, bewilderment . . . eventually relief and maybe a glint of excitement. Experiencing these emotions together was validating. Through these moments of validation, we slowly built resilience. Today, while those emotions still come and go, we feel we can navigate publication and its required revisions with more distance and perspective. (Of course, that also comes along with both of us being faculty now.)

We close with a fun coda to these revision stories—and further confirmation of how significant horizontal mentoring can be for revision. Alisa had mercifully let her article go after it received a second revise-and-resubmit from *CCC*. Originally, we thought this chapter would highlight that revision journeys can be significant even when one article ends in publication and the other does not. However, writing this very chapter required Alisa to revisit all of her article drafts, emails, and feedback after a year and a half's distance. Most significantly, it meant talking to Dana again about the draft. After opening that horizontal mentorship back up, Alisa decided to revise her article one more time and submit to *Composition Studies*. It was accepted—a full five years after drafting the original.

REFERENCES

Adams, Lauren L., Megan Adams, Pauline Baird, Estee Beck, Kristine L. Blair, April Conway, Lee Nickoson, and Martha Schaffer. 2020. "Crossing Divides: Engaging Extracurricular Writing Practices in Graduate Education and Professionalization." In *Graduate Writing Across the Disciplines, Identifying, Teaching, and Supporting*, edited by Marilee Brooks-Gillies, Elena G. Garcia, Soo Hyon Kim, Katie Manthey, and Trixie G. Smith, 269–90. Fort Collins, CO: WAC Clearinghouse.

Aitchison, Claire, Barbara Kamler, and Alison Lee. 2010. *Publishing Pedagogies for the Doctorate and Beyond*. Abingdon: Routledge.

Anderson, Virginia, and Susan Romano. 2006. *Culture Shock and the Practice of the Profession: Training the Next Wave in Rhetoric and Composition*. New York: Hampton.

Belcher, Diane. 1994. "The Apprenticeship Approach to Advanced Academic Literacy: Graduate Students and Their Mentors." *English for Specific Purposes* 13 (1): 23–34. https://doi.org/10.1016/0889-4906(94)90022-1.

Bloom, Lynn Z. 2007. "Mentoring as Mosaic: Life as Guerilla Theater." *Composition Studies* 35 (2): 87–89. https://www.jstor.org/stable/43501705.

Bommarito, Daniel V. 2015. "Collaborative Research Writing as Mentoring in a U.S. English Doctoral Program." *Journal of Writing Research* 8 (2): 267–99. https://doi.org/10.17239/jowr-2016.08.02.04.

Eble, Michelle F., and Lynée Lewis Gaillet. 2008. *Stories of Mentoring: Theory and Praxis*. Anderson, SC: Parlor Press.

Lee, Ena, and Bonny Norton. 2003. "Demystifying Publishing: A Collaborative Exchange Between Graduate Student and Supervisor." In *Writing for Scholarly Publication: Behind the Scenes in Language Education*, edited by Stephanie Vandrick and Christine Pearson Casanave, 53–60. Abingdon: Routledge.

Liu, Lu, Irwin Weiser, Tonya Silva, Janet Alsup, Cindy Selfe, and Gail Hawisher. 2008. "It Takes a Community of Scholars to Raise One: Multiple Mentors as Key to My Growth." In *Learning the Literacy Practices of Graduate School: Insiders' Reflections on Academic Enculturation*, edited by Christine Pearson Casanave and Xiaoming Li, 166–85. Ann Arbor: University of Michigan.

Lunsford, Andrea. 2018. "Are You a Mentor?" *Macmillan* (blog), June 2018. https://community.macmillan.com/community/the-english-community/bedford-bits/blog/2018/06/21/are-you-a-mentor.

Ribero, Ana Milena, and Sonia C. Arellano. 2019. "Advocating Comadrismo: A Feminist Mentoring Approach for Latinas in Rhetoric and Composition." *Peitho Journal* 21 (2): 334–56. https://cfshrc.org/article/advocating-comadrismo-a-feminist-mentoring-approach-for-latinas-in-rhetoric-and-composition/.

Simpson, Steve, and Paul K. Matsuda. 2008. "Mentoring as a Long-Term Relationship: Situated Learning in a Doctoral Program." In *Learning the Literacy Practices of Graduate School: Insiders' Reflections on Academic Enculturation,* edited by Xiao Ming Li and Christine Pearson Casanave, 90–104. Ann Arbor: University of Michigan Press.

VanHaitsma, Pamela, and Steph Ceraso. 2017. "'Making It' in the Academy through Horizontal Mentoring." *Peitho Journal* 19 (2): 211–33. https://citeseerx.ist.psu.edu/viewdoc/download?doi=10.1.1.1060.3803&rep=rep1&type=pdf.

Wells, Jaclyn M., and Lars Söderlund. 2018. "Preparing Graduate Students for Academic Publishing." *Pedagogy* 18 (1): 131–56. https://doi.org/10.1215/15314200-4216994.

9
REVISING SCHOLARLY PEER REVIEW
Don't Be a Dick

Raúl Sánchez

> *We need a new language, one that doesn't convince us of our unutterable and ongoing differences, one that doesn't force us to see one another as competitors. We need a language that allows us to imagine respectful and reciprocal relationships that acknowledge the degree to which we need one another (have needed one another) in order to survive and flourish.*
>
> —Malea Powell

In the above passage from 2004, Malea Powell is addressing a specific situation in rhetoric and composition: the field's inability (or refusal) to imagine itself as multirhetorical to its core and to instead relegate so-called nontraditional practices of writing, rhetorics, and literacies to the margins, orbiting around an Aristotelian or otherwise Western center. Answering a call by Victor Villanueva and others to center the rhetorics of this hemisphere, Powell offers a revision of the field, urging us to make it one that welcomes, nurtures, and values "respectful and reciprocal relationships" among our field's scholars and the traditions they study, practice, and represent (41).

The problem extends—has extended—from the question of recognizing multiple traditions and practices to the issue of understanding the various ways they might be studied. Consider the epigraphs with which Aja Martinez begins the first chapter of her 2020 book, *Counterstory: The Rhetoric and Writing of Critical Race Theory*. In three separate passages, three separate scholars reviewing for three separate journals tell Martinez to justify her decision to use narrative as her method and methodology. While all three endorse her decision, each one thinks nonetheless that it must be explained. This prompts her to wonder "when or if these academic gatekeepers will arrive at a point of admission that all work, especially in the humanities, is story" (Martinez 2020, 2). Similarly, in his review of *Counterstory*, Louis M. Maraj notes that such comments "attest to widespread ignorance" of methods that "have been around for decades" before himself offering similar and in fact even less generous examples of reviewer comments that "all too often greet people of color's storying methods" (Maraj 2021, 197).

Given the sixteen years between Powell's and Martinez's observations, it seems that much work remains to be done, especially—but of course not exclusively—around scholarly peer review. I am particularly concerned with how these venues address manuscripts that deepen and widen the field empirically, theoretically, and methodologically. As manuscript reviewers, how can we extend—or begin applying, as the case may be—the values of respect, reciprocity, and relationality that Powell describes above? How can we embed them more firmly into our disciplinary mindsets? How can we better attend to the *processes* of scholarly production?

Many of us, perhaps especially those who come from other fields and bad experiences, like to imagine rhetoric and composition as welcoming, tolerant, humane, and collegial. And it is, in some cases and for some people, maybe even in many cases for many people. And I am sure few, if any, of us would espouse or condone a notion of scholarly peer review that was not somehow constructive, affirming, and focused on improvement and cooperation rather than gatekeeping and competition. But how can we make sure our own reviewing practices actually do this kind of work?

When discussing drafts with students, I often ask them to distinguish between what readers can find on the internet and what they can get only from the piece of writing at hand. I tell them that the latter constitutes their valuable contribution to the topic. So it is for me in this essay: I may say some things you already know or have already considered about the process by which our publication venues develop and assess their submissions. But in sharing my perspective, I hope to give you something useful just the same, something specific with which you might compare your own experience and practice. The first draft of this essay contained a literature review of work in and outside of composition studies that shows how flawed, even broken, scholarly peer review is. The editors of this book told me to cut it and to focus instead on "practice/doing" rather than making a traditional scholarly argument. This made sense, until one of the reviewers noted that it would be "helpful to acknowledge that there is a growing effort in the field to change the way we approach review." Splitting the difference, I point to the 2021 document "Anti-Racist Scholarly Reviewing Practices: A Heuristic for Editors, Reviewers, and Authors." Its contributors—scholars in technical communication—offer a detailed outline for "a system of inclusivity, rather than gatekeeping and disciplining" ("Anti-Racist," 2) that underscores the responsibilities of editors, reviewers, authors, and others and "anyone involved in academic publishing" ("Anti-Racist," 3). If you haven't yet read "Anti-Racist Scholarly Reviewing Practices," stop reading this essay and do so. Placed in the context it provides, what follows here will make more and better sense.

I have three modest goals amounting not to an argument but to a sharing of my perspective, based on my experience, my observations, and my practices. They are: (1) to show graduate students and junior faculty how I—and others—think manuscript review *should* work, so that they will know what they can rightly expect as authors and as reviewers, (2) to remind my fellow senior colleagues that our job as reviewers is—first and only—to help others do their work, and (3) to encourage these senior colleagues to resist the sometimes strong, sometimes unconscious urge to behave poorly. As my absent literature review shows, scholarly peer review has been undergoing revision for some time. In the pages that follow, I will share my perspective as a very minor participant in this process. In that sense—and as Powell, Martinez, and other scholars often remind us—this is a story. In particular, it is a story about how I try—guided by the wisdom of others—not to be a dick.

A TECHNICAL TERM

I employ the term *dick* here in a way consistent with its use in contemporary US culture. This use is outlined in the online *Urban Dictionary*, which offers a set of related definitions. One entry, submitted by a user named "it is not your business" in 2019, reads as follows: "an obnoxious, uncooperative, and dishonest person." Another, from "das_it_mane" in 2016, contains four definitions, the second of which is most relevant here: "A mean, aggravating, or otherwise just disliked person." Similarly, the third definition submitted by "cash master" in 2009 claims that the term is "used to describe people as an asshole." And perhaps most pointedly, "sirdefenition" in 2017 tells us that dick means "you." We all stand accused.

I think sirdefenition has a point. Because we are human beings, we can act like dicks. I don't know if the capacity is innate or learned, but it seems safe to say that however it begins, it is reinforced and refined through years of formal and informal training. In fact, there are times when we must work *not* to be dicks, despite our otherwise good intentions. I don't want to say that we cannot help ourselves, because I think we can—that is the point of this essay—but I do want to say that helping ourselves is *work*: perhaps difficult work, but important and necessary. Dickish behavior is certainly not unique to rhetoric and composition, but this is where I dwell professionally, and it is where I have seen some dickishness in the last three decades. Of course, I have also seen—and have benefited from—behavior that was the very opposite: generous, encouraging, instructive, and even transformative.

We need much more of this very good behavior. In fact, it needs to be the unquestioned norm, a value firmly embedded in our disciplinary consciousness. To reach such a goal, I think we must make *ongoing* the work of describing, modeling, and fostering such behavior. And I think the responsibility of doing this rests mainly—though not only—with scholars, teachers, and mentors like me: people who have been in the field for a while, who have achieved some measure of job security, and who are often called upon to assess the work of colleagues, especially junior colleagues, and most especially our growing ranks of colleagues from historically underrepresented groups. If we are not making use of our relative professional privilege to do *precisely* these things, then we are wasting that privilege. And that is dickish, indeed.

MY PERSPECTIVE

What I am saying, then, is that I have an ethical, professional, and moral obligation not to be a dick. And in practice, I am often confronted with the option not to be a dick, which I should *always* take. This should go without saying, for me and for everyone else. "Don't be a dick" would seem to be the most obvious and most commonsense directive one could imagine. Yet, Reviewer 2 memes exist because enough people decline the option not to be a dick. Perhaps their dickish behavior is unconscious. Perhaps a reviewer is going through some difficulty and lashes out at others. No doubt, the reasons vary. But ultimately, the reasons do not matter, because in the field that I want to be part of, scholars and researchers value rigorous kindness, thoroughgoing generosity, and a spirit of cooperation *at all times* and above all else. I see these values as part of the larger and ongoing revision of the field, in which the historical narrowness of its ideologies and epistemologies is broadening to include the widest possible range of experience and understanding regarding the study of writing, rhetorics, and literacies. Not only are we studying more things more deeply; we are also changing the ways we talk to each other about the things we study and the ways we study them.

This revision of the field includes, as well, the field's understanding of revision itself. While we have long understood writing as a collaborative process, I think we have—in practice at least—mistakenly understood collaboration to take place within certain ontological and procedural limits. That is, you get feedback on your writing, perhaps even at multiple points of intervention from teachers and peers and reviewers, but then *you revise on your own.* This amounts to a privatized, blackboxed theory of revision, one in which reviewers' investments extend no farther than their critiques, and in which the agency of the singular writing subject is preserved. But a more socialized, "open-source" approach to revision—especially in the case of scholarly peer review—might prompt us to see the write-review-revise process as distributed: more people doing more things more often. This seems truer to how we understand writing processes to actually work, and it might reduce the perverse incentives built into the current system that encourage dickish behavior: anonymity, emphasis on critique, credit accruing only to the designated writing subject (the "author") who survives the process, and so on.

For example, I am the designated author of several documents, including one dissertation and two so-called monographs. Yet during each process, I received feedback and guidance from people who opted, when dealing with me, not to be dicks. That is, they resisted or ignored the incentives that obtain in our current approach to revision and review. For this, they deserve acknowledgment beyond the "acknowledgments" pages on which their names appear. My dissertation advisor, Gary A. Olson, disagreed with—as he once put it somewhat jokingly—"almost every single word" in that document. But he recognized that I was using what I had learned from him and taking it in unexpected (to him) directions, and he understood that his job was not to make me revise the dissertation in his image. Susan Miller was a constant interlocutor during the arduous process of thoroughly revising that dissertation into my first book, *The Function of Theory in Composition Studies* (Sánchez 2005). She and I often disagreed on specific points, but these differences always served the project, even when it questioned her own previously stated claims (Sánchez 2005, 86). Similarly, another University of Utah colleague, Howard Horwitz, provided perceptive, generative, and generous readings that prompted some of the book's more adventurous (at the time) theoretical claims (Sánchez 2005, 99). Finally, Victor Villanueva's encouraging but detailed editorial advice on my second book project, *Inside the Subject* (Sánchez 2017), helped to better attune that book to its audience (making me a better "author" in the process). In all these instances, "reviewers" saw their analyses as contributions to the larger goal of advancing the project at hand, a project that would ultimately bear my name alone. This is how authorship works, for now. But their efforts were collaborative, and our agency was shared. It certainly was not mine alone, since without them those projects simply would not exist.

In addition to this, I have benefited from watching others in the field behave well toward others, thus modeling ways for me to proceed. Since 2014, I have been a small part of the Cultural Rhetorics Consortium, a group of scholars in rhetoric and writing whose goal is to "create space in which folks can find engagement, encouragement, support, and collaboration with each other" (Cultural Rhetorics Consortium 2022). I have sat in meetings where colleagues such as Malea Powell, Phil Bratta, Gwendolyn Pough, and Marilee Brooks-Gillies have strategized paths toward a different kind of discipline, one explicitly oriented not only toward the idea that cultures and rhetorics are inevitably intertwined but also toward values of scholarly cooperation, relationality, and inclusion. Helping organize the 2016 Cultural Rhetorics Conference—and working with colleagues such as Andrea Riley Mukavetz, Alexandra Hidalgo, Terese Guinsatao Monberg, Erin Schaefer, and Hannah Espinoza—I saw the Consortium's goals and values enacted in various practical and administrative ways, from the vetting of proposals to the planning of the program.

In addition, I currently serve on the editorial board of the Consortium's journal, *Constellations: A Cultural Rhetorics Publishing Space*. From its founding, *Constellations* has pursued what Powell calls "a mentoring-focused editorial practice" (Powell 2022, 208). It asks certain reviewers to mentor the authors whose manuscripts they have reviewed, to help those authors make revisions that will get their manuscripts ready for publication. It consciously and intentionally uses the peer review process to promote inclusivity, minimize gatekeeping, and provide an alternative to "the cruelty and violence"—what I have been calling the dickishness—"of a profession that holds high rejection rates as a standard of prestige" (Powell 2022, 209). I have done some of this mentoring for *Constellations*. It mirrors the informal mentoring work I—and many others—do with up-and-coming scholars, but here it is purposefully built into the review and editorial process. And I have wondered why every journal in our field does not work this way right now. While some of them do—as indicated, for example, in Cruz Medina's contribution to this volume—I don't pretend to know about everything going on in every corner. But it seems to me that if we want to have a field in which many voices are not only heard but encouraged, valued, and nourished—a goal set for us decades ago—then this is one specific way to do so. As Powell notes, traditional publishing venues use the "revise and resubmit" option to allow for a manuscript's continued development and eventual publication (Powell 2022, 209). We see this option play out in Dana Comi and Alisa Russel's contribution to this volume, as they develop their own horizontal mentoring approach to helping each other. But "revise and resubmit" is different, in substance and tone, from the "accept with mentoring and revision" response preferred by *Constellations* (Powell 2022, 209). The latter is not only an invitation but a concrete offer of help. It is the procedural and administrative enshrinement of what we already know: that our field's scholarship emerges through relation, collaboration, and cooperation.

PROCESS

While a given journal or press may not use a review process like that of *Constellations*, a reviewer can nonetheless adopt and approximate that ethos in any venue. Above, I mentioned Reviewer 2, and I know most of us find that kind of behavior unacceptable. To me, it is so unacceptable, unnecessary, and toxic that the fear of *inadvertently* acting that way preemptively affects my behavior, prompting me to reaffirm my commitment to *not* act like a dick and instead to be helpful, kind, and possibly instructive. This commitment plays out most thoroughly, most meticulously, when I revise my manuscript reviews before submitting them. I am not trying to appear especially virtuous or conscientious, but I am acknowledging that the impulse to act like a dick is never entirely absent, certainly not in me.

I cannot use one of my actual manuscript reviews as an example, which puts me at a something of a disadvantage. I cannot ethically point to a real sentence I have written to show how I revised the dickish elements out of it and turned it into a perceptive and helpful comment that the author might find useful. So, instead I'll explain my state of mind and thought process as I take particular steps and do the intellectual work of trying to respond intelligently, constructively, and collegially.

First, I read the manuscript all the way through without jotting down any marks or comments, apart from a few reminders about the content of a particular passage. I do this for philosophical and practical reasons. By helping me get a sense of the project's scope, flow, and contours, it goes a long way toward preempting any dickish remarks I might otherwise make. I will be better prepared, for example, to comment on a point that appears on page 2 if I know it resurfaces on page 22, perhaps in a consequentially different context that informs its earlier appearance. This saves me time in the long run, of course, because I won't have to go back and revise my possibly dickish comment on page 2, equipped now with what I learned on page 22. But it also enacts the generosity of attitude that Powell's epigraph called for. I should not stand poised, as it were, to pounce on what I perceive as my colleague's omissions, errors, or infelicities. So, even though I will spend time later trying to revise any residual dickishness from my review, that work will go more smoothly, successfully, and easily if I can avoid the dickishness in the first place.

This step resembles the instructions many of us give to brand-new TAs: read the work, first, without a literal or metaphorical pen in hand. As such, I am invoking Peter Elbow's believing game, which he describes, in part, as "trying to get inside the head of someone" (Elbow [1973] 1998, 149), and Carl Rogers's recommendation, made over seventy years ago, "to see the expressed idea and attitude from the other person's point of view . . . to achieve his [sic] frame of reference in regard to the thing he [sic] is talking about" (Rogers 1952, 84). Of course, the believing game and Rogerian rhetoric are more complex and nuanced than my cursory references indicate. But I am helped by remembering them even in such a cursory way. That is, I am reminded that before I make any critical or evaluative statements, I must know, as best I can, what the author is trying to do.

The first draft of my review, then, is a summary of the manuscript: whatever it is arguing, reporting, or relaying to readers. My goal is to faithfully render the author's line of thought: to hold a mirror to the text and reflect it back to the author. This is more than a cursory overview; it is not something I "get out of the way" before moving on to the supposed substance of my review. My summary is integral to the review, and it takes up considerable space. To do this work carefully and accurately, I often reread key passages and paragraphs several times, making sure the sentences I am writing are as accurate as I can make them. As with student writing, sometimes this means pointing to implied rather than stated connections between ideas in the text and thereby possibly helping the author better see their own text. This parallels what happens when we work with students' writing: we tell them what we see in their drafts, in turn letting them better see what they are trying to do, or not to do.

Steve Parks describes a similar situation, one in which a writer in a Syracuse labor union group insisted that Parks "help him understand how to effectively present his vision to an audience" rather than offer vaguely positive assessments. Doing so, Parks came to understand, would help the writer "produce the best articulation of his unique vision," and it "showed respect for his writing" (Parks 2019, 281). This kind of interaction and relationship creates a positive context for recommendations and constructive criticism, because it lets the author know that their work is being carefully read and encountered on its own terms. Just as I should not stand ready and eager to "pounce" on an author's perceived errors, peer review as a whole should not function as a trial, especially not for scholars from groups whose standing in the field has already been persistently scrutinized, policed, and denied. Peer review should not be a process by which you must prove you belong. Instead, it should be a process by which colleagues make each other's work better. This process begins by reading manuscripts carefully, accurately, and respectfully—by taking the believing game seriously.

After the summary, I then explain that if I have missed the mark, both author and editor should feel free to stop reading the review, since it will be based on my flawed observations and assumptions. If I have gotten it wrong, in full or in part, there's little point in pursuing my subsequent recommendations. Nor will I be insulted or offended if either the author or the editor decide I am off base. (If, months later, I see the article published without my recommendations having been taken into account, I will not take this as a sign that something went wrong, that I was ignored, or that the process is corrupt.) Next, I write that if my description is accurate, I hope the author will read my recommendations as efforts to help them reach and refine their goals. I say this because I do not want what I recommend to be interpreted as an attempt to bend their project toward my vision. That is, I am not trying to get them to write the manuscript I would have written or that I think should have been written. Rather, as Parks notes, I'm interested in "opening opportunities" for them to better achieve their vision, rather than making demands upon them (Parks 2019, 282).

For example, if an author is using narrative as a methodology—as Powell and Martinez do, as many scholars in our field do—my job is not to suggest ways they might "shore up" this work by citing research and scholarship that an imagined reader will find more familiar and, in that sense, comfortable. This is something I might do, but again, I am not the author of the manuscript. Furthermore, my job is not to drag the author's work into the Burkean parlor, which Jacqueline Rhodes refers to, ironically, as "our treasured metaphor" and which, she notes, "is governed by a logic of mastery, of individual attainment, and of disciplinary assessment of that attainment" (Rhodes 2019, 162). Rather, my job is to recognize that the author is consciously situating their work in certain epistemological contexts, contexts that they are inviting readers to learn about, if they don't already know them, because doing so deepens and widens the discipline's knowledge base. And, having recognized this attempt, my job is to help the author succeed at it.

Again, the parallels with teaching practice abound. Every semester, students in my advanced composition courses assume there is something like a Burkean parlor, to which I have the key and in which they will find academic success and a good grade. Early in the term, I spend considerable time and energy convincing them that no such parlor exists and that I do not expect their writing to conform obligingly to scholarly, argumentative, or stylistic expectations. Instead, I want them to arrive at their own voices and visions, whatever those might be, and I want to offer whatever help I can while they do so. Of course, I know some things about writing and rhetoric that they do not—thanks to my training and experience—and I share these things with them. But, to borrow another familiar trope, my goal is not to make them invent the university that already exists; rather, it is to help them imagine new ones. So it is with scholarly peer review.

Once I have added my recommendations to the summary, I have completed the draft of the review. Then, if time permits, I set it aside for a while, perhaps several days. As we tell our students, some cognitive and emotional distance can create useful perspective that can, in turn, productively inform the revision process. In this case, the distance allows me to reflect upon the manuscript itself and my response to it. It allows me to approach similar questions—have I read it carefully? did I summarize it accurately? do my recommendations help both author and editor?—from a slightly different perspective. This helps curb any "hot take" reactions that might have accompanied my first readings.

The revisions to my review focus on substance, but mostly they emphasize style. I try to make sure, of course, that what I have written—either in summary or by way of recommendation—remains relevant and useful. But I also work on how my message reads. For example, I frame the review as a letter addressed to a colleague, one who has devoted significant time, energy, and thought into the manuscript. I open and close the review by thanking my colleague for the chance to read and learn from their work. And throughout the review, I assume a friendly tone that resembles a conversation we might enjoy at a conference over drinks or coffee.

All of this might seem "touchy-feely" and thus inappropriate, or at least unnecessary, to some. Earlier in my career, I would have agreed. But the older I get, and the more I find myself in a position of responsibility and mentorship toward younger scholars, the more clearly I see that the peer review process is no place (in fact, is one of the worst places) for competition, egoism, animosity, pettiness, and other forms of aggression that we dignify as "rigor." This does not mean that I do not review manuscripts carefully, critically, and with an eye toward publishing the best possible research. But it does mean that I try not to be a dick about it.

REFERENCES

"Anti-Racist Scholarly Reviewing Practices: A Heuristic for Editors, Reviewers, and Authors." 2021. https://tinyurl.com/reviewheuristic.

Cultural Rhetorics Consortium. 2022. "Home." https://cultrhetconsortium.org/.

Elbow, Peter. (1973) 1998. *Writing without Teachers.* Twenty-fifth anniv. ed. New York: Oxford University Press.

Maraj, Louis M. 2021. "Review of *Counterstory: The Rhetoric and Writing of Critical Race Theory*, by Aja Y. Martinez." *Composition Studies*, no. 49, 196–99.

Martinez, Aja Y. 2020. *Counterstory: The Rhetoric and Writing of Critical Race Theory.* Urbana, IL: National Council of Teachers of English.

Parks, Steve. 2019. "From Fear to Collaboration: Working with Academic Journal/Series Editors." In *Explanation Points: Publishing in Rhetoric and Composition*, edited by John R. Gallagher and Danielle Nicole DeVoss, 280–82. Logan: Utah State University Press.

Powell, Malea. 2004. "Down by the River, or How Susan La Flesche Picotte Can Teach Us about Alliance as a Practice of Survivance." *College English*, no. 67, 38–60.

Powell, Malea. 2022. "Making Space for Diverse Knowledges: Building Cultural Rhetorics Editorial Practices." In *Behind the Curtain of Scholarly Publishing: Editors in Writing Studies*, edited by Greg Giberson, Megan Schoen, and Christian Weisser, 202–12. Logan: Utah State University Press.

Rhodes, Jacqueline. 2019. "Queer/ed Research: Disrupting the Unending Conversation." In *Explanation Points: Publishing in Rhetoric and Composition*, edited by John R. Gallagher and Danielle Nicole DeVoss, 161–65. Logan: Utah State University Press.

Rogers, Carl R. 1952. "Communication: Its Blocking and Its Facilitation." *ETC: A Review of General Semantics*, no. 9, 83–88.

Sánchez, Raúl. 2005. *The Function of Theory in Composition Studies.* Albany: State University of New York Press.

Sánchez, Raúl. 2017. *Inside the Subject: A Theory of Identity for the Study of Writing.* Urbana, IL: National Council of Teachers of English.

10
REVISION AS PROTECTING WHAT IS IMPORTANT

Cruz Medina

This is a story about drafting and revising an article manuscript for an ill-fitting "top-tier" journal while trying to protect the important student writing at the heart of the piece. In 2015, I began researching the translingual practices of multilingual students in a first-year composition (FYC) course at my Bay Area university. When I submitted the manuscript to an National Council of Teachers of English (NCTE) journal, I revised the format of the manuscript for a more empirical model in line with the journal's guidelines, and the manuscript was ultimately rejected after revision and resubmission. Even though I had envisioned this piece as addressing the decolonial potential of multilingual students performing translingual practices, I made needless revisions to sound more empirical, because I was drawn to the allure of the "top-tier" journal. This chapter is about finding my way back to the correct methodology and how generous *Composition Studies* journal editors helped to restore my confidence in an article that would ultimately be published and selected for the *Best of the Journals of Rhetoric and Composition 2020* (Medina 2021).

When I first started writing what would become "Decolonial Potential in a Multilingual FYC" (Medina 2019), I was motivated by the negative experiences that my multilingual students had written about in their literacy narratives in the bilingual first-year writing course I taught. The internalized inferiority or isolation that my students had experienced because of their multilingual abilities felt important for me to share; for example, one student wrote: "Throughout my education, I always viewed English as a superior language to my native Spanish language due to the constant separation of students into classrooms of different English levels" (as cited in Medina 2019, 81). Many of my multilingual students had concluded, after having discussed their feelings of isolation, that they would adapt their English to meet the linguistic expectations in the area, to improve their job prospects. Having written about decoloniality in terms of Latinx pop culture (Medina 2015), digital archives (Medina 2016), and student writing (Medina 2013), I felt that the students' experiences and their conclusions came from internalized standards of the dominant monolingual ideological and economic forces. Simply put: the whiteness of settler colonialism in Silicon Valley made my students feel that they would be measured against an impossible standard that framed their multilingual abilities as deficient.

However, when it came to writing about these literacy narratives, I targeted selective NCTE journals and found myself similarly feeling as though I had to write with rigid expectations on behalf of my imagined audience. First, I felt unsure whether the audiences would be receptive to scholarship on translingualism, so I felt an additional concern about applying a decolonial approach, because Indigenous forms of knowledge-making like storytelling are not always accepted in NCTE journals, which can skew towards more "objective" approaches. The students' writing, their translingual experiences, and the decolonial approach were the most important aspects for the article; however, due to allowing myself to contort my writing to something it wasn't and omitting this method in the initial drafts, the revision process took much longer (*years!*) than it should have.

The initial draft I began writing in 2016 included a lot of material about my university's context of the Bay Area, some mention of California English-only politics, and the influence of Silicon Valley. Keeping the field of writing studies in mind, I framed the analysis around David Bartholomae's (1985) "Inventing the University" because I imagined my writing studies audience firmly identifying with canonical references, which would then ideally help to make the material on translingualism more situated in relation to familiar academic discussions. The original abstract was:

> This article is about the practical application of translingualism in a first-year writing course, examining the responses of students in this course through the data collected in literacy narratives that speak to linguistic difference, the myth of linguistic homogeneity, and translingualism; however, I begin with a contemporary exhibit that satirizes the context for where this research comes from because of the dominant role that the technology industry plays in the U.S. economy, not to mention the affordances technology provides for those of us in writing studies.

Although I can clearly see how the central focus on market forces of the tech industry was my desire to address capitalism's role in colonialism, the "satirizing" aspect stood in place of the decolonial critique and detracted from the focus of my analysis of translingual practices. In the introduction, I included quotes from the HBO television show *Silicon Valley*, where different app developers all say that they "want to make a better world" whereas the central focus of everyone in the show is to make the most money. The critique of *Silicon Valley* was rooted in capitalism's impact on how language difference is viewed, but the mention of the show detracted from my original motivation: the students' writing.

Although I did not initially incorporate a decolonial methodology, I drew on Suresh Canagarajah's (2012) discussion of autoethnography as a way to frame the value of lived experiences. I explained how Canagarajah draws attention to emotions experienced when language differences are central to an experience. I paraphrased his work when I described the literacy narrative assignment where "I ask students to think about experiences that connect to an emotion because these emotions connect to how we think about people's response to our use of language." When I submitted this early draft, it was desk-rejected by the editor at an NCTE journal with minimal feedback, noting that the journal had recently published something on translingualism (which I knew, encouraged that the journal published scholarship in that area.) To be fair, the editor's feedback got at my omission of decoloniality in relation to translingualism when the editor wrote that my submission needed to "thicken the conversation about it in some substantive way." In wanting to remain somewhat central to the conversation, I had not pushed the academic conversation much further because of my hesitancy to include a decolonial approach.

It wasn't much later that I attended a roundtable of journal editors at the College Composition and Communication Conference (CCCC) and heard the incoming editor of a different NCTE journal announce a new section about pedagogical innovation to which I decided to submit my article. Though pedagogically oriented, the description for this new section emphasized empiricism; the section "showcases primary classroom documents and empirically documented practices that translate disciplinary expertise into the instructional practice" ("*College English* Submission Guidelines"). To fit this focus, I cut some of the Silicon Valley context and moved up references to the journal's recent special issue on translingualism. The revised abstract read:

> Based on the data collected from student writing, I posit that translingualism taught alongside critique of monolingual ideology to critically raise student awareness of how they can begin to understand their place in inventing the university (*à la* Bartholomae); additionally, translingualism, as a concept, reframes linguistic diversity, which has traditionally been

portrayed as a deficit (e.g., "broken English"), as an additional literacy resource and rhetorical mode available to them.

Rereading this abstract is painful, in no small part because of my attempt to sound extra empirical, but also because I was putting the form of the article before the content, which provoked an entirely different format. The reviewers offered thorough feedback that called for a more empirical methodology than what they considered to be a more interpretive lens of translingualism. With the emphasis on empiricism, I talked myself out of incorporating a decolonial methodology. The journal's section seemed in many ways antithetical to decolonial knowledge and practices that seek to redress the colonial paradigm that relies on the collection of data. But I couldn't break from the internalized expectations I put on myself to align with the journal.

Writing this is hard, perhaps in part because revision can be hard work, but more so because returning to the reviewers' comments is also painful. Reading reviewer feedback can often be nerve-wracking, but looking at reviewer suggestions from a journal that was not meant for work like mine feels more like peeling off a bandage that covered a scar from unnecessary surgery. Reading the list of "comments" and the "changes" or "rebuttals" that the editor asked me to include with my resubmission, I found comments that seemed to suggest that a reviewer at times might not have been reading too closely. Their comments seemed to support their assessment more than to offer revision guidance:

> Comment: "It promises to develop a shared vocabulary, again something that the article really can't fulfill."
> Rebuttal: The "shared vocabulary" refers to the introduction of terms such as monolingual ideology, myth of linguistic homogeneity, translingualism, multilingualism in the articles that precede the literacy narrative assignment. ("Revision Suggestions for Your Article" 2017)

In the next draft, I still added longer definitions for some of these terms. However, the tone of the reviewer's recommendations suggested that no amount of revision would meet expectations, like a failing grade that the feedback had to defend.

In other instances, the phrasing of the feedback continued to discourage revision. Both reviewers seemed to make suggestions in relation to journal criteria, although this did not stop one reviewer from slipping in negative commentary that they then backpedaled from as they seemed to be thinking through their explanation. The reviewer commented, "The article itself is truly disorganized; I didn't see an underlying structure that would help a reader follow everything coherently.

Maybe 'disorganized' isn't quite the right word—it's just very narrative, not structured." And to their credit, the initial draft that I submitted began with more narrative that was meant to situate the research:

> After having taught first year writing at the University of Arizona, a large land-grant state university in the Southwest, I witnessed how conservative state legislatures dismantle the Mexican American Studies program at the Tucson High School, despite the fact that it contributed to increased state test scores and graduation rates (Cabrera et al.; Medina). . . . So, when I returned to my native state of California to begin my first tenure-track job teaching at a private liberal arts university in the Bay Area of Northern California, I kept in mind that my home state had also been affected by policy such as Proposition 63, which made English the "official" language in 1986.

In the reviewer's initial comment, they called the manuscript "disorganized" before revising their description in the comment to call it "very narrative." Unfortunately, comments like this confirmed my original reluctance to include a decolonial methodology, because decolonial practices include storytelling, or narrative, as a legitimate form of knowledge-building (King, Gubele, and Rain Anderson 2015). Again, it was my own mistake not to include decoloniality in this draft, although it can be difficult to get past reviewer comments that read more like punitive intrusive thoughts rather than constructive feedback.

Even though the motivation for writing this article was to criticize the colonial force of monolingual ideology impacting my multilingual students, I begrudgingly added critical discourse analysis as the method in an attempt to appease the journal and remain critical of social power dynamics. I very much felt what Joseph Harris articulates in this collection when he writes that "we often revise to meet the demands of others" (Harris, 27). My revision choices were somewhat ironic, because I was responding to social forces similar to those I was critiquing in my article, as exemplified by revisions to the first line of the introduction that made it read more like an abstract: "Scholars across composition studies (Baca; Banks; Canagarajah; Cushman; Haas; Selfe; Shipka) have widened the scope from the monolingual perspective about writing in English to arguing for valuing and teaching multilingualism, non-alphabetic modes and composing with multiple modes." I addressed the organization suggestion by framing the article in a traditional IMRaD format (Introduction, Method, Results, and Discussion). I continued to go against what was important by second-guessing the decolonial argument and pushing the student voices into the analysis or discussion section of the IMRaD format. All of this ran in opposition to the original motivation of showcasing multilingual voices that are negatively framed by English-only rhetoric. This revised manuscript was ultimately rejected.

Fortunately, during this submission and revision process, I had a short piece published in *Composition Studies* (Medina 2017) as a part of the "Where We Are" section on Latinx Compositions and Rhetorics. It was that short piece and the inclusive leadership of Laura Micciche that inspired global revisions and reworking the translingual piece with a decolonial methodology. Still under the influence of the most recent NCTE journal's reviewer feedback, I revised and submitted a manuscript that followed something similar to an IMRaD format. The first line had the grand summative statement about Englishes: "Within rhetoric and composition, African American, American Indian, and Latinx scholars have questioned the extent to which the field can, across university contexts, operate within higher education and against colonial paradigms undergirded by racism, sexism, classism, and other systems of oppression that impact whose voices or English(es) are valued." Though the line contains fewer references than the previous version, the next few lines remained somewhat dense as I introduced important ideas about decolonialism.

One of the biggest turning points in my revision came after I submitted my revised manuscript based on the editorial and reviewer feedback. Micciche asked if I would be interested in working with Bob Mayberry, a former editor of the journal. Micciche explained that doing so could make the manuscript that much stronger before the reviewers reread it. I was somewhat exhausted by the thought of another go-round with more feedback, but I knew Micciche's recommendation came from a place of genuinely wanting to help, especially when compared with my previous editorial and reviewer experiences. Mayberry was such a good reader for this article that he even read an earlier article of mine, "Nuestros Refranes" in *Reflections* (Medina 2013); Mayberry said that reading my earlier article helped him see connections between both pieces. He helped me declutter my prose from some of the theoretical jargon that I was still hiding behind in the same way that the IMRaD format depersonalizes the writer and subject for supposed empirical neutrality.

One of the major revisions that I made was forefronting the student voices, which provided the exigency that helped the reader to see why the decolonial potential of this program should be considered. Mayberry offered me the same advice that Cristina Kirklighter, then editor of *Reflections*, had also given me, about beginning with students' voices. My article "Nuestros Refranes" begins: "In the words of a high school student in Tucson, 'Words of wisdom, from those who survived their grimmest days, speak in proverbs, or dichos, to live by' " (Medina 2013, 53). Kirklighter explained that with articles about students' writing, it only made sense to begin with the students' voices. Mayberry's editorial advice led to beginning with a student whom I coded as "Selena":

> A multilingual student, Selena, describes in her literacy narrative the feeling of vulnerability she experienced in elementary school when she moved from Mexico City, Mexico, to Toronto, Canada: "I would rather be in a tank full of hungry sharks than once again be vulnerable to a language barrier that had barely been trespassed months before." (Medina 2019, 74)

Beginning with student voices set the right tone to humanize the experiences in the students' writing, more so than in my previous, more empirical-sounding drafts. It was unfortunate that, in previous versions of my article, I had lost sight of what had originally motivated me: the student voices and experiences.

One of the main differences between the early reviewer feedback and what Micciche and Mayberry offered was the sustained editorial back-and-forth that helped me regain my focus. While this is not standard across journals, peer reviewers and editors could make their feedback more effective by building relationships with authors. Mayberry and Micciche worked with me to reorganize, offering generative ideas about shifting the student writing to earlier in the piece and moving the theoretical discussion to later, as opposed to the earlier feedback about being disorganized without offering any suggestion for revision. Their editorial work embodied what Raúl Sánchez envisions as a noncompetitive peer review that is "constructive, affirming, and focused on improvement and cooperation" (Sánchez, this collection, 118).

I should clarify that I assume all blame for not following my initial impulse to incorporate decolonialism. As a Chicano scholar, my thinking and writing is rooted in the genealogy of Gloria Anzaldúa's (1987) work, which offers criticism of colonialism while focusing on Indigeneity and the struggle for land. Cana Uluak Itchuaqiyaq and Breeanne Matheson deftly articulate my desire for transparency in the revision process with decolonial work when they write, "We believe that by talking about and modeling transparency regarding the complexities we've faced as scholars attempting to do decolonial work, we provide space for other scholars to acknowledge and . . . rectify the messiness involved in their own work" (2021, 21). If anything, I think this piece reveals some of the messiness of continually working to resist what we have been inculcated to believe that we desire from our work.

Perhaps because there is something of a happy ending, I feel more comfortable sharing my numerous (and repeated) mistakes during the revision process of this article that was ultimately published in *Composition Studies*. I am additionally honored that "Decolonial Potential in a Multilingual FYC" was also included in the *Best of 2020 Rhetoric and Composition Journals* collection (Medina 2021). Quoting the materials generated during the editorial process, I tried my best to acknowledge the editorial work that, as I explained, "restored my faith in my writing" (Medina 2021, 82). Though the audiences we imagine might change and shift for good reasons, protecting what motivates us to write can be the most important aspect of writing, because it is what keeps us writing.

REFERENCES

Anzaldúa, Gloria. (1987) 1999. *Borderlands / La frontera: The New Mestiza*. San Francisco, CA: Aunt Lute.

Bartholomae, David. 1985. "Inventing the University." *When A Writer Can't Write*, edited by Mike Rose, 134–65. New York: Guilford.

Cabrera, Nolan L., Jeffrey F. Milem, Ozan Jaquette, and Ronald W. Marx. 2014. "Missing the (Student Achievement) Forest for All the (Political) Trees: Empiricism and the Mexican American Studies Controversy in Tucson." *American Educational Research Journal* 51 (6): 1084–118.

Canagarajah, A. Suresh. 2012. "Autoethnography in the Study of Multilingual Writers." In *Writing Studies Research in Practice: Methods and Methodologies*, edited by Lee Nickoson and Mary P. Sheridan, 113–24. Carbondale: Southern Illinois University Press.

"*College English* Submission Guidelines." National Council of Teachers of English. Accessed October 25, 2021. https://ncte.org/resources/journals/college-english/write-for-us/.

Dyste, Connie. 1989. "Proposition 63: The California English Language Amendment." *Applied Linguistics* 10 (3): 313–30.

Itchuaqiyaq, Cana Uluak, and Breeanne Matheson. 2021. "Decolonizing Decoloniality: Considering the (Mis)use of Decolonial Frameworks in TPC Scholarship." *Communication Design Quarterly* 9 (1): 20–31.

King, Lisa, Rose Gubele, and Joyce Rain Anderson. 2015. *Survivance, Sovereignty, and Story: Teaching American Indian Rhetorics*. Logan: Utah State University Press.

Medina, Cruz. 2013. "Nuestros Refranes: Culturally Relevant Writing in Tucson High Schools." *Reflections: A Journal of Public Rhetoric, Civic Writing, and Service Learning* 12 (3): 52–79.

Medina, Cruz. 2015. *Reclaiming Poch@ Pop: Examining Rhetoric of Cultural Deficiency*. New York: Palgrave MacMillan.

Medina, Cruz. 2016. "Poch@: Latin@ Blogs in the Decolonial Archives." In *Decolonizing Rhetoric and Composition Studies: New Latinx Keywords for Theory and Pedagogy*, edited by Iris Ruiz and Raúl Sánchez, 93–107. New York: Palgrave Macmillan.

Medina, Cruz. 2017. "Identity, Decolonialism, and Digital Archives." *Composition Studies* 45 (2): 222–25.

Medina, Cruz. 2019. "Decolonial Potential in a Multilingual FYC." *Composition Studies* 47 (1): 74–95.

Medina, Cruz. 2021. "Composition Studies: Decolonial Potential in a Multilingual FYC." In *Best of the Journals of Rhetoric and Composition 2020*, edited by Jessica Pauszek, Kristi Girdharry, Charles Lesh, David Blakesley, and Steve Parks, 58–84. Anderson, SC: Parlor Press.

SET 4

Revision Meets the World

Allison D. Carr

As this book is being produced, state governments are working overtime to ban speech and other forms of expression, none more aggressively than the Florida state legislature, which in March 2022 passed HB 7 (the "Stop WOKE" Act), prohibiting the inclusion of materials in Florida's public schools and workplaces that would accurately detail the "legacy of racism" in the United States (SPLC 2022). In Iowa, where contributor Mike Garcia directs the writing center at Luther College, a private liberal arts college in the northeast corner of the state, the legislature has passed similar measures. House File 802 (HF802), known locally as the "divisive concepts bill" (King 2022), signed into law by Republican governor Kim Reynolds in June 2021, applies to public workplaces, K–12 schools, and public colleges, and lists ten so-called "divisive concepts" that are prohibited, including "that the United States and the state of Iowa are fundamentally or systemically racist or sexist" (Iowa State Legislature 2021). In addition to relying on *willful misunderstandings* to criminalize inclusive or culturally responsive programming, measures such as these open the door for nefarious and litigious groups such as Turning Point USA to target individuals and organizations for legal *and* extralegal action (such as doxxing, online harassment, or smear campaigns).[1]

Such is the minefield Garcia finds himself navigating at the outset of his chapter in this volume. Though Garcia's institution is private, and therefore *technically* outside the reach of the state legislature's animus, his chapter vibrates with an anxiety simmering beneath, and in many instances shaping, the discussions he has with his writing center staff in their work to write and revise an antiracism statement shortly after HF 802 was signed. Further texturing Garcia's revision work with his staff: descriptions of the harassment and press faced by Asao Inoue after his writing center at UW Tacoma published a similar statement, an early model for others; and reminders that when the Luther College office for Diversity, Equity, and Inclusion circulated a first draft of *their* antiracism statement for feedback, some members of the faculty called it "dystopian" (Garcia, chapter 11). As he and his staff continue to review comparable statements as well as community reactions to them, they determine that avoiding mention of the words *white* and *whiteness* and instead centering equity may enable them to assert their conviction without attracting unwanted attention. It is a compromise, of course. Would this elision be perceived as undermining the writing center's antiracism goals? Is it possible to be "antiracist" without naming the structures that enable racism? Or, would the (unfinished) work Garcia and his staff undertook be seen as "a strong version of a document that has never existed before—a mark of meaningful progress and a commitment to specific, near-future action" (150)?

Each of the chapters in the next set highlights moments in the revision process where the story of revision pivots, or comes to life, at the fulcrum of a single term or concept that seems to encapsulate writers' overall projects but also threatens to derail them altogether. For Garcia, that term is "white/ness." For Fulford and Frigo, "radical adaptability." For Basgier, "mandates" and "requirements." In the last set, we saw a similar dynamic with Medina's uncertainty over whether the inclusion of his students' voices belonged in an article he hoped to place in a top journal. (In the end, of course, with supportive mentorship, Medina was able to diffuse that worry and protect what felt most important to him.)

It's funny—how, in the process of revising statements, research, curricular overviews, and other documents, the full rhetorical power of individual signifiers can be found to carry so much weight. Such was the case with our work on this book, which provoked surprisingly animated disagreements about whether to use the noun or gerund form in the title: *revision* moves, or *revising* moves? What subtle but not insignificant details came into view as we flipped between these grammatical forms? Which did we want to prioritize? Likewise, with our titular insistence that revising (or revision) *moves*? If we were committed to that conviction, we would need to build a book that, itself, *moved*.

Poet Devin Kelly writes in his weekly *Substack* newsletter, *Ordinary Plots*, about movement, describing the very practice of reading poems as a practice teaching "that feeling can be the operating energy of a piece of writing, that a piece of writing can move by force of feeling alone. [. . .] That, when we say we are moved by something, we quite literally are. We are moved." It is this "force of feeling" that helped us find an emergent structure for this volume, and what propels the narratives in this set.

Set 4: Revision Meets the World   139

Collie Fulford and Stefanie Frigo's chapter begins in such a way as to suggest it will reveal the idiosyncratic details of asynchronous coauthorship. Yet, before their dialogue really settles into its groove, readers (and authors) are bombarded by news that Ahmaud Arbery has been murdered while out for a jog. Collie, then, can hardly get a word in before a staccato-like intrusion of emergency proclamations and more police-perpetrated violence sweeps, like wildfire, through the narrative. No doubt, anybody reading can recall the escalation of bewildering, traumatic, enraging, worrying news in early 2020; many readers will probably recall additional reports from their own communities which would fit neatly in line with the news Fulford and Frigo process in Durham. It's no wonder, as the world burns around them, that their reconstruction of their writing and revision process would be characterized by their effort to hold onto the piece of it that felt, perhaps, like an oxygen mask.

And while Christopher Basgier's narrative of revising curricular documents for his institution's WAC programs doesn't situate itself in such socially tense context, it is difficult to read his essay without noticing the growing sense of risk or precarity that attends his revision process, as upper administrators signal their preference that the documents move away from the version that Basgier and his collaborators, in their disciplinary expertise, are striving to advance. Through his narration and side-by-side comparisons of key moments in each draft, we can observe in slow motion Basgier's deft maneuvering between conflicted stakeholders and his internal negotiation of how each adjustment comes to bear on his sense of himself as WAC director. These moments recall Sills and F. Sánchez's experiences working on job documents, and even Wenger's years-long work to make her WPA labor visible in her annual review.

In the end, Garcia, Fulford and Frigo, and Basgier manage to let go of the thing that initially anchors their ideas. Their decisions aren't uncomplicated and certainly aren't made without an accompanying sense of loss or compromise. I think it's common to think of revision as something like forward propulsion, always iterating *toward* an ideal, seeing and reseeing until the vision is clear, crisp, in focus. (I can't stop hearing the cheerful voice of my optometrist as I write this: "One or two? One or two?") As you read the stories in this set, you may observe that, at some points, the drafts seem to be moving backward, away from the thing their authors have set out to do. We know by now that binaries like forward/backward are reductive, and it is the case that these stories offer another view altogether: that revision is (re)calibration, an iterative undertaking that adjusts over time to changing circumstances, changing stakes, and our own changing relationship with our work and our capacities to do that work.

NOTE

1. In our production timeline, a full year has passed since writing this opening, and things are only worse. As we prepare to submit this manuscript for copyediting, transphobic and queer-erasing legislation is winding its way through several state legislatures, and in Florida, the governor has escalated his fascist campaign to destroy higher education entirely. If the above described "Stop WOKE Act" was a lit match, his most recently introduced higher education bill—which among other things bans gender studies majors and minors as well as any initiatives or curricula aimed at increasing diversity, equity, and inclusion—is a blowtorch. I shudder to imagine what things will look like when this book is in readers' hands.

REFERENCES

Kelly, Devin Gael. 2022. "Sean Thomas Dougherty's 'Grief's Familiar Rooms.'" *Ordinary Plots* (newsletter). *Substack*. May 29, 2022. https://ordinaryplots.substack.com/p/sean-thomas-doughertys-griefs-familiar.

King, Grace. 2022. "Iowa Law That Bans Teaching 'Divisive Concepts' Has 'Chilling Effect' on Equity, Education Experts Say." *Cedar Rapids Gazette*, February 21, 2022. https://www.thegazette.com/k/iowa-law-that-bans-teaching-divisive-concepts-has-chilling-effect-on-equity-education-experts-s/.

SPLC (Southern Poverty Law Center). 2022. "SPLC Files Amicus Brief in Suit against Florida's Stop WOKE Act." May 26, 2022. https://www.splcenter.org/news/2022/05/26/splc-files-amicus-brief-suit-against-floridas-stop-woke-act.

11

REVISING AN ANTIRACISM STATEMENT FOR KNOWN AND UNKNOWN AUDIENCES

Mike Garcia

Five tutors, one writing director, and a large, empty whiteboard. Our task was to write an antiracism statement on behalf of the writing center. But we were already getting writer's block at the whiteboard stage. We were stuck on enormous conceptual questions: *What are we trying to do here? Are we activists? Are we criticizing our own college? Are we taking a position on Standard English? Who's reading this, and what will they expect?* We weren't close to knowing the scope and purpose of our statement or the language we would use for it.

In retrospect, this shouldn't have been surprising. Sure, we had no shortage of models: there are plenty of antiracism statements in circulation online, including several written by writing center staff. However, there wasn't a set format we could look up, and it would be a stretch to say there was (or is) consensus on the definition or purpose of the genre. It seems that writing centers develop their statements by adapting the ones that already exist. So it goes with new genres. At this point, all we could do was set up our own goals and start writing.

This was the first of a series of meetings I had set up with a group of five tutors with the goal of producing a statement. All of the tutors were undergraduates in their second or third years (we do not have graduate students at our college), and one of the five was a student of color. The group simply comprised whoever was available for the project at the time in our writing center staff of seven. None of the tutors had studied antiracism as a concept—at least not by that name—and, until I proposed this project, were unaware of the genre of an antiracism statement. I led the project as a faculty member of color but also as the writing director at the college, hired to bring expertise from the discipline of composition to our writing programs.

Our blank whiteboard and big questions prompted us to take a step back. We left that whiteboard blank for a while and ran the next couple of meetings like a minicourse, reading a handful of pieces on antiracism (especially in education), looking at other statements, thinking about our potential audiences, and defining what we wanted to accomplish. We asked ourselves: How do we write a statement that articulates a real, active antiracist vision?

THE "ZERO DRAFT"

We began trying to define the genre and task. We considered the fact, mentioned above, that writing centers appear to write their statements mostly by adapting others'. This suggested to us that one of the purposes of such a statement is to show *solidarity* with other writing centers—to join them in a shared mission. So as a starting point in drafting, a couple of us attempted to synthesize several statements into a single document: the zero draft (this is a term carried over from first-year composition courses). Ours was a patchwritten, cut-and-pasted, redundant collection of quotations with a few freewritten notes alongside—a far cry from an actual draft of our statement. But from there, we were able to analyze patterns in content and rhetorical moves and figure out how writing centers were defining the genre for themselves.

This process helped us to articulate an early set of definitional questions: What is the "bare-minimum" coverage of an antiracism statement? What are the things that, if not accomplished, disqualify the statement from being an antiracism statement? And is there a difference between this bare-minimum coverage and *typical* coverage in a writing center context?

As we examined statements and constructed the zero draft, we wrote a list of definitional observations on the whiteboard. Here's a sampling from our list:

Antiracism statements . . .

- make claims about language and privilege.
- suggest training on these topics for writing center tutors and staff.
- suggest specific antiracist action items for the center.
- acknowledge the writing center's role in privileging languages and dialects.
- comment on the broader society (?)
- position writing center tutors as activists and the writing center as a center of activism (?)
- call out whiteness / white supremacy by name (?)

As you can see, we started to become less certain about the must-have status of our items as we proceeded down the list. There are two reasons for this. First, we noticed that some writing center statements didn't cover all of the later items. Also, we wondered whether an antiracism statement might be able to accomplish its overall goals without doing some of these specific things.

In the second or third meeting, a tutor grabbed a marker and divided the whiteboard into four sections:

1. General def. of statement / purpose of our statement
2. Topics to be covered: CLAIMS
3. What are we committing to do? ACTIONS
4. Language / phrasing dos and don'ts

Our definitional observations went into section 1. We then wrote down the claims and actions made in other statements in sections 2 and 3, and we left section 4 for later. For a moment, our zero draft and whiteboard lists seemed to be working well together, and the rest of the process looked like a reasonably linear one: we'd produce a draft, make sure the lists in sections 2 and 3 on the whiteboard were covered, and then revise the draft with increased attention to section 4.

DEFINING THE PROJECT: AUDIENCE AND CONTENT

However, this vision of the future became complicated in our fourth and fifth meetings as we paid closer attention to the potential audiences of our statement. Normally, when a writing center releases a document to the "public" (e.g., an annual report), the document finds a home somewhere on the college website, and the actual readership is small. For writing center directors like myself, that limited, familiar audience makes our writing and revision processes fairly uncomplicated. However, the rules are different for public documents related to diversity, equity, and inclusion (DEI). In recent years, as our group discovered, right-wing journalistic outlets have sought out such pieces and created a pipeline for them to reach a new audience. They point their readers toward DEI projects at schools and colleges, portraying them as antidemocratic endeavors meant to suppress opposing views. Though the hit pieces produced by these organizations involve a lot of random cherry-picking, they've been given the appearance of coherence through a right-wing campaign against critical race theory, which has become a scapegoat used to demonize the DEI "agenda" (see Wallace-Wells [2021] for more information on the intentional nature of this campaign). This perceived threat to American values has created high-stakes working conditions for educators: increased surveillance of curriculum and readings by school boards and local governments; suspensions and firings; and even personal threats of violence from angry parents and random agitators. Legislation has followed. In Iowa, the state where I teach, a 2021 bill (HF 802) has made it illegal for public schools and universities to teach content or offer training that describes the state or the US as "systemically racist or sexist." The law also bans what it calls "race scapegoating." In response, the Office of the Provost at Iowa State University (2021) has asked faculty to "evaluate the language" in their course materials—that is, to check for any phrasing that might trigger an investigation by the state. These events suggest that those who write antiracism statements in a higher education setting need to consider a wider audience. Though our small, private college is hardly under the same microscope as Iowa State, we were compelled to keep the possible consequences of our work in mind and to factor that consideration into our writing and revision process.

To develop this line of thinking, I told my tutors the story of writing center director Asao B. Inoue, at the University of Washington–Tacoma, who cowrote and publicized an antiracism statement with his tutors. Like many statements of this type, the UW Tacoma statement articulated commitments to create a welcoming environment in the writing center, to embrace linguistic diversity, and to "be sensitive" to tutor behaviors that might make students from various linguistic backgrounds feel "uncomfortable or . . . inferior." The statement prefaced its commitments with a statement of beliefs, including a claim that "racism is pervasive." The statement named "standard English," as well as actions based on assessments of standard English proficiency, as products of systemic racism (Inoue 2017). Soon after the UWT Writing Center statement was published, it began to circulate among various right-wing outlets, which responded mostly to the statement's broader claims about structural racism. *The Daily Wire*'s response by Curl (2017) was titled "Grammar Is Racist? You Bet It Is, You Racist." On *Breitbart News*, Ciccotta's (2017) article was titled, "University of Washington Declares Proper Grammar Is Racist." On the surface, these distorted portrayals of the statement are snarky and benign rather than threatening—but because they fed into a larger narrative about indoctrination of students, Inoue and UWT received emails and letters containing obscene, racist language and literal threats of violence. As Inoue said to me in an email, the threats have "only gotten worse" as he has moved to a different institution and continued to work on antiracist projects. We discussed Inoue's story at length because we, too, were looking to articulate our commitments as our small way of combatting inequities in our educational system. The idea that simply identifying these inequities could be so provocative was an important point for us to consider. We were also aware of a recent attempt by our own college's Office of Equity and Inclusion to draft an antiracism statement for the college as a whole. The first full draft went to faculty, and some of them responded that it painted a "dystopian" picture of the college and failed to acknowledge the progress it has made toward inclusion. The document was shelved afterward.

As we considered these reactions, we thought about how to avoid provoking them in the first place: this would involve keeping our statements vague and noncommittal or skipping them altogether. We weren't worried about our college's defunding by the state, but we knew that any state or federal financial aid could be put at risk if those in power chose to make our institution's perceived politics an issue. And even if this didn't happen, we felt that we could do without negative reactions from faculty and staff or harassment from random readers of right-wing websites.

Despite these considerations, our research for this project had made us even more committed to writing a meaningful, truly antiracist document. First, we wanted a space to commit ourselves to specific actions on paper. We looked at our mostly white-staffed center, which used fairly traditional tutoring practices, and we asked ourselves how we could commit to change. Second, we acknowledged the problem, identified in the UW Tacoma statement and others, of using "Standard English" as a means of evaluating students. We understood it as both a product of "whitely ways" of thinking (to use Inoue's term [2021]) and a means of perpetuating that thinking, especially when the notion is given weight and legitimacy by institutions. We read Greenfield, who writes that "'Standard English' is a qualifier ascribed to many ways of speaking (and by extension, though differently, writing) by privileged white people, or perhaps more accurately, any variety of English that has not been associated historically with resistance by communities of color" (Greenfield 2011, 43). We knew that problematizing standard English in the writing center would entail resisting traditionally white values.

However, we also knew that acknowledging these truths in our meetings was different from specifically naming whiteness in a public statement. Inoue acknowledges that our use of such language can lead to accusations that we're calling all white people racist, even if that isn't our intention (Inoue 2021, 30). That assumption certainly seems to be at the heart of the Iowa law mentioned above as well as many others ostensibly designed to block "race scapegoating." As writing center staff, we asked ourselves, *Is it possible to discuss racism, and to make a strong statement against racism, without specifically calling out whiteness—and even if it is possible, is that what we want?* We saw evidence that other writing centers had probably had this discussion. For example, the word *white* does not appear in the Drexel Writing Center's (2021) excellent and detailed antiracism statement; instead, the writers target standard English and structural racism. However, the current antiracism statement at the University of Washington–Tacoma Writing Center (UWTWC 2021)—which has been revised since Inoue's departure—names "white linguistic supremacy" once, while the original didn't use the word *white* at all.

These observations led us to conclude that sections 2–4 of our whiteboard—which dealt with claims, commitments, and language—would themselves undergo revision as we moved from zero draft to first draft. The drafting process would force us to make decisions about how far we were willing to go with the content and phrasing of our statement, and that negotiation of boundaries happened in our background discussion for quite some time as we produced the statement.

WRITING THE DRAFTS

The consideration of whether to address whiteness directly was just one of many: the word whiteness jumped on and off our whiteboard a few times. As we revised our zero draft into a first draft, we used such considerations mostly to decide on the content for our statement; in other words, we narrowed the claims and actions we found most important to cover (sections 2 and 3 on our whiteboard) and then drafted the entire document from scratch, making it our own. We erred on the side of boldness, knowing we could revise in the future. As we wrote the second draft, which we hoped would be published on our website after edits, we began to look more closely at language, thinking carefully about how to balance our message with considerations of audience. In the effort to achieve this balance, we developed a concept on our whiteboard called "revision rules" (an expansion of "dos and don'ts" for language and phrasing). I don't have the space to cover all of these rules, so I'll compare three specific passages from the first and second drafts to show how we used three rules to revise our statement.

In the first passage, we took the lead of several of our writing center peers and threaded the needle between racism and whiteness (see Table 11.1). In our research, we found that the most hostile right-wing

Table 11.1. Introduction / statement of beliefs. Revision rule: Name racism and acknowledge its past and present effects; avoid naming whiteness.

Draft 1	Draft 2
We believe that racism is ingrained in institutions and that it profoundly affects the way those institutions are structured. For example, the concept of "standard English" derives from white academic forms of expression. Therefore, any institution that assesses students on their standard English proficiency inevitably disadvantages students whose upbringing did not incorporate traditional white academic values and ways of communicating.	We believe that racism is ingrained in institutions and that it profoundly affects the way those institutions are structured. We want success to be equally possible for all students at our culturally and racially diverse institution to achieve. However, sometimes, when we look closely at the seemingly good or well-intentioned concepts that underlie formal education, we see that those concepts are defined or applied in a way that clearly disadvantages many of our students.
We believe that failing to acknowledge and confront white supremacy only serves to perpetuate it. Specifically, when a writing center sets up fluency in standard English as the ultimate goal for all students who visit the center, it is perpetuating a white academic way of thinking at the expense of many of our students.	"Standard English" is one of those concepts. Students at our institution are frequently judged on the basis of their proficiency in standard English regardless of whether they are effective communicators. These judgments can have significant and lasting effects. At the writing center, a place that serves all students, we feel obligated to question the overvaluing of standard English and the disparities this overvaluing can create in our students' grades and academic progress.

reactions in the media were directed toward statements that specifically called out white values and white supremacy (i.e., that used those specific terms). They were less hostile to (or made no comment on) statements that focused on the equality and opportunity of all students at the center. For example, the *Breitbart* article mentioned earlier, which caricatured Inoue's statement, actually does a pretty good job of summarizing the statement's commitments to inclusive practice. So we made a decision: among ourselves, we would continue to discuss the overlap of white supremacy and standard English but would refrain from using such phrasing in the statement. In other words, *white* came off the board and out of the draft. Instead, we would focus on our desire for equitable treatment.

The result is a passage that still sends a strong message about standard English but that, honestly, addresses race less directly. One could argue that it nearly abandons the topic of race in the second paragraph. We found ourselves torn about this decision (especially since we specifically set out to write an antiracist statement!), and we imagined an audience of our peers who might be disappointed at our lack of boldness. But we made peace with our decision after stepping back and looking at the clear statement about linguistic privilege that remained in this part of the draft.

Table 11.2. Articulating the writing center's place in the discussion. Revision rule: Be direct and uncompromising about how antiracism differs from "nonracism."

Draft 1	Draft 2
At the writing center, we try to be aware of any sign that racist ideas and practices are either present on our campus or in the parts of the world that impact our campus. However, we realize that simple awareness is not enough; actions must be taken to combat racism. Similarly, we acknowledge that "tolerance" or "acceptance" of difference is important, but those values alone will not stop us from upholding the status quo.	We try to be aware of any sign that racist ideas and practices are either present on our campus or in the parts of the world that impact our campus. However, we realize that simple awareness is not enough; actions must be taken to combat racism. Similarly, we acknowledge that "tolerance" or "acceptance" of difference is important, but those values alone will not stop racism, which thrives on the upholding of the status quo. If we and our institutions do not make concrete, antiracist commitments, we risk perpetuating racism. We are responsible for dismantling racism where we find it; racism will not dismantle itself.

In the second passage, which is echoed elsewhere in our statement, we found it important to make a strong distinction between antiracism and the absence of racism (see Table 11.2). This, to us, was one of the bare-minimum criteria for an antiracist statement and was a way of holding ourselves accountable for the actions we would propose later in the document. Like Medina (in chapter 10), we remembered our original purposes and motivations for writing the statement in the first place, and we were unwilling to let those go. Perhaps we also considered the audience we might have disappointed by eliding the concept of whiteness earlier in the statement. We suggest that the status quo is linked to racism—which is perhaps the boldest statement we make. Yet we stay mostly at a level of topical generality ("racist ideas and practices") that, in our minds, sets up less of a potential target for decontextualized soundbites.

In my opinion, the third example shows the strongest stretch of revision between drafts 1 and 2 (see Table 11.3). While the items in draft 1 reflect a necessary change in mentality at the writing center, they also contain some of the bold-but-risky terms (i.e., "social justice and white supremacy") that might prove to be lightning rods for criticism. More importantly, however—for all their boldness on the topics of racism and standard English—the draft 1 items are short on actual *commitments*: things that we can resolve to do and hold ourselves accountable for. "Discuss[ing] social justice" and "challeng[ing] conventional thinking on 'standard English'" are important goals, but their impact on the day-to-day work of the writing center is not especially clear. In this case, the "bold" language might actually be an *obstacle* to specificity. The draft

Table 11.3. Action items. Revision rule: Focus on tangible actions.

Draft 1	Draft 2
We resolve to	We resolve to
• Actively resist the overvaluing of standard English at our institution. • Discuss social justice and white supremacy as it relates to language, language instruction, and writing instruction. • Help writing center visitors see the importance of rhetorical situations over "correctness." • Challenge conventional thinking on "standard English" and "academic discourse." • Be sensitive to our own language practices, avoiding those that might make others feel unwelcome or inferior. • Create a more welcoming environment in the writing center. • Compile resources to educate others about racism.	• Create a more welcoming environment in the writing center. • Revise our recruiting and hiring practices to build a more diverse group of writing tutors. Attach this document to hiring materials and make it a topic of discussion in the hiring process. • Develop teaching and tutoring materials on biased language in writing. • Help writing center visitors identify effective rhetorical choices in their writing tasks—even when those choices might conflict with the rules of "standard English." • Compile resources that reflect the rhetorical choices mentioned above, not just resources related to standard English. • Be a voice for the underrepresented students we serve, bringing their concerns and challenges to the faculty.

2 items are less bold on the surface but potentially more impactful in practice.

Before we release the statement, we might take the opportunity to assess our audience's response to this language—specifically the students at our institution who we allude to in the statement. Do our students want us to focus on broad linguistic concepts (and if so, why?), or would they be attracted to our more localized commitments in version 2?

CONCLUSION: THE WORK OF REVISION

This drafting and revision process has taught me and the tutors a lot—not just about how we articulate our values but also about what those values actually are. Through the process, we've developed a fuller understanding of our role in challenging racism, and we're clearer about what it means to do antiracist *work*: to use our growing awareness to motivate actions. I think the word *work* also means something deeper to us. As I mentioned earlier, it's easy to see these written products by writing centers as work with a clear revision process and identifiable end point, like an undergraduate paper: we do the research, write the paragraphs, clean it up a bit, share it with a small audience, and then let it be. By contrast, this piece could end up working in ways we can't foresee and don't intend, a possibility that has motivated us to do harder work on it now, especially as we prepare to bring it across the threshold from private to public.

As I write this chapter, I feel that our antiracism statement is not quite ready for that move into the public. With the revised statement in hand, we still have decisions to make. Have we made it too timid? Should a statement with a broader, more public audience define racism more clearly and take a stronger stand, even in the face of potential backlash from our audiences? Or should we be content with a strong version of a document that has never existed before—a mark of meaningful progress and a commitment to specific, near-future action? We haven't decided yet, but the process of getting to this point has already changed our writing center for the better. We've revised our own thinking, and some of that has shown up in our revision to the statement. There might be more revision to come.

REFERENCES

Ciccotta, Joseph. 2017. "University of Washington Declares Proper Grammar Is Racist." *Breitbart News*. Last modified February 22, 2017. http://www.breitbart.com/tech/2017/02/22/university-of-washington-declares-correct-grammar-is-racist/.

Curl, Joseph. 2017. "Grammar Is Racist? You Bet It Is, You Racist." *Daily Wire*. Last modified February 1, 2017. https://www.dailywire.com/news/grammar-racist-you-bet-it-you-racist-joseph-curl#.

Drexel University Writing Program. n.d. "Drexel Writing Center." Accessed October 15, 2021. https://drexel.edu/coas/academics/departments-centers/english-philosophy/university-writing-program/drexel-writing-center/.

Greenfield, Laura. 2011. "The 'Standard English' Fairy Tale." In *Writing Centers and the New Racism*, edited by Laura Greenfield and Karen Rowan, 31–60. Logan: Utah State University Press.

Inoue, Asao B. 2017. "Is Grammar Racist? A Response." *Asao B. Inoue's Infrequent Words*. Last modified February 7, 2017. http://asaobinoue.blogspot.com/2017/02/is-grammar-racist-response.html.

Inoue, Asao B. 2021. *Above the Well: An Antiracist Argument from a Boy of Color*. Logan: Utah State University Press.

Iowa State University Office of the Senior Vice President and Provost. 2021. "Frequently Asked Questions, Iowa House File 802—Requirements Related to Racism and Sexism Trainings at Public Postsecondary Institutions." Last modified August 5, 2021. https://www.provost.iastate.edu/policies/iowa-house-file-802-requirements-related-to-racism-and-sexism-trainings.

University of Washington Tacoma Writing Center (UWTWC). n.d. "Inclusion and Antiracism." Accessed October 15, 2021. https://www.tacoma.uw.edu/tlc/inclusion-and-anti-racism.

Wallace-Wells, Benjamin. 2021. "How a Conservative Activist Invented the Conflict over Critical Race Theory." *The New Yorker*. Last modified June 18, 2021. https://www.newyorker.com/news/annals-of-inquiry/how-a-conservative-activist-invented-the-conflict-over-critical-race-theory.

12
FEELING OUR WAY THROUGH COLLABORATIVE REVISION WHEN THE WORLD IS ON FIRE

Collie Fulford and Stefanie Frigo

In fall 2019, a call for proposals comes out for a journal that is doing a special issue on nontraditional approaches to undergraduate research. It seems as if the call has been written precisely for us. We are two white faculty who work at a historically Black university (HBCU). Grant funding for our recent project, Learning from Adult Learners, has enabled us to form close working relationships with several nontraditional undergraduate research assistants whose identities, insights, and work ethic bring significant value to the project. Involving adult learners as both researchers and participants, the project addresses the experiences of adult learners pursuing undergraduate degrees. The research assistance from insiders who are adult HBCU students themselves helps us directly address potential cultural, racial, and institutional power differences between faculty investigators and student participants. It is an experience we very much want to write about. We hope our work will result in more nontraditional undergraduate researchers being invited onto projects at sites where involving them is not yet a conscious or common practice.

We also look forward to doing another collaborative project because that's what we do. Although we are trained in different fields—linguistics and composition—we have happily partnered on projects for the entire decade that we've worked together. We serve on committees, consult each other about curricular design, and present together at conferences. We even coedited a special issue of *Across the Disciplines* before we landed this grant to jointly investigate the reasons adult students leave and return to college, and to involve students as research partners with us. We anticipate that responding to this highly relevant call will result in an opportunity to coauthor our first piece derived from this research. We are eager to offer principles and strategies to other faculty who may not have discovered yet how mutually beneficial it is to work with nontraditional students as research partners.

https://doi.org/10.7330/9781646425501.c012

But our writing conditions are mismatched right now. With our past projects, we've juggled similar workloads. When this call for articles about undergraduate research is announced, however, our writing worlds cannot be more different.

Collie: When the call comes out, I am on a visiting faculty fellowship that offers me an extremely different workload than I experience in my normal life as a professor and writing program administrator at an HBCU. On fellowship, my main job is not to teach. It is to do scholarship, and I have abundant time to do so for the first time in my life. I am in the thick of data collection for a new research project, and the journal's call pertains to my methods. I already have a different article in the works about undergraduate research, so I figure taking a new angle on it will be efficient. This CFP is announced during fall 2019 with a February 2020 deadline. The topic is relevant to collaborative interdisciplinary research teams that Steff and I have co-led in the past, so I ask if she wants to coauthor.

Steff: And I do want to coauthor. Collie and I have always had a fruitful and rewarding writing partnership. This is a no-brainer. However, while Collie's fellowship affords her space, both physical and metaphorical, to write, I am teaching a 4/4 load at our institution and administering our burgeoning Interdisciplinary Studies program. Space, metaphorical nor not, is rather thin on the ground. Our writing styles, though, complement each other, and our back-and-forth drafting and editing approach has always paid off, so space is going to make itself.

Collie: Luckily, the journal is only seeking a brief proposal to get the process started. We meet once in January 2020 to discuss the points we want to raise, then I "crap draft" the first version.

Steff: Our method for starting off has remained the same over the last few things we've worked on together and is often the only portion that we do in the same physical space. This is an easy one to pull together; we have been developing this longitudinal study of the lived experiences of adult learners at HBCUs for quite a while. In the article we propose, we discuss ways of ensuring access to undergraduate research opportunities for these students, who are so often excluded from traditional undergraduate opportunities. The fundamental aim of the piece is to develop concrete strategies to reduce barriers to participation by leveraging existing institutional structures.

February 23, 2020: AHMAUD ARBERY MURDERED BY THREE WHITE MEN WHILE JOGGING

Collie: We think about equity and representation, and about being flexible and having to radically adapt what's been designed without adult students in mind. After a couple of back-and-forths, we are satisfied with the proposal and settle on a working title, "Radical Adaptability: Alternative Opportunities for Interdisciplinary Research with Nontraditional Adult Learners." In February 2020, we learn it is accepted, and we begin a new round of turn-taking to write the article we have envisioned.

March 10, 2020: NC GOVERNOR DECLARES A STATE OF EMERGENCY RE: COVID-19

March 13, 2020: BREONNA TAYLOR KILLED BY POLICE

March 13, 2020: DUKE CAMPUS GOES ON "CONTROLLED ACCESS" AFTER 3 STUDENTS TEST POSITIVE FOR COVID-19

March 20, 2020: NCCU (AND THE UNC SYSTEM) SUSPENDS IN-PERSON CLASSES; DUKE CANCELS ON THE SAME DAY

March 26, 2020: DURHAM COUNTY ISSUES STAY-AT-HOME ORDER

Collie: The last restaurant meal I order in 2020 is the takeout lunch Steff and I share at my office two days before Duke is shuttered for the pandemic. Over sandwiches, we discuss the draft and make plans for next steps.

Steff: The office is eerily quiet, with lots of available parking. Collie's texts to me that week talk about the fact that any minute the building we are meeting in might shut down—in the event, working from home is voluntary at that point.

Collie: Steff is then swept up in the massive shift to emergency online teaching and holding her students, her program, and her family together. Meanwhile, I am still on research leave. I am freaking out and doomscrolling like everyone else, but it is without the impossible task to somehow appear calm, professional, and prepared for my students.

How do we draft an article during the first months of the pandemic? My brain is numb when I try to remember this. We submit the article three weeks after our university suspends in-person classes. It is three weeks before Derek Chauvin murders George Floyd. It's a blur.

Steff: It's a blur to me too. Looking at our messaging during this period, it's obvious that neither of us have much time nor mental energy to focus on the piece in the way that we normally would. "I'm up to my eyeballs in remote advising," I text Collie in late March. A few days later, she texts, "I'm completely wiped out without a speck of intelligence left to talk about [the article] tonight. I'm sorry!" This is also the first time that we are writing collaboratively in two separate locations. Prior to this, Collie's office had been just downstairs from mine. That physical closeness had made it easy to keep each other on task, to collaborate informally with impromptu meetings, to exchange ideas in a casual way.

Now, the physical distance and the danger between us means that we have to be much more deliberate about carving out time to spend on the work, yet it also means that our lives and time are being consumed with navigating lockdown and quarantine, me homeschooling an elementary- and a middle-schooler, balancing classes, helping students manage the first months of the pandemic, cope through their family illnesses and deaths, and deal with the stresses of having to show up for a minimum-wage frontline job in the days before vaccines.

We do, however, complete the piece, submitting with fifty-five minutes to spare on May 1, 2020.

> May 25, 2020: GEORGE FLOYD KILLED BY POLICE
>
> May 30, 2020: BLM PROTESTS BEGIN IN DURHAM
>
> May 31, 2020: THE NATIONAL GUARD IS DEPLOYED IN MORE THAN TWENTY-FIVE STATES TO ASSIST OVERWHELMED POLICE DEPARTMENTS
>
> August 27, 2020: RALEIGH LOCAL NEWS STATION, WRAL, REPORTS DURHAM POLICE PULL GUNS ON THREE BLACK BOYS PLAYING TAG IN THE STREET

Steff: When we meet over Zoom or FaceTime to work in the same space, tapping away at our Google Doc, our conversation is as much about the events of the world as about the work at hand. There is a great deal of pain. We each work at an HBCU, and our students and colleagues are directly under attack. The BLM protests are beginning, and as I work at the table in my kitchen, I hear drums and chanting on weekends throughout the summer. This all at a time when congregating together holds not only the danger of racial and police violence but also the unseen violence from the virus.

> September 23, 2020: PROTESTS BEGIN IN DURHAM AFTER LOUISVILLE, KY GRAND JURY DECIDE NOT TO INDICT OFFICERS IN BREONNA TAYLOR'S DEATH

Collie: Reentry to my "normal" teaching life after a fellowship year for research would have felt abrupt no matter what. But in fall 2020, there is no normal to return to. I collide with the workload at a velocity I could not plan for, troubled and raw, in a persistent state of alarm. In October, five months after sending in our article, we receive a revise and resubmit notification with detailed reviewer comments and a one-month turnaround date. My initial reaction is anger. All I can see are the criticisms: "Unfortunately, [. . .] the manuscript is not acceptable in its present form for publication [. . .] The reviewers have delineated several deficiencies and recommend major revisions that may render the work suitable for publication."

I feel slammed by that word, "deficiencies." I'm sure I take this more personally than I would have in any other October; it is my first semester teaching online, and I have just accepted an emergency interim gig as writing center director on top of teaching four classes. And the world is still on fire. "Deficiencies" cuts because deficiency feels like every. damn. day. on. the. planet. Maybe reading these comments a year from now, I will see that they are simply advice for making the article different. It's not personal. Right now, though, these reviewers' criticisms feel like little stabs: "What is the radicalism of the adaptability being posited? This is a sound approach but it seems better described as merely sensible." "It feels as if it was edited from a larger piece, making it difficult to follow, and pushes well beyond the journal's length requirements." "If no IRB was obtained, then you absolutely must remove the personal identifying information and names of each student."

Steff: I feel like our two reviewers have each read a different paper. One comes across as hypercritical and the other feels like they see the value in what we have done and written about—to an extent. I am also stymied by the fact that our first reviewer wants us to remove all reference to the students that form such a vital part of what we do . . . And this for a submission to a journal that is supposedly all about undergraduate research. I feel that their comments insinuate that we should erase our students from the work that we have done. These students are the whole point.

Collie: Despite our strong feelings about the reviewers' comments, we attempt to deal with the R&R within the month. After all, it remains an opportunity to publish about our work with student researchers, something we value. Jennifer Ahern-Dodson, my writing group convener, tells me she takes the sting out of R&Rs by transferring editors' and reviewers' comments into a task spreadsheet.

Steff: Collie is the one who uses spreadsheets; I am a list kind of person when it comes to editing my writing. I've always needed to print spreadsheets out because they don't work for me visually. This time around, though, the spreadsheet approach works. Using the feedback from the reviewers and the journal editor's comments, two main types of entries appear in the spreadsheet and task list:

1. Minor editing: These comments have mostly come from the journal editor and really come down to fixing punctuation and rephrasing for clarity here and there.
2. Longer, more complex criticisms: These come from our two reviewers, and they still feel critical, to be honest, although these feelings are soon to be tempered by the input we get from a trusted reader, Adam Rosenblatt.

The spreadsheet organizes the revisions that need to be done, who is going to do them, and yes, it does go some way towards taking the sting out of the R&R comments.

Collie: From the complex criticisms, we face three major revisions: (1) reduce the word count, (2) reluctantly eliminate named references to student researchers, and (3) either double down and provide evidence that our adaptations are radical forms of mentored undergraduate research or frame our approach in a way that will be more palatable to these reviewers.

> November 3, 2020: US PRESIDENTIAL ELECTION
> November 10, 2020: NCCU *CAMPUS ECHO* PUBLISHES STORY ABOUT PANDEMIC STRESS ON STUDENTS

Collie: A one-month turnaround is not realistic for us. Our editor responds to our request for an extension with generosity, indicating there might still be a home for this piece given adequate revisions, but we will miss the deadline for the special issue. Having an unspecified end date is initially helpful. Then it becomes a problem. October and November 2020 pass. Then December. We are so depleted. In a desperate attempt to salvage our work, I ask a friend from my writing group for advice. In February 2021, Adam sends audio feedback accompanied by handwritten notes on the manuscript.

Steff: I've never had a person send a voice memo reflecting on my or our work. I don't know Adam personally. His voice, however, soothing and reflective, dissolves the frustration that I felt with our initial reviewer comments. It is easy to list changes that should be made, and to be honest, at this point, I am just so ready to be done. Although he notes that he sides with the reviewer and with Collie "in that the radical vocabulary is just getting in the way," he also describes our work as "committed, caring, responsive, and creative." That feels good.

Adam does two key things that really transform how I think about our piece and how I feel about the reviewers' comments—he also has a great sense of humor (suggesting that Collie see if she can "get Steff to back off of Radical Adaptability" makes me laugh out loud). These two things shift how I interpret the reviewers' perspectives on our work and make it much easier not to take them personally:

1. Adam notes that our piece is "in this liminal, uncomfortable place between a few genres." And he is totally right—we are both trying to be that "really punchy, hard-hitting commentary piece," as Adam describes it, while simultaneously writing a "longer, more scholarly version" of the same thing. By expressing the length issue this way, Adam makes it very easy to just decide which option we should go for and then go for it.

2. Adam also questions our use of the term *Radical Adaptability* but does it by drawing a parallel with disability studies and equity and inclusion. This leads us to totally transform the angle that we have initially taken, moving from Radical Adaptability to a philosophy of equity for adult learners who are often unintentionally excluded from undergraduate research because of various factors. Adam refers to what he calls our "really savvy, equity-based use of institutional structures." We can roll with that . . .

March 8, 2021: DEREK CHAUVIN TRIAL BEGINS

Collie: After we have both listened to and read Adam's feedback, we meet early in March 2021 to plan our next revisions. My page of notes from this meeting includes a lot of action words: "cut," "excise," "clean up," "rethink," "shave," "move," "refine," and the decisive "ax." Most of them are about radically reducing the word count. Steff takes the first leg of these hard cuts.

Steff: I am not sure where the fire in me comes from the night that I sit down to work on the edits. I am so tired of this paper and so ready to be done. So tired, too, of the year of teaching online, of being shut in, of railing in frustration at the inequities and injustice of the American system of policing. It is easy to look at the number of words we have and the number of words they want and scrape and slice away until it fits. I address the paper as a piece with which I have no relationship—it is orphaned from me and needs a caustic, editing eye. I have been so involved in it and so passionate about the radical adaptability, and yet here I am, ruthlessly editing and fine-tuning to order. In a lot of ways, it is cathartic. There has been such a long gap since I've last worked on the paper that the connection I've had with it is gone.

This is really a first for me, using this concept of the orphaned text; imagining it as a lost child that has come into my care, needing nourishment and love, perhaps a little discipline. I stop thinking of this writing as something I have written, and instead as something I need to edit. The idea stems from a lecture I'd attended as an undergraduate, years before; this is the first time that I have applied it to my own work. We get attached to what we write and we are protective of our words and ideas. Initially, I had been offended by the reviewers' comments questioning the "radicalism" of the piece, annoyed that they couldn't see what I could. With the distance of time and the generous comments from Adam, I now look at the article like it isn't actually mine anymore. This makes it easy to take a scalpel to it—I don't care for it at this point, but I do care about publishing it; I can see the bigger picture for both Collie and myself. The bigger picture is tied up in some things like the pressure to publish, but for us both, mostly this need to get it out there reflects how we feel about the work we are engaged in. Adult learners are often neglected in the university system, and the collaborative work we are doing with our students has impact and importance for these learners. We want this work out there, changing things for these students.

This lesson is probably the most important one I learn during this hard year of hard things. Sometimes, good enough is good enough; it doesn't have to be perfect. We are all stretched so thin during this emotional, pandemic time. We need to give ourselves grace.

April 20, 2021: DEREK CHAUVIN FOUND GUILTY ON ALL COUNTS

Collie: A week after our meeting, Steff texts, "Alright, I've slashed and burned my way through the morning, and we've gone from 4373 to 3470 words. I'm going to run a last search for radical adaptability, but we've got rid of the whole concept and have a new title . . . I'll send it your way in a moment." She sends me a track changes Word version, a *much* slimmer draft with every instance of the term "radical adaptability" excised. She also texts, "Have you had a vaccine yet? Central just sent out the schedules for next week if not . . ." It should be easy for me to pick this up and run, but I do NOTHING with the draft until more than two months after Steff's dramatic revisions.

At the end of May 2021, I attend a writing retreat with people I connected with during my fellowship. I use this focused space, time, and community to pick up Steff's baton. I work on more firmly foregrounding the equity principle both in our title and in descriptions of our work with adult student researchers.

Steff: When I get the piece back from Collie, there really is little to be done. The length is right, the edits have been completed, and I offer to review and double-check our references, and promptly don't.

We really are out of steam at this point. Summer teaching rears its head, and as we move towards the fall semester of 2021, we are still preparing two syllabi for each class in case of a last-minute move to online teaching because of the ongoing pandemic. Academic advising begins for me.

Finally, on September 18, 2021, on the sidelines of a Saturday morning soccer game, my oldest son learns how to do a reference check with his academic mum, marking off names and dates as the Razorbacks warm up for their game. The paper is done, only nineteen months after we began our work. America feels like a totally changed country given the ravages of those months.

Collie: Under layers and layers of duress, Steff and I chose to abandon the concept of radical adaptability for the piece we write about in this chapter. Yet we are embodying the practice we had attempted to articulate. It's one that refashions possibilities for worthwhile action from a hodgepodge of available tools designed for other purposes. The entangled collaborative revision process Steff and I patched together during a nearly unendurable period could be mutually sustaining under better circumstances, as well.

Even during more peaceful times, with the most tactful reviewers, the revise and resubmit process is fraught. We cannot help but experience some mix of self-doubt, defensiveness, and anger in the process of reworking writing that we have already put intense energy into. And the language around publication is hardly humane. That awful word, "submit," sets us up for a power struggle. To "resubmit" is to yield twice, reluctantly, to someone else's power to determine whether a piece is worthy or not. And per common practice, these reviewers are "blind" to us, blind to our contexts. Academics rail against the ubiquitous "Reviewer 2" not because their advice is necessarily wrong but because we feel fundamentally unseen, and we cannot have an open back-and-forth to work out *with* these readers why we made the writing choices that they question.

Steff: Part of this self-doubt, defensiveness, and anger in the process stems not from the writing process itself, not even from the reviewers, not from the publication process, but from the relentless push from our institutions and our tenure requirements to produce. Nothing we write from an academic perspective really exists outside of this paradigm. We are always seeking approval from Reviewer 2, not because they are Reviewer 2 but because we are under contract to publish—not create, or write, or innovate, but to publish . . .

Collie and Steff: Collaborative writing with people we genuinely care about offers a humanizing way to work during dangerous times. Pandemic, political upheaval, and violence are the contexts under which we labor for this project, with no guarantee of the outcome. Yet we have found ways to shoulder the words that we feel responsible for writing. Even during less fraught times, revising together helps us endure the depersonalized aspects of anonymous peer review. We vent. We weigh the costs of revision. We debate with each other when we can't with the reviewers. The turn-taking practice that we use, of one person delving into a hard part of revision then releasing it to the care of the other, is an act of trust that gives each of us a chance to set the work aside without neglecting it. It is like amicable joint custody. When we get stuck, we can expand collaboration beyond our coauthorship by handpicking a third reader, entrusting a draft to them for a while to help us see a way forward. Although we care about the writing, we care about each other—friends, coauthors, other collaborators, and trusted readers—above publication. Every choice about the work is nested in our awareness that what matters more is who we are and how we are surviving. The article, the chapter, the book—it can wait. Nobody is going to die if we don't finish it. But we need life-affirming social contact so very much, thus the gift of a collaborative revision process is that it gives us reason to be in each other's presence working on something that matters enough.

And it is this gentleness between us as collaborators that keeps the soul in our work, beyond the reach of the opinions of our reviewers and the pressures of tenure. This is what keeps us writing and returning to each other as co-writers, as co-conspirators. During the isolation of COVID lockdowns, the dramatic shift to teaching to an online environment, and the multiple traumas experienced by our university community, our collaboration remains more important than the article.

That is fortunate, because our efforts to revise do not have the results we expect. Not only have we missed the moment of the original special issue, but (unbeknownst to us) by the time we finish our painstaking revisions, the editor who gave us an open extension has been replaced, and the journal's direction changes. March 2022, six months after we resubmit the piece, the boilerplate response we receive from the new editor: our paper "is not suitable for publication in its present form."

Yet, as other contributions in this collection make refreshingly clear, we are not alone. Our mixed and mangled feelings, our collaborations and contortions, and our struggles to find an end point where there may not ever be one, are experiences shared by many other writers. We are in good company with those who have found that inviting trusted others into our work can help us puzzle through uncertainty and bear the sting of criticism. Dana Comi and Alisa Russel's mutual mentoring friendship is, like ours, a humane way to see each other into new phases of academic projects and professional identities.

Our friendships, our families, and our myriad commitments have an uneasy relationship with our academic writing. Jule Wallis-Thomas documents the untidy seepage of family life into her writing life, finding that she is still revising by the end of her chapter. Like her, we are "constantly shifting" (196) between our intimate, academic, and public worlds as social strife and lockdown roil normality. The "personal and often brutal nature of academia" (204) that she describes is also omnipresent in the writing environment in which our piece was birthed. And writing is like parenting: at times we do need to be firm with our text children, to discipline them, making sure that they fit the world's parameters for them.

We are also not alone in the experience of laboring and contorting only to have a project that does not yield, at least not in the ways we had intended. Like us, Karen R. Tellez-Trujillo has no clear end point to her labors. She finds that revision resists a time frame, and it is not "failproof." Reflecting about her abandoned but beloved project, she claims that "work that is worthwhile requires patience and discomfort, even when it appears that it is physically and emotionally impossible to find a way forward" (217). Sometimes we don't finish what we start, yet we can achieve different ends that are worthwhile to us. Perhaps the final rejection is what we needed; in the end, like Tellez-Trujillo, we realized we were not going to be afforded "enough time or words to convey" (217) what our piece had to say. That rejection prevents us from publishing a version that misrepresents our commitments to student-researchers as partners. Tailoring too closely to someone else's criteria shortchanges our text-child, and our students, leaving out most of what actually matters to both of us. Having thoroughly reflected on this belabored failed revision, we can now imagine different approaches to addressing the kinds of feedback that compromise our core intentions; Joseph Harris's chapter in the present volume provides us the encouragement to stand more firmly in our authority about what matters in a piece.

13
WHOSE EXIGENCE?
The Social Dynamics of a Writing Across the Curriculum Plan-in-Process

Christopher Basgier

As an educational reform movement, writing across the curriculum (WAC) requires careful attention to complex social dynamics of an institution. Campus politics, departmental structures, language ideologies, curricular requirements, and even interpersonal relationships form a complex web of purposes, desires, and motives—exigencies—that can create tension during the planning, implementation, and assessment of WAC programs. I experienced many such exigencies in spring 2021, when I set about composing a plan for the next phase of University Writing, a comprehensive WAC program and writing center at Auburn University, reporting to the Office of the Provost.

A key element of our office's work in the previous decade had been working with the University Writing Committee (UWC, a Senate committee) to review and approve writing plans, which departments were required to create for every undergraduate major on campus. In many ways, this initiative was a success, with nearly universal compliance and many meaningful conversations about writing among departmental faculty. By the time I began leading University Writing, however, administration sought a new direction for our office that aligned with Auburn's strategic plan and emerging initiatives on campus.

One such initiative was a new infrastructure that tracked and measured graduating seniors' experiences with high-impact practices (HIP), which are educational interventions that boost academic success and postgraduate outcomes for students, especially underrepresented and minoritized students (Kuh 2008). During a meeting with my immediate supervisor, Norman Godwin,[1] Associate Provost for Academic Effectiveness, I suggested that writing intensive courses were another HIP that might be worth pursuing, because they could allow us to track student experience and assess student writing ability more directly.

Godwin was immediately interested. He suggested that we call them "writing-enhanced" courses, a term he found more inviting, and asked me to write a plan for how they could be developed, implemented, and assessed.

As I wrote the plan between February and April 2021, I shared drafts with colleagues who had sometimes vastly different perspectives on what my office's work ought to entail. Based on their feedback, which often conflicted, I revised the plan from a narrow focus on writing-enhanced courses into a writing-enriched (WE) curriculum plan, called WE Write, with WE courses as one component. The final document is four single-spaced pages, and it includes an overview, a justification, a process outline, details on support and incentives for students and faculty, an assessment plan, and a proposed implementation timeline. The final version aimed to convince several different audiences of my vision for the next phase of University Writing at Auburn, especially Godwin and Cathleen Erwin, associate professor in health administration and my UWC co-chair; their input was key in this intensive, two-month revision process and figures prominently in this chapter. More pragmatically, I also sought a go-ahead from the provost and an affirmative vote from the UWC, both of which I needed in order to implement the plan with institutional support. Complicating the matter, the UWC had not always seen eye-to-eye with the provost, with whom I had little direct contact. Thus, embarking on this endeavor, I felt the tension of many competing exigencies.

What follows are my reflections on how I navigated those exigencies and revised the document into a coherent plan. Rather than proceed chronologically, I will focus on four key themes that will throw my revisions into sharp relief: service language, recognition of the past, process and engagement, and assessment planning. In these four areas, I had to account for multiple, competing exigencies in my revisions, including feedback from specific individuals, institutional dynamics, and scholarship in WAC.

SERVICE LANGUAGE

Although University Writing always offered faculty development and student support services, the original writing plan mandate had created resentment among some faculty, who saw it less as a meaningful articulation of their commitments to writing pedagogy and more of a bureaucratic hoop. Of course, the writing plans functioned both ways, sometimes simultaneously. Nevertheless, Godwin believed that my time would be better spent supporting academic units' needs rather than hounding them to document courses. He wanted me to offer services to faculty, not enforce a mandate.

At first, I disagreed. I was not ready to perform what Wenger (chapter 6) calls "mindful revision," which entails "paus[ing] judgment" and "hold[ing] space" for our own and others' needs (79). I was keenly aware that writing is too often marginalized at institutions, because service metaphors ignore the rich intellectual and pedagogical work of rhetoric, composition, and writing studies (Kopelson 2008; Miller 1991). The field's intellectual work was the basis for the writing plan mandate, which emphasized disciplinary and professional audiences, purposes, genres, and processes. That same intellectual tradition—WAC scholarship—also underwrites writing-intensive course mandates and requirements, which are commonplace in WAC programs.

Therefore, I pushed through, rather than paused: in my first draft of the plan, I referenced writing-intensive "requirements" frequently. After I shared that draft with Godwin, he and I discussed the challenges entailed by mandates at length. I explained my worry that without a mandate, faculty would not participate in a writing-intensive course initiative, and students would be reluctant to take such courses, thwarting the shared responsibility of writing instruction that is so central to WAC (Anson 2015). I had a lengthy conversation about Godwin's request with Amy Cicchino, associate director of University Writing, during which I shared my fear that the plan would crash and burn without a graduation requirement. We discussed ways to highlight benefits without a mandate, and I tried some simple changes to that effect. For instance, in the introduction, I wrote:

> **Original (version 1):** A WE requirement at Auburn will also enable University Writing to demonstrate and measure impact in a coherent, evidence-based manner.
>
> **Revision (version 2):** WE courses at Auburn will make high-impact writing experiences more visible to students and faculty in the departments that choose to adapt them. The courses will also enable University Writing to demonstrate and measure impact in a coherent, evidence-based manner.

This early change represented a shift away from a campus-wide requirement and toward an option with benefits—namely, visibility—for the programs that participate. Based on Cicchino's feedback, I also explained that the courses could be responsive to evolving disciplinary and professional standards (as opposed to just institutional mandates) if they were revised every three years. This move was one way in which I attempted to maintain a space for foundational WAC theory, namely that instructors who are immersed in disciplinary discourse communities are in the best position to teach the expectations of those communities to students. Still, these changes did not signal clearly enough for Godwin that the program was voluntary. Especially as I began to articulate the WE Write process in later drafts (more on that below), Godwin explained that it still resembled the writing plan mandate too much. When he read version 5, he suggested select wording in the introduction that would underscore the optional nature of the program from the beginning:

> **Original (version 5):** University Writing has developed a new plan that builds on the success of the writing plan initiative and the ePortfolio Project: a writing-enriched (WE) curriculum process, called WE Write, through which we will (1) consult with select academic programs about their expectations for student writing, (2) guide them in the creation of WE courses that meet those expectations, (3) support their local assessment of writing, and (4) plan next steps. WE Write will allow us to expand direct support for students attending the MWC and deepen relationships with academic programs who are integrating significant writing experiences into the major. The newest feature of this plan is WE courses—a new, official course designation—which will make programs' commitment to writing more visible to students and faculty.
>
> **Revised (version 6):** University Writing has developed a new, *opt-in service* for academic programs: a writing-enriched (WE) curriculum process, called WE Write. Through WE Write, we will (1) consult with *interested* academic programs about their expectations for student writing, (2) guide them in the creation or redesign of courses that explicitly teach those expectations, (3) support their local assessment of writing, and (4) plan next steps for ongoing implementation and support. WE Write builds on the success of the writing initiative and the ePortfolio Project while expanding direct support for students and deepening relationships with academic programs *seeking to engage* students with high-impact writing experiences across the major. *When academic program leaders elect to collaborate with University Writing on the WE Write process,* programs will earn a new course designation—WE—which will make their commitment to writing more visible to students and faculty. (emphasis added)

Although I was reluctant to give up a mandate, I agreed to take up the service ethos Godwin wanted, which is emphasized in the italicized portions of the revised version 6. According to Adler-Kassner and Roen (2012), service can be problematic when it is relegated to committee work or attached to a particular course (i.e., first-year composition), but it can be incredibly rewarding when it stems "from a set of principles": it can become "an opportunity to build alliances with others on campus and within the community, thus enlarging our experiences (which contribute to our research and our teaching) and, ultimately, the experiences of our students." With this more capacious definition of service in mind, I emailed Godwin, noting that I had "threaded in more language about opt-in, elect, service, etc." in hopes that the provost, who read the final version, would see that I wanted to partner with faculty, not to enforce my vision of writing on their curricular spaces. Thus, this set of revisions reflected the tensions Godwin and I had to negotiate among the power of institutional mandates, bureaucratic resentment, and what I hoped would be an intellectually rich, principled service to the faculty at large.

RECOGNIZING THE PAST

Although I did not consider it at the time, early drafts of the plan introduced a new set of tensions with Erwin (the UWC co-chair), to whom the plan read like a drastic departure from the past, especially the initial impetus for the writing plan initiative. She had invested many years in the UWC and in supporting writing in her own program, which had resulted in national recognition of her students' writing. When she first read my plan, she explained that it seemed like a step backwards: it risked departments loading all writing into a single WE course, rather than integrating meaningful writing experiences throughout the major, which had been our core focus. My good working relationship with Erwin, as well as the history and mandate given to the UWC, all became pressing exigences for my next revision.

I felt guilty for not having considered the program's history in early drafts, and I turned to Heather Stuart, who was senior program administrator with our office at the time. She had been with University Writing longer than I had, so we had multiple conversations in which we reflected on the past and considered how to fold it into the new plan. Cicchino, too, gave valuable feedback on the document. For example, she pointed out that the exigence for WE courses was less than clear because I had language pointing to a significant number of writing-focused courses already embedded in the disciplines. She wrote, "As a reader I'm thinking if this already exists largely, then what does WE accomplish?" After these conversations and feedback, I revised the plan, using several strategies to recognize the past while explaining the need for change. Early in the introduction, I began by acknowledging the success of the writing plan initiative:

> **Original (version 2):** Building on our office's work with writing over the last decade, upper-division Writing Enhanced (WE) courses offer an effective focal point for University Writing to improve undergraduate

students' writing and offer faculty effective teaching strategies. WE courses at Auburn will make high-impact writing experiences more visible to students and faculty in the departments that choose to adapt them.

Revision (version 3): Building on *Auburn's decade-long success integrating significant writing experiences into every major,* University Writing will promote Writing Enhanced (WE) courses as an effective mechanism for improving undergraduate students' writing and supporting faculty's teaching. *Departmental writing plans will continue to ensure writing is integrated throughout the majors at Auburn.* (emphasis added)

The first change gave more credit to the university broadly, and by inference to the UWC, which was my direct response to Erwin's critique that the plan did not recognize the good work that had already been done by the committee or by the former director of University Writing. The second change reintroduced the writing plans, which Erwin wanted to preserve as a mechanism for ensuring programs integrated writing at multiple points in the curriculum, but eliminated discussion of specific courses, per Cicchino's feedback. Thus, a new section in version 3, called "Rationale," explained:

Addition (version 3): In many ways, Auburn's writing plans have been a success: the University Writing Committee has 98 writing plans on file for undergraduate majors, representing nearly-universal compliance. The writing plans ensure writing experiences are embedded in every major, making explicit how students communicate across occasions for different audiences germane to the discipline. In the best cases, departments use their plans as a focal point for reflecting on curriculum, and programs like Health Administration, Interior Design, and Biology use them to represent innovative teaching and communicate about writing with external stakeholders like accrediting bodies. For these reasons, **Auburn should maintain the undergraduate writing plan requirement**. (emphasis in original)

This addition demonstrated how programs used the writing plans in the best-case scenarios. I also elaborated the visibility problem: in my experience, many students and faculty were "unaware of their departmental writing plan's existence," and the new course designation could help alleviate that problem.

At this point in the revision process, I felt myself caught between competing visions for University Writing: Godwin's desire for a new direction that would evidence impact, and Erwin's interest in continuing to work from our core principles. Moreover, when Godwin read version 3, he was frustrated that I had reintroduced the writing plans; he would have been content had the plan requirement been eliminated completely. I had several impromptu meetings with Cicchino over the course of about a week, in which I bemoaned the situation. Godwin and Erwin's perspectives felt irreconcilable.

Those conversations with Cicchino, and additional ones with Stuart, helped me find ways to reconcile these two competing perspectives. For instance, I revised the Rationale section and retitled it "Why WE Write?"—a section devoted to recognizing the value of the writing plans and justifying the need for meaningful, sustained work with faculty teams to teach writing in the major:

> **Revision (version 6):** In many ways, Auburn's writing plan initiative has been a success: the University Writing Committee has 98 writing plans on file for undergraduate majors and has conducted regular reviews with academic programs. *We have learned a great deal from this process about programs' practices and needs with regard to writing, so we no longer need to require regular review and revision of writing plans university-wide. Instead, we need to act on what we have learned from successful programs,* such as Health Administration, Interior Design, or Biological Sciences. In these and other cases, faculty have used their plans as a focal point for reflecting on curriculum, *as an opportunity to represent innovative teaching, and/or as evidence of impact for external stakeholders like accrediting bodies. The best writing plans are the result of ongoing, concerted, collaborative effort of faculty to deliver meaningful, discipline-specific writing instruction to students. WE Write will allow University Writing to replicate that work systematically with interested academic programs.* (emphases added)

The first italicized revision represented a negotiation between the two competing perspectives on the writing plans: rather than simply eliminate or keep the writing plan requirement, I argued that we could keep existing writing plans on file, engage new programs in planning, and eliminate regular reviews because we were seeing the same progress and limitations over and over. The second italicized revision then argued for my vision: to engage interested academic programs in deep, ongoing curricular work. As a result, I reasoned, they could revise their writing plans when it made the most sense—after they had participated in the WE Write process and had new ideas for what they wanted to accomplish with writing. No doubt, histories impact our revision processes; as I revised, I found I had the challenging task of negotiating between divergent historical experiences with my program and devising a compromise that acknowledged both.

PROCESS AND ENGAGEMENT

The WE Write process was also a result of such negotiation. As the plan took shape, I had to think carefully about how to cultivate participation, especially without an institution-wide mandate, and I needed to design a program that was systematic and sustainable over time (Cox, Galin, and Melzer 2018). Early in the plan's evolution—before I had conceptualized WE Write as a process—I recognized that faculty would want support in teaching WE courses. University Writing had already had success in leading faculty through multiday workshops, which we called Academies for Writing, so I included them in the plan:

> **Original (version 2):** Based on our good reputation for high-quality work with faculty across campus, University Writing is prepared to support faculty in the creation and teaching of WE courses. We can easily re-tool our existing summer Academies for Writing to support WE faculty who want to create or revise syllabi, assignment sheets, peer review activities, rubrics, and other elements to enhance students' writing.

Shortly after this version, I met with faculty who had participated actively in the ePortfolio Project, the Quality Enhancement Project for Auburn's Southern Association of Colleges and Schools Commission on Colleges (SACSCOC) accreditation, which we also ran in University Writing. The Project had had a strong faculty community of practice who attended workshops and lunch discussions, enjoyed priority consideration for workshops and grants, and received regular newsletters. Although these colleagues understood the impetus behind the plan, they believed it lacked community. They suggested that faculty community-building might promote more participation than the Academies alone, so I revised the next version accordingly:

> **Revision (version 3):** *Taking what we learned about faculty development from the ePortfolio Project, University Writing will reallocate our current resources to create a new faculty community of practice, called WE Write. Faculty who join WE Write will get priority registration* for summer Academies for Writing, which University Writing can easily re-tool to support faculty in creating or revising syllabi, assignment sheets, peer review activities, rubrics, and other elements to enhance students' writing . . . During the academic year, *WE Write faculty will get priority registration* for workshops on specialized topics (e.g., writing about numbers) or on adapting our existing resources (e.g., literature reviews) to teach their courses, and *they will be eligible for in-class workshops delivered by University Writing personnel . . . Overall, WE Write faculty will have ongoing opportunities to learn, interact, and collaborate with colleagues across the university who are invested in the teaching of writing in the disciplines.* (emphasis added)

These revisions emphasize the collaborative nature of WE Write, as well as the opportunities and incentives faculty would enjoy when participating in the community of practice. Still, I was not sure a faculty community of practice would be enough incentive for a critical mass of participation. Godwin had a similar question: what exigencies would drive faculty to (re)design courses and curricula with writing?

To answer this question, I turned to the writing-enriched curriculum (WEC) philosophy, which holds that WAC ought to be embedded at the departmental level, faculty-led, and developed inductively out of local expectations and curricular needs (Flash 2016, 2021). I met with Pamela Flash, who directs the WEC program at University of Minnesota, to discuss the challenges at play in my planning, and she helped me understand how I might adapt the WEC process to manage some of the competing exigencies I described in the previous section. After our discussion, I decided WE Write ought to be a process, not a faculty community, with WE courses and writing plans as possible outcomes. I also changed WE to "writing-enriched" instead of "writing-enhanced" to align the initiative's name with larger trends in the discipline.

In the plan overview, I added a summary and brief justification of the WE Write process. Cicchino asked numerous clarifying questions about the process, especially about the nature of departmental discussions and their relation to data collection. Based on her feedback, I revised the faculty-focused section substantially by including a more detailed explanation of the WE Write process:

Addition (version 4)
1. Programmatic consultations: Surveys of students, faculty, and industry partners will form the basis of initial consultations with academic programs about their goals and needs for addressing students' discipline-specific writing needs. Based on faculty-wide conversations about these needs, programs will develop or refine writing-focused student learning outcomes.
2. WE course creation: Faculty will identify existing courses or create new courses in which significant writing experiences will achieve their desired outcomes. We will encourage programs to identify multiple WE courses arranged in a vertical sequence or a menu of courses offered horizontally at a certain level (i.e., the 3000-level). University Writing will offer structured programs to help faculty create or revise syllabi, assignment sheets, peer review activities, rubrics, and other elements (e.g., writing about numbers) to enhance students' writing.
3. Assessment: University Writing will help programs plan a regular assessment cycle for writing and support their efforts to complete those assessments. (See below for more information on assessment).
4. Review and Plan: After faculty design courses, the UWC will approve the courses and revised writing plans on a 3-year cycle.

I shared version 4 with Erwin, who was pleased with the idea. She agreed that the shift from writing-intensive courses alone to a WEC process that included WE courses was more in keeping with the original vision of the writing initiative to integrate significant writing experiences throughout the major. At the same time, she appreciated the new possibilities of deepening relationships with academic programs rather than pushing for widespread review of writing plans. We shared the plan with the UWC, who approved of it as well, with the understanding that their role would shift to creating WE course criteria and certifying WE courses. Godwin, too, saw the benefit of this process, and, as I discussed above, was happy to support it so long as we continued to emphasize the optional, service-focused nature of the program, which is also part of WEC's ethos. With WE courses as an outcome of the process, rather than a requirement, WEC thus became a fundamental anchoring philosophy for the plan.

ASSESSMENT

Assessment was another point of tension in the development of the plan. Before I began the plan, our office had already begun creating a new set of learning outcomes for students participating in our programs and services. I recognized that WE courses, and eventually WE Write, could also allow us to demonstrate impact via direct assessment of student writing.

In the initial version, I proposed collecting student work products from WE courses and "conduct[ing] a regular Assessment Institute with faculty and MWC peer consultants to evaluate that work," a process I argued would offer "a measure of student writing ability derived from authentic course experiences." However, Godwin had other priorities, and he asked me to speak with Katie Boyd, director of Academic Assessment, about this assessment plan. Both Godwin and Boyd urged me to find a way to plug into the university's existing assessment infrastructure, rather than create a wholly separate one. This infrastructure included a survey about experiences with HIPs, standardized evaluations of Auburn's core curriculum outcomes (including writing), and a survey of seniors' "first destinations," such as job placement or graduate school. The Office of Academic Assessment had used the ETS HEIghten to assess graduating seniors' writing abilities. When we met, Boyd suggested that direct assessment of student work products from courses using a standardized rubric might not be valid, because students' writing would represent drastically different tasks. Additionally, she offered one benefit to the standardized assessment: that we would be able to disaggregate results and see relationships among scores, participation in HIPs, and employment or graduate school plans.

Once again, I felt caught between two different exigences. I recognized that this assessment infrastructure was important for the institution, but I was also aware of rhetoric, composition, and writing studies' emphasis on locally owned assessment of writing, and skepticism of general, university-wide writing assessment (Anson et al. 2012; Broad 2003). When I shared my concern with Flash, she told me she had encouraged her administrators to think multidimensionally about assessment, which inspired me to take a "both-and" approach. First, I revised the plan to include new materials specifically mentioning the university's approach to assessment:

> **Addition (version 3):** To assess the effectiveness of WE courses as a means for improving students' writing abilities, we will leverage Auburn's existing assessment infrastructure. During summer 2022, the Office of Academic Assessment will conduct the ETS HEIghten exam with all incoming students . . . and they will do so again four years later . . . University Writing will work with the Office of Academic Assessment to disaggregate results by college/school, MWC attendance, and faculty engagement in WE Write.

While Godwin was pleased with this shift, I remained cautious about using a standardized test as our only measure of writing ability, so I sought another means to supplement it. As the plan evolved, I saw an opportunity to support departments' locally owned writing assessment more directly as WE Write became a process:

> **Revision (version 5):** As mentioned above, in the years between 2022 and 2026, University Writing will support WE Write academic programs in the assessment of writing according to their own outcomes. This process has several benefits. First, it will promote valid, department-driven assessments that are responsive to local curriculum and discipline-specific writing conventions. Second, it will provide another means through which University Writing can respond to departments' emergent needs for writing support. Third, the UWC can encourage departments doing an especially good job assessing writing to highlight their process in revised writing plans and nominate the best ones for awards.

Here, I attempted to emphasize local ownership of processes, which is one of Godwin's key values, and one I have grown to value even more through this revision process after reflection on disciplinary theories of both WEC and assessment. The combination of local, departmentally owned assessment with university-wide assessment will facilitate more dialogue within the UWC and across campus about what we mean by writing, who we might best assess it, and how we might best teach it.

CONCLUSION

Revision is a complex process shaped by a shifting, ever-emerging network of exigencies, many of which are in tension with one another. In some ways, my experience resembles Garcia's ongoing revisions to a writing center antiracism statement, which required the staff to attend to their values and commitments while considering how audiences would react to it amidst the shifting local, statewide, and national political landscape. Garcia and I both learned that what may seem like a constraint in one moment—or even an impossible obstacle—may become a generative opportunity for revision and persuasion. Garcia and his tutors saw how language of welcome and rhetorical choice might be "less bold" than that of social justice and white supremacy, but it might actually be "more impactful in practice" (149). Similarly, I came to see how slow, sustainable change might be "less bold" than a mandate, but it could lead to deeper relationships across campus and therefore a bigger impact. Like Wenger (chapter 6), my revisions to an institutional document also entailed a revision to my sense of myself as a writing program administrator, one committed to a meaningful, intellectually grounded service ethos.

Programmatic plans like the one I wrote so often bear the imprints of social dynamics that raise questions about who owns institutional genres. Revisions to such genres are often as much about people as they are instrumental adjustments to design a more effective program. Godwin, Erwin, Cicchino, Stuart, Boyd, and others all affected the final document—more than I have been able to represent in this chapter. Of course, rhetoric, composition, and writing studies have long critiqued the myth of sole authorship. My experience with the WE Write plan illustrates that critique in action: our revisions to institutional genres are the products of intersecting exigencies and multiple voices.

The next time I undertake such a plan, I will gather multiple stakeholders in the same room for a discussion, which I believe will bring various commitments to the fore. While I would not expect tensions to go away in a larger meeting—indeed, it may amplify some—I would be able to promote collaboration and move toward consensus that comes, if not through shared exigencies, then at least by forging connections among exigencies. I would then use one-on-one meetings with individuals to work out kinks, smooth tensions, polish plans, and generally work to ensure that many stakeholders' perspectives, and even their voices, are represented in revisions. I will also make more use of my professional network. Flash's advice was helpful, and her WEC Institute would have helped, as would the WAC Summer Institute sponsored by the Association for Writing Across the Curriculum. A network of experienced peers can go a long way towards managing the anxiety that comes with institutional projects that must take up the needs of so many different stakeholders across a campus. Readers who find themselves engaged in composing and revising plans with an institutional purview would do well to investigate those intersecting exigencies head-on. If the perspectives of faculty partners and administrators go unspoken, they cannot influence the creation of a successful document and, more importantly, a successful program.

NOTE

1. All individuals gave me permission to name them in this chapter.

REFERENCES

Adler-Kassner, Linda, and Duane Roen. 2012. "An Ethic of Service in Composition and Rhetoric." *Academe* 98 (6). Accessed October 18, 2023. https://www.aaup.org/article/ethic-service-composition-and-rhetoric#.Y8GOrnbMJD8.

Anson, Chris M. 2015. "Crossing Thresholds: What's to Know about Writing Across the Curriculum." In *Naming What We Know: Threshold Concepts of Writing Studies*, edited by Linda Adler-Kassner and Elizabeth Wardle, 203–19. Logan: Utah State University Press.

Anson, Chris M., Deanna D. Dannels, Pamela Flash, and Amy L. Housney Gaffney. 2012. "Big Rubrics and Weird Genres: The Futility of Using Generic Assessment Tools across Diverse Instructional Contexts." *Journal of Writing Assessment* 5 (1). Accessed March 5, 2022. http://journalofwritingassessment.org/article.php?article=57.

Broad, Bob. 2003. *What We Really Value: Beyond Rubrics in Teaching and Assessing Writing*. Logan: Utah State University Press.

Cox, Michelle, Jeffrey R. Galin, and Dan Melzer. 2018. *Sustainable WAC: A Whole Systems Approach to Launching and Developing Writing Across the Curriculum Programs*. Urbana, IL: National Council of Teachers of English.

Flash, Pamela. 2016. "From Apprised to Revised: Faculty in the Disciplines Change What They Never Knew They Knew." In *A Rhetoric of Reflection*, edited Kathleen Blake Yancey, 227–49. Logan: Utah State University Press.

Flash, Pamela. 2021. "Writing-Enriched Curriculum: A Model for Making and Sustaining Change." In *Writing-Enriched Curricula: Models of Faculty-Driven and Departmental Transformation*, edited Chris M. Anson and Pamela Flash, 17–44. Fort Collins and Boulder: WAC Clearinghouse; University Press of Colorado. https://doi.org/10.37514/PER-B.2021.1299.2.01.

Kopelson, Karen. 2008. "Sp(l)itting Images; Or, Back to the Future of (Rhetoric and?) Composition." *College Composition and Communication* 59 (4): 750–80.

Kuh, George. 2008. *High-Impact Educational Practices: What They Are, Who Has Access to Them, and Why They Matter*. Washington, DC: AAC&U.

Miller, Susan. 1991. *Textual Carnivals: The Politics of Composition*. Carbondale: Southern Illinois University Press.

SET 5

Revision Spirals

Jayne E. O. Stone

This final set of chapters reverberates with the themes and attitudes about revision that have emerged over the course of this collection thus far. However, these final stories of revision don't necessarily end with tidy resolution in the form of the coveted "final" draft or even a sense of finality or certainty, as some others have. The writing projects central to this set challenge, in varied ways, the idea that there even *is* a final form to be reached. Will Duffy, for example, writing of the ongoing and endless need for revising definitions, suggests that definitions "grow stale" if they aren't revised alongside the ever-evolving scholarly discourse. For her part, Jule Wallis-Thomas tells the story of the complex scenes of revision surrounding a grant, which she is still revising by the end of the chapter, many questions still lingering. Likewise, Karen Tellez-Trujillo's project is still (and has only ever been) in flux; in fact, Tellez-Trujillo suggests that while there is still hope for her "sleeping" project, it may *never* find a form meant for public eyes. Finally, Ian Golding reminds us in his artist's statement of what we editors have been reminded time and again throughout this project: just as we begin to think that we've landed on the "final form," another voice, thought, need, constraint, opportunity arises and shakes us awake from the dream that we can ever reach a point where further revision couldn't possibly improve things in some way.

Still, the authors in this set nevertheless desire and make moves toward a final form; however, their roads are more lengthy, less certain, or conveyed with more vulnerability than we've yet seen. Further, these at times uncertain revision journeys *all* require, as Wallis-Thomas writes, a "letting go" of what their authors find themselves holding onto during revision, a circumstance quite familiar to plenty of contributors whose revision stories have led us here (Fulford and Frigo's excisement of "radical adaptability," for example). What "letting go" means for each author in this set is different, of course, but what further bridges their stories is an open engagement with emotion and, at times, a display of deep vulnerability as they navigate that letting-go.

The emotionality evident in this last set and throughout this volume has us thinking about Kelly Myers's recent work in which she takes up the concept of *metanoia* and applies it to revision, coining the concept of *metanoic revision*. She writes,

> As an approach to writing, metanoic revision involves actively turning toward "missed opportunities" with the goal of seeing and creating new ways to navigate content, context, opportunity, and time. While turning toward missed opportunities can spark new insight, it also stirs feelings of regret, disappointment, and fear—a complicated and challenging endeavor . . . , and one that cannot be taken lightly. A metanoic revision process, then, must begin with a reimagining of regret. Instead of a stagnant and repressive force, *metanoia* helps us reframe regret as an entry point that can lead to reorientation on both intellectual and emotional levels. (2016, 387)

We see sparks of this concept at work in these chapters—when Duffy details the work he and his collaborator put into a revision only to have to "start over" (185) when they felt unequipped to negotiate the "rigorous and sometimes contradictory feedback" (185) from reviewers; when Wallis-Thomas uses her past experience of the sudden and erroneous loss of her full-time status to propel an ethnographic revision of her grant; when Tellez-Trujillo finds that writing her contribution to this collection about a missed opportunity has "roused the possibilities" (220) that have been there all along; and when Golding finds himself convinced that there is no way to revise his carefully constructed comic depicting revision lest it all come unraveled, only to ultimately take a breath and go—quite literally—back to the drawing board.

Through these contributors' stories, we also recognize emotion in the stops and starts of revision—a theme prominent in the third set but one that takes on new significance in this set where multiple contributors have carried their revision projects for nearly a decade. The stops and starts represent a cycle that, though at times it may draw intense feelings of inadequacy or frustration, can ultimately lead to growth and success, a conclusion each of this set's contributors reaches over the course of their journeys. This growth mindset reminds us of Nancy Sommers's reflections on revision: "It is deeply satisfying to believe that we are not locked into our original statements, that we might start and stop, erase, use the delete key in life, and be saved from the roughness of our early drafts. Words can be retracted; souls can be reincarnated" (26). This set explores the depths of Sommers's sentiments.

The stops and starts of revision that are recurring here are prompted by new opportunities, audiences, or exigencies and met with promise and excitement, but are ultimately halted or slowed in part by the authors' own questions of whether their revisions result in an accurate representation of their ideas and the subjects of their writing. Therefore, the emotion wrapped up in these stories doesn't stop at the authors' own sense of self—their identity or state of mind. It is also heavily influenced by the subjects and concepts about which they are writing. The task of figuring out how to revise toward accurate representation is intensified for each author by individual start-and-stop factors: reviewer feedback (Duffy), influence of family life (Wallis-Thomas), recurring self-doubt (Tellez-Trujillo), and editor demands (Golding). These unique and external factors which the contributors grapple with during their revision process offer supporting examples of Chris Mays's (2017) suggestion that revision might be effectively "[cast] simultaneously as a deeply personal process that inspires intense feelings of ownership as well as an impersonal function of a complex system neither owned nor created by any one person or agency" (65). Hannah, in "Set 1: Revision Takes a Stand," references this same quote to help us see how competing wills (from both human and nonhuman sources) shape revision. From this final set of chapters, we can once again identify the will and complexities of the "system" Mays identifies, including those actors and forces that become imbricated in the revision process alongside the will of a text or project. In this set, we especially experience the feel of the "deeply personal" as contributors highlight emotionality and growth in narrating their revision experiences.

In this final set, we slow down. We get personal (like we did in the third set). While Duffy opens this set with a chapter that isn't as emotion-forward as the others, his persistence, patience, and dedication to revising a single definition, and the lessons he takes from that lengthy process, evidence—in subtle ways—the entanglement between the personal and the academic. His revision journey, which finds movement through known and unknown collaborators, becomes a volleying act, one that upholds Sommers's reflections on revision's personal nature. Sommers, excited for the possibilities of revision, asserts that "it is in the thrill of the pull between someone else's authority and our own, between submission and independence that we must discover how to define ourselves. In the uncertainty of that struggle, we have a chance of finding the voice of our own authority. Finding it, we can speak convincingly . . . at long last" (31). These words hold true for the other contributors in this set as well. Wallis-Thomas, for example, pushes the boundaries of the grant genre in which she's writing, building confidence to do so through her unwavering commitment to the subjects of her research and her fight for greater awareness of the personal nature of academic work.

Despite the uncertainty and tension that can be found prowling among these final chapters, there is undeniable growth. After all, as Golding reminds us, "Revision is—if nothing else—an extremely productive process of transformation and growth." (222) While we see Golding's sentiment reflected in the chapters throughout this collection, in this final set, the personal nature of transformation and growth that comes from revising toward an accurate representation of the heart of a project comes through in bold. This set reminds us, as does the collection as a whole, that revision is never simply textual; it is embodied, emotional, personal, complicated, collaborative, and, at times, uncertain.

REFERENCES

Mays, Chris. 2017. "Revision as Heresy: Posthuman Writing Systems and Kenneth Burke's 'Piety'." In *Kenneth Burke + the Posthuman*, edited by Chris Mays, Nathaniel A. Rivers, and Kellie Sharp-Hoskins, 61–79. University Park: Penn State University Press.

Myers, Kelly A. 2016. "Metanoic Movement: The Transformative Power of Regret." *College Composition and Communication* 67 (3): 385–410.

Sommers, Nancy. 1992. "Between the Drafts." *College Composition and Communication* 43 (1): 23–31.

14
DEFINITION AS INVENTION
Turning a Familiar Concept into a Critical Keyword

William Duffy

Collaboration is a mutual intervention and progressive interaction with objects of discourse. At least that's how I define it in *Beyond Conversation*, a book I wrote about collaborative writing. In fact, that definition is critical to understanding the theoretical framework for collaborative authorship I propose. As I write in the book's introduction, "taking up my own definition of collaboration as a mutual intervention and progressive interaction with objects of discourse, I position coauthorship as labor that hinges on the ability to anticipate remedies to the various limit-situations"—all of the things that impede our writing—"that all cowriters face, not the least of which is how to account for the development of a draft that does not 'belong' to any single writer, or agent, within the collaboration" (2020, 22).

For context, the book is a revised version of my dissertation, the latter of which opens with an epigraph from Steven Johnson's *Where Good Ideas Come From*: "The trick is to figure out ways to explore the edges of possibility that surround you" (2010, 41). A nonfiction trade book adjacent to the self-help genre, *Where Good Ideas Come From* is a collection of journalistic case studies that examine how innovation is almost always the result of people working together in various ways. What I liked most about the book was how Johnson invented concepts with which to explain the different phenomena he was writing about, concepts like "slow hunches" and "liquid networks," terms he coined to describe the social dimensions of rhetorical invention, a term he doesn't use but very well could.

I was trying to do the same thing with my dissertation, albeit in a register that was decidedly more scholarly and for an audience specifically interested in collaborative authorship as a site for writing pedagogy. While I wasn't necessarily coming up with glitzy names for phenomena academics have already discovered (Johnson's theory of "the adjacent possible" is similar to what Vygotsky [1978] identified as the "zone of proximal development," for instance), I knew I needed to offer a definition of collaboration that aligned with the theoretical framework I wanted to construct for the project. Little did I know how challenging this seemingly straightforward task would turn out to be. Nor did I anticipate that I'd be revising my definition for years to come. Indeed, my initial attempts at defining collaboration resulted in definitions that are quite different from the one that opens this chapter.

In fact, during the time between when the first version of this essay was written and when the version printed here was, I've had the opportunity to hear from readers whose responses have prompted me to reconsider some of the components informing my understanding of collaboration. One of these responses, which I'll discuss momentarily, has been helping me think about revision as the process of expanding the rhetorical ecology of an emergent text. As a draft develops from concept to object—as its rhetorical properties take shape—it becomes an object around which others can engage with its development. Revision is all the work that goes into attuning the overlapping signals of this engagement. Before I tackle that idea, however, let me share the story of how my definition of collaboration initially developed.

WHERE'S THE INVENTION?

Definitions are tricky, because academics are trained to be precise with our language, yet most of us are suspicious of any standard that is arbitrarily prescriptive. Maybe this isn't true of all academics, but it certainly is for those of us who work in the humanities and adjacent disciplines. Language is fluid and malleable, just like the grammars we use that make language transportable. While they don't come with an expiration date, definitions grow stale if they aren't revised to reflect how our understanding of those terms develops as other scholars engage with our work and vice versa.

My experience with collaborative writing began in graduate school with my friend and fellow student, John Pell. We started writing together because one of our professors suggested we do so for a particular project, but after that we were hooked. We sought opportunities to coauthor wherever we could. In particular, we were drawn to how coauthorship allowed us to capitalize on each other's strengths as readers and writers, but we also loved how coauthorship gave us the courage to try things in our writing that we might have been too sheepish or inexperienced to try individually. Indeed, having a coauthor can make a writing project less intimidating, if for no other reason than you have someone helping to process and make sense of your writing as it develops.

When the first-year writing program in our department decided to publish its own in-house textbook, John and I volunteered to write a chapter about collaborative writing. Even though neither of us had written for an audience of first-year college students, we knew we wanted to present collaboration in a way that challenged conceptions that equate it with group work, especially group work team members will likely divvy up and complete individually. We wanted to emphasize collaboration wasn't just a way for us to hold each other accountable; it also enhanced the pedagogical benefits of the writing process itself. In other words, we were coming to terms with the significance that coauthors are their own first audience and that having such an audience expands the rhetorical potential, broadly speaking, for what we set out to write. To invoke the subject of this edited collection, cowriting gives us the opportunity to experience revision as an iterative process that begins the moment we start writing.

But how do you capture these complex ideas in a single definition, one appropriate for an audience of first-year writing students? To be clear, we didn't set out to retheorize collaboration; we simply wanted to present its advantages to first-year writers while encouraging them to give it a shot if the option was available. I don't recall much about the drafting process, but I do remember John and I talking about wanting to present collaboration primarily as a set of attitudes rather than procedures. This goal is visible in the definition of collaboration we wrote for our essay, one that emphasizes the attitudes that help coauthors discover unanticipated possibilities for their writing. In that piece, we work up to our definition by explaining that effective collaborators develop a "particular kind of stance, not just in relationship to the work at hand, but toward the people with whom you are collaborating. This stance needs to be one in which generosity and a sense of inquiry come together through reflexive dialogue." Then we get to our definition: "Put simply, collaboration is both an inventive process and reflexive relationship in which two or more writers synthesize their individual ideas and create new ones in order to compose texts" (Pell and Duffy 2008, 40).

Not long after we finished that in-house textbook chapter, we decided to expand and adapt it for a submission to the latest volume in the *Writing Spaces* series of open-access first-year writing textbooks. While our revision strategy was to simply expand on what we had already written, John and I deliberately used this opportunity to revise our definition of collaboration. At the time, we were enrolled in a research methods course and were collaborating on a small ethnographic research study of several sections of composition taught by fellow TAs who were utilizing our chapter as part of a low-stakes collaborative writing assignment. While the students we interviewed weren't antagonistic to collaboration, they also weren't that interested in it as a mode of writing either, a point I mention because that became one of the things John and I focused on as we wrote the *Writing Spaces* piece. We figured we could keep the same outline as the chapter we wrote for our department's first-year writing textbook, but we could incorporate more examples of how writers can benefit from coauthorship. When revising the definition itself, we decided to emphasize what collaborators do to harness these benefits.

In our first definition, the one for the in-house textbook, we said collaborators "synthesize their ideas," but I recall both of us discussing how this sounded more passive than we intended it. Which is to say we were starting to realize (thanks in part to the ethnographic research we were doing) that telling students that collaboration requires them to "synthesize" their ideas might be confusing without detailing not just what this means but also what it looks like in practice. The more coauthors talk to one another and identify the overlaps in their respective ideas, we wanted to say, the better positioned they would be to work through the various starts and stops that all writers experience, not just coauthors. In revision, for our definition, we drew on those observations informed by the students themselves, who wanted more direct advice for collaboration in practice. Collaboration, as we ultimately defined it in our *Writing Spaces* submission, "refers to the inventive process through which two or more individuals engage in reflexive dialogue in order to synthesize their individual ideas to create new ones." Our revised definition emphasizes dialogue, a term we didn't use in our first definition but one we thought can stand in for the mutual back-and-forth talking that marks the beginning of most collaborative projects. By that point we were actively pursuing collaborative projects with others in addition to our work together, experience that was teaching John and I the importance of fostering space where coauthors can talk without any preconditions for where that dialogue leads.

Unlike the internal review process for the first essay we published in our writing program's textbook, the *Writing Spaces* editorial team had a more formalized process that involved sending manuscripts to outside readers. When we got those reports back, one review said our "advice remains very general" and that "there is a lot of time spent developing definitions." Pointing specifically to our engagement with the idea of reflexivity, this person "wondered how much experience with reflexivity students would have. That concept needs attention as something students develop individually, and then in groups." But the belief that writers must *first* develop certain critical capacities *before* they can write collaboratively is exactly the kind of thinking we hoped to challenge. That is, we wanted to suggest that collaborative authorship doesn't require individual writers to first master some arbitrary set of skills. Now that I think of it, my earlier comment about imagining revision as the process of expanding a rhetorical ecology is an idea that no doubt has roots in experiences like this one—the messy work of trying to attune an emergent draft to the ideas and desires of its authors *and* those of its reviewers. Nevertheless, what mattered in the moment was that this was our first time engaging with feedback from "real" peer reviewers.

I won't bury the lede: we didn't publish our *Writing Spaces* manuscript. The review process was difficult, because we didn't have experience interpreting and implementing rigorous and sometimes contradictory feedback from multiple reviewers. We also were frustrated with what felt like a lack of editorial guardrails overseeing this process, especially given our status as graduate students, which is something I note not as a criticism but to highlight my own inexperience. With that said, one recurring challenge we faced during that process was finding a voice appropriate for our intended audience (first-year students) that also appeased the reviewers (*not* first-year students). In short, we couldn't figure out how to balance a clear, accessible register—one free of unnecessary jargon and description—with the more abstract ideas about the attitudes and dispositions collaborators foster in order to write together.

Once it was clear we needed to set aside the *Writing Spaces* piece, we decided to lean in on the reviewers' various points about how we were seemingly writing more for an audience of fellow composition specialists than we were novice writers. We decided to start over, in other words, and compose something for a scholarly audience. It turns out we didn't have to wait long for an opportunity to follow through with this plan.

A CFP focused on faculty as writers came across our radars, one that asked for essays that consider "theoretical, philosophical, and pedagogical approaches to faculty writing support." This seemed like the perfect opportunity to wrangle some of the abstract ideas about collaboration John and I wanted to articulate for other teachers and scholars. We also knew this was another opportunity for us to revise our definition. While the collection's framework would allow us to focus more on theory than specific techniques, our writing and revision of what became "Imagining Coauthorship as Phased Collaboration," just like that of our *Writing Spaces* manuscript, ended up turning on the same kinds of questions:

Does this sound too ephemeral? Will readers be inspired or confused by our focus on attitudes? Which concepts need to be better qualified and illustrated?

That is, writing this latest piece ended up showing us how revision can be a site for tracking our growth as writers, just as much as it is for tracking the improvements of a specific piece of writing. Yes, this is an idea foundational to contemporary composition theory, but this was the first time John and I got to experience this fact for a piece of non-school-based writing. Indeed, I remember thinking as soon as we put the *Writing Spaces* essay aside that we no longer needed to be *as* concerned for issues related to clarity and accessibility.

I wouldn't have described it this way then, but as I look back on the editorial feedback for what became "Imagining Coauthorship," I see the reviewers encouraging us to be mindful of our readers' needs *as readers*. "There are places where you could explain explicitly why faculty writers or administrators reading this collection would find your chapter useful," one of the editors suggested after reading our first draft. "It is important to us that each chapter, while presenting 'practices,' also works to theorize those practices. You did that, but we urge you to be more deliberate and open about that, connecting your experiences with the reality and then offering a new way to attend to the complications of collaboration." This is the kind of feedback that really pushed John and me to wrestle with how we marshaled our own experience as cowriters. Sitting at John's kitchen table with both our laptops open, we dedicated several writing sessions to working out the "so what?" we wanted to give readers as a takeaway. The strategy that guided this revision work rested on looking for models—essays written by scholars who draw on their personal experiences in ways that resonated with John and me as writers and that we could in turn imitate. The text we ended up using as a model, Donna Qualley's (1997) *Turns of Thought: Teaching Composition as Reflexive Inquiry*, also became a resource for developing our definition.[1]

In fact, you can see the influence of Qualley in our revised definition of collaboration. As we write in that essay, "we call collaborative writing an inventive process and reflexive relationship through which two or more writers synthesize their individual perspectives to create a new, shared voice through which to compose texts" (2013, 251). We were still committed to highlighting collaboration as a method for rhetorical invention, but we thought grounding this argument in an appeal to the shared voice coauthors create would give our definition a more narrative quality, which is what we liked most about Qualley's writing and what we felt would answer that editor's suggestion to better connect our own experience with the "new way to attend to the complications of collaboration" that our piece proposed.

By the time we were revising "Imagining Coauthorship," John and I were each working on our respective dissertations. Informed in large part by our experience as cowriters, I decided to write a dissertation about the history and development of theories of collaboration in rhetoric and composition, a project that gave me another exigence to refine the approach to collaboration John and I were hacking together as we pursued the abovementioned projects. Guided by the oversight of my committee and the experience I was accruing with John, I decided to use my dissertation and several subsequent writing projects to explore what collaborators share that allows them to produce writing that neither writer would produce individually, which was and still is a popular reason coauthors give for why they pursue collaborative projects.

NOT TALK, BUT THE OBJECTS OF TALK

Fast-forward to my dissertation defense; I had a definition of collaboration that had obvious links to the one we wrote for "Imagining Coauthorship," but I rounded out the definition by stating what collaborators do with their dialogue. Describing this definition as "pragmatic and consequential," I defined collaboration in my dissertation as "the ways in which interlocutors use reflexive dialogue to intervene in and enhance the progression of their interaction with an object of discourse" (2011, 92), a definition that I retained when I developed an article manuscript from my dissertation that I submitted to *College Composition and Communication* (*CCC*), which received an invitation to revise and resubmit. As is often the case with "R&Rs," one referee recommended publication and one referee didn't. It turns out the reviewer who recommended publication especially liked how I define collaboration:

> The writer offers a definition of collaborative writing that gives the discussion in the field a great deal more clarity; this is [a] very useful contribution all by itself. On its theory of collaboration, I think the field has been suffering from an inability to transgress its own conceptual boundaries. As this writer conceives it, the source of this inability is that we've been unable to dislodge the equivalence we have set up between collaboration and conversation. This is a vital insight, and, too candidly, I am embarrassed that I've been unable to see the problem in just these terms, myself.

I share this excerpt from "Reviewer 1" because this one paragraph alone gave me the confidence-boost I needed at that stage of my career. I was in my first tenure-track job, barely a year out of grad school; I was still new to the process of publishing; and I was desperately curious to see if my dissertation work could attract the interest of a "big" journal.

I revised the manuscript and resubmitted the article, but it was ultimately rejected for reasons I won't linger on here since they didn't involve my definition of collaboration. But Reviewer 1's comments persuaded me to revise the article and submit to a different journal, this time *College English* (*CE*). In that revision, I leaned into the theoretical qualities Reviewer 1 complimented in my *CCC* manuscript, which included amplifying my definition by dedicating an entire section of the article to it. In this new draft, I explained the need for a definition of collaboration "that is object-oriented and flexible to potential adaptations," one "not constrained by a narrow definition of technique or method," which leads into a more streamlined definition: "Collaboration is the engagement between interlocutors who deliberate to intervene in and enhance the progression of their interaction with objects of discourse."

While I won't belabor the theory informing this revised definition, I landed on that phrase about intervening and enhancing the progress of how collaborators interact with objects of discourse because it better communicated what I wanted to express with the idea of "reflexive dialogue," a term I dropped from this latest definition. Namely, I wanted it to highlight the phenomenon of discovering new dimensions or wrinkles of meaning (to borrow a phrase I once heard) in the various ideas and observations we share with an interlocutor when we deliberate. By that point in my own professional development, I was prepared to argue that there is no such thing as collaboration in the abstract, just the interactions we share whenever we deliberately draw on someone else's skills or positioning to help us accomplish something. I therefore wanted a definition that invited adaptation, so to speak, one that couldn't be applied without qualifying the scale or extent to which a team of collaborators name for themselves the differences that make a difference for the cowriting they undertake.

Like the *CCC* version, my *CE* submission got an R&R; unlike the *CCC* version, it was eventually accepted. When I got the official acceptance, I was sent some additional notes from one of the reviewers, just minor suggestions for enhancing my prose. In the last paragraph, however, this reviewer turned explicitly to my definition, the first time a reviewer had done so since my initial *CCC* submission: "You give us something we all like on page 11: a definition. But I would really like to see you cut out part of this definition. Instead, I like this much more: *Collaboration is a mutual intervention and progressive interaction with objects of discourse.*"

And there it was, the definition I had been trying to write, the one John and I had set out to write more than five years earlier. And it was delivered to me with the assistance of an anonymous referee whose own intervention with the objects of discourse populating my definition not only improved it but modeled how collaborators use their discourse to invent ideas and articulations that can't be exclusively claimed by one writer individually. Put differently, this reviewer modeled how my argument could be scaled to fit the different roles collaborators play, even as peer reviewers.[2]

The *CE* article was published in 2014, after which I started working on my book. While it would take several years before I was ready to submit a proposal to potential presses, and another couple of years to finish the book, my definition of collaboration hadn't changed when *Beyond Conversation* was eventually published.

CONCLUSION

What I hope this microhistory of a definition reveals is that just like collaboration itself, inventing a definition can be challenging, long-term work. When John and I came up with that first iteration of a definition, I had no idea that more than ten years later that ambitious articulation would have developed into the sleek one-liner I now use. Even though the idea of reflexivity was dropped from the definition, the practice of "turning back to discover, examine, and critique one's claims and assumptions," as Qualley put it in *Turns of Thought*, is what kept us pushing forward and, when necessary, starting over when we hit a roadblock.

All of this thinking and writing pursued alone and together with John, not to mention the scores of drafts and reader reports and abandoned manuscripts, all of this discourse finally "fit together in a productive, more seamless way," as the referee put it who recommended against publishing the manuscript I submitted to *CCC*. And true to the epigraph from Johnson I discuss in the introduction, my understanding of collaboration, especially the definition I now use, was possible only because I had a team of colleagues who helped me explore the edges of possibility that unfurled with each attempt at a mutual intervention and progressive interaction with our ideas about what happens when we write together.

A couple weeks ago I got an email from someone who just finished reading *Beyond Conversation*. They pointed specifically to how the ideas in one particular chapter were helping them conceptualize ways to incorporate collaborative writing into a technical communication course. But this person also pointed me to an article they had published that focused on a related topic and noted how we were similarly engaged with a particular set of theoretical questions. After reading the article, I was astounded by the clarity of this scholar's insights. Recent and obviously limited, I bring up this exchange because I can anticipate accounting for this scholar's ideas as I continue to advocate for the pedagogical value of coauthorship. I can also anticipate how this scholar's ideas might prompt me to revisit my definition if given the opportunity to do so in an expanded context.

I have one final thought.

The occasion of thinking about the impact of this recent exchange while working on *this* revision of an essay about revision, the one you are reading (are you still following me?), pushes me to appreciate when readers engage with texts as objects distinct from their writers, as something I might have helped make (my book, this book chapter, etc.) but not something I own or control. Moreover, I am struck by how the ideas in this person's article are intermingling with my own in a process that is now in situ, expanding the depth and breadth of the rhetorical ecosystems we both navigate in our work. Needless to say, this wasn't what I imagined I would be thinking about at the conclusion of an essay about the development of a definition.

Depending on the context, it may be enough to cite existing definitions for the keywords writers deploy in a manuscript. For me, though, it took the experience of trying to write a detailed, scholarly definition to realize that definitions, just like writing more generally, require revision as we deploy those terms in critical ways.

NOTES

1. We especially liked how Qualley defines reflexivity as "the act of turning back to discover, examine, and critique one's claims and assumptions in response to an encounter with another idea, text, person, or culture" (1997, 3). As I detail later in this piece, though, I eventually decided to remove the idea of reflexivity from my definition of collaboration.
2. To be clear, I don't consider this anonymous peer reviewer a collaborator in the same way I view John as a collaborator. However, I do believe the way the reviewer engaged with my definition as an emerging object of discourse is similar to the ways experienced collaborative writers engage an emerging text. While I didn't have such language at the time, here is how I explain this in my book: "If we recognize collaborative writers are like all writers insofar as they must renew and sometimes reinvent the processes through which they compose each time a new exigence presents itself, it becomes clear that overgeneralized claims about the social nature of writing rooted in the idea of collaboration elide the very thing we can say with relative confidence about collaboration itself: it almost always slows down the work of writing and in that slowdown reveals more of the resistances all writers confront" (2020, 50).

REFERENCES

Duffy, William. 2014. "Collaboration (in) Theory: Reworking the Social Turn's Conversational Imperative." *College English* 76 (5): 416–35.

Duffy, William. 2020. *Beyond Conversation: Collaboration and the Production of Writing*. Logan: Utah State University Press.

Duffy, William, and John Pell. 2013. "Imagining Coauthorship as Phased Collaboration." In *Working with Faculty Writers*, edited by Anne Ellen Geller and Michele Eodice, 246–59. Logan: Utah State University Press.

Johnson, Steven. 2010. *Where Good Ideas Come From: The Natural History of Innovation*. New York: Roverhead Books.

Pell, John, and William Duffy. 2008. "Where Two or More Are Gathered: Writing Collaboratively." In *Writing Matters*, 4th ed., edited by Brandy Grabrow, Laurie Lyda, and Melissa J. Richard, 38–44. Dubuque, ID: Kendall Hunt Publishing.

Qualley, Donna. 1997. *Turns of Thought: Teaching Composition as Reflexive Inquiry*. Portsmouth, NH: Boynton/Cook–Heinemann.

Vygotsky, Lev. 1978. *Mind in Society: The Development of Higher Psychological Processes*. Cambridge, MA: Harvard University Press.

15
UNCOVERING THE VEIL
Revising the Dichotomy between Motherhood and Academic Personas

Jule Wallis-Thomas

SCENE ONE: REVISING AND RETELLING THE STORY

I am sitting in my sunroom, and my new puppy is zooming around the house like he has spring fever from the living room to the sunroom and back. I do all I can to ignore the dog hair on the floor and the cobwebs that glisten in the sunlight and focus on my College of Liberal Arts and Sciences (CLAS) Assessment Grant. I wrote the grant for a very specific audience of deans, administrators, and assessment teams at my institution, Wayne State University (WSU). I had stepped outside of the typical genre of writing center research by quantifying the impact of WSU's writing center. For years, I'd requested additional, ongoing funding for an assistant director, technology and social media support, and discipline-specific tutors. Yet I knew, since the writing center was funded by the English Department, my requests would never materialize. I had also become acutely aware that in a time of continued budget cuts, I needed to provide deans with irrefutable evidence of the academic impacts of writing centers on student retention. With a fierce desire to justify my requests, I applied for, and was awarded, one of the five CLAS grants. I was ecstatic. Completion of the grant, and all my evidence, surely meant that my requests could no longer be denied. I framed the grant by using Salem's groundbreaking 2016 qualitive analysis of student use and nonuse of writing centers. Her research described the importance of quantitative research for exploring how and why students used writing centers for academic support, and presented evidence that writing centers were instrumental in student success. In the grant, I would attempt to replicate the study at WSU, an urban university with a diverse student body and competencies like Salem's at Temple University. In those two long years, I learned to shift my mindset from a qualitative to a quantitative lens. And in many ways, I was proud of my ability to step out of my comfort zone and dive headfirst into a new approach to research. I had proved the naysayers wrong. I had gathered massive amounts of outcome-driven, numerical data documenting use of the writing center by students from various fields of study. I had irrefutable proof that would dismantle the prevailing belief that our writing center worked primarily with students within the field of humanities. I finally had a strong argument for requesting monetary support campus-wide.

In the end, I, along with the other four grant recipients, was recognized at a ceremony attended by deans, colleagues, and family. I was given a fancy plaque to hang on the wall in my office. Sadly, it became a constant reminder that I had received grant money that I had hoped would result in support for the writing center, but instead, all I received was recognition and no support for our writing center's needs. Conversations with deans about my findings did not, as I had imagined, convince them to increase budgetary support. Rather, it was suggested I limit tutoring services to CLAS students only. That way I could make the most of my current budget. I felt like a knight who had failed to complete their quest. Worse, I had spent countless hours on a failed grant, hours that could have been spent with my family. I vowed that I would use the grant for an article publication. If no one would hear me at my institution, I'd make sure I was heard beyond the walls that had been stacked up around me. In between my teaching, service to the university, and role as a mother, I tinkered with the grant. Yet I felt no inspiration. The more I played around with new versions, the more the very nature of the grant troubled me. It seemed to silence the profoundly personal nature of writing centers, writing center work, and the complex frameworks designed to support students.

With hesitant starts and stops, and beaten down by defeat, my grant-writing sat in limbo. I hated the grant. It was a constant reminder that all my hard work had amounted to nothing. I fell into a void of complacency and defeat until I read the *Revising Moves* call for demonstration of academic revision strategies. Here was the push I needed. I would use the call as my motivation for revising my grant and, in the process, write a chapter for publication. However, I was no longer interested in repurposing the grant. No. I had played the game, and I had still lost. Instead, I would breathe new life and voice into the grant I so despised by transforming it into a new genre. I would shift the rules of the game by sharing my story and defeat. I would interweave the process of quantitative research into a narration of the complex and personal experiences of conducting that work. My goal was to shift the gears of how we typically present research into the format of a story that might resonate with other writing center directors who might also feel beaten down, exhausted, and unsure of how to prove that their work mattered. If anything, my retelling might be a cautionary tale of the pitfalls of relying solely on quantitative data to demonstrate our influence on student success.

And so, here I sit, in spaces of my house that provide me with a semblance of an office, if it can be called that. Even prior to the pandemic, I rarely had time to sequester myself in my office, in blissful silence, honed in on my own research. Rather, if I did find time for writing, it was in between checking in students at the writing center, the exhausting meetings that peppered my daily schedule, or late at night when my family was finally settled and in bed. Similar to Fulford's and Frigo's struggle in this volume, I too found it difficult to navigate what had now become my new reality. I could no longer retreat to my office on campus and leave my personal life for a while. Rather, all aspects of my multiplicities of wife, mother, friend, and professor had become even harder for me to find the time, let alone the space, to work on my project since I began working remotely. Initially I thought I'd finally be able to carve out time for myself. I didn't have to commute, I could attend meetings from my living room, and my work schedule had become more fluid since teaching online. But instead, the delicate balance between my academic and personal life became blurred. I simultaneously attended meetings or taught while keeping an eye on my youngest's virtual classes. Or I found myself preoccupied by the mundane expectations of being a wife that I had been able to shed when briskly walking into the writing center, ready to tackle what the day might bring. Now, the multiplicity of my two personas collided together like electrons where the separation between the two became almost obsolete. I no longer knew where one ended and the other began.

In an attempt to navigate the fusion between my two identities, I set up shop in places of the house where I am less distracted by the constant reminders of my life outside of academia. And so, in a rare moment of successfully pushing my personal life down into the deep recesses of my mind, I once again attempt to translate my grant into an ethnographic narrative. I take one final glance at the living room littered with toys, Post-it notes of to-dos on the coffee table, and the pile of laundry waiting to be washed and attempt to remember where I left off with my revisions. *Get it together, Jule, you don't have much time! Ugh, what was I even trying to say in this paragraph. Right. I remember now, establish your audience. Focus!* My fingers hover over the keyboard as I will myself to slip into the somewhat automatic nature of writing. I let my thoughts and ideas spill onto the page. I call out to my readers, asking them to follow me on a reflective journey of the uneasy and often unfruitful nature of quantifying our work and our students. *Maybe I should write in the first-person. That way I can establish a sense of "we are in this together" with my readers.* It is important for me to let my readers know that I understand their struggle, as I too have found myself drowning in a sea of frustration, doubt, and despair. I want to honor the burden of knowing that while we have evidence that is valid and important, it is often discounted:

> As writing center directors, we know that our impact far exceeds the number of appointments, outreach, and cross-campus support provided. Further, we know that most of the important work we do cannot be quantified. Student reviews of their experiences, tutors' growth as learners and academic professionals, and the feeling of community and collaboration that is often documented in qualitative research highlights the multifaceted significance of writing centers. Yet, that research does not often lead to continued and increased buy-in or increased financial support.

Reading through the changes I've made to the original grant, I begin to understand that my revisions are not really a new journey of exploration but rather an ongoing struggle of trying to disconnect the daily and often ordinary experiences of life from academia. Yet, by refusing to narrate the messy and personal nature of our work, we dishonor ourselves and those we hope to support. Numbers cannot describe our interactions with students, who often come to our centers scared, overwhelmed, and lost. Numbers cannot explain the impacts tutors have on students by simply listening, supporting, and collaborating in the messy nature of writing. And I certainly cannot ignore the influences my role as a mother and wife have on my own writing and revisions. I am a mother of three boys, and to put it mildly, my life is hectic and my academic work is sporadic. And yet, somehow, I must find a path through the messiness that inextricably enfolds my work and my identity.

My youngest son, Felix, just started kindergarten, and I often receive phone calls from the school asking me to come pick him up. It's always jarring and interrupts me just as I'm getting into the flow of researching, of writing, of revising. And so I jump up from my desk, drive to the school, and listen as the teacher describes what's happened. I can hear Felix screaming in the office. I stand outside because of COVID protocols, even though all I want to do is rush in and comfort him.

"We've had another incident," the teacher explains. "Felix was on the playground and tackled another child. We couldn't calm him down and we think it is best that he goes home for the rest of the day."

I sigh and ask the teacher if they tried removing him from the situation, if they tried to find out what happened, if they tried to give him some space. Ignoring me, her words dripping with judgment, she responds: "You need to understand that we do not have the staff to remove him from class. And as you know, we cannot tolerate this type of behavior. We think Felix might need additional support, like counseling." I remind her that Felix has autism, often finds it impossible to share or describe his emotions, is constantly bombarded by sensory overload, and *is* in various types of therapy. I schedule a meeting with the principal, and the teacher finally releases Felix, who runs sobbing into my arms.

I pick him up and carry him to the car. I tell him that I love him, and when he is ready, he can tell me what happened. Once he's on the couch, tablet in hand, he says: "I'm ready to tell you. A boy was being mean to me on the playground. I did what you said; I used my words and told him he was being mean and to leave me alone. But he didn't stop and I didn't know what to do. I just wanted him to stop. So I pushed him down." I hug him and once again discuss and demonstrate how we use our words, not our hands. He nods, we watch an episode of *SpongeBob*, and I eventually open my laptop, hoping for a few moments of quiet so that I can resume my work. As I struggle to remember where I'd left off in my revisions, I glance at my notes in the margins to reorient myself and sigh as I see the reminder to pay the after-school care bill (see figure 15.1). Great; it's already two days late. And now I'll have to pay late fees for a service that we only sporadically end up utilizing. My life is a constant mess of trying to remember everything, get everything done, yet no matter how hard I try to juggle it all, I still manage to disappoint the people in my personal life, my colleagues, and myself.

The reminders in the margins are concrete examples of the intertwining of the everyday nuances of life within my work. I am constantly shifting between Felix's world, my world as a mother, and the world of academia. And the remnants leave their mark within a space that fails to accommodate interruption, messiness, scrambled thoughts, and disjointed revisions. I am forced to have a clandestine relationship between my personal and academic life. And I am tired of it. I want to expose the mess. I want to integrate the very nature of my life into the work I do as an academic. Similar to Pantelides's "Embracing Interruptions in the Personal and the Professional," I must remind myself that interruptions and the juncture of "personal and professional goals can be more about mindful persisting" (2018, 101), as well as about where interruptions may become an impetus for change and growth (2018, 110). Even now, in this rare moment of quiet, I glance at the clock, checking if I have a few more minutes to revise before heading to Felix's gymnastics class. In the

Student Level. <u>When conducting</u> qualitative <u>research of</u> undergraduate <u>students, I found</u> that students in undergraduate tutoring (don't forget to pay afterschool bill) <u>were</u> more comfortable in seeking out support <u>than Graduate students.</u> <u>It is not known if that comfortability comes from instructor support and guidance, from students' self-motivation, or both. From my own experience, undergraduate students often make choices based upon word of mouth. Students pick instructors that have high rankings from their peers. Thus, it would be possible that undergraduate students</u> choose <u>to utilize a writing center based upon their peers' experiences. While</u> Graduate students were almost as likely to seek writing support, they had specific goals for revision: (submit flex-spending receipt to Discovery Benefits or you'll be locked out again!). discipline-specific writing, effective summary and paraphrasing of other's words, and academic persona in writing.

Figure 15.1. Screenshot showing the revisions and personal notes and reminders.

end, I complete a disjointed paragraph before I am forced to stop. We leave; I quiet the internal voice that cries out in protest about the chaos I have left on the page. I jump into the car, turn on *NPR*, and barely listen as I imagine myself methodically typing out new ideas, new revised sentences in my grant that magically transform the mess that I currently have into a shining beacon of innovative and impactful insights:

> What is needed is an approach to assessment that not only matches the needs and goals of those who fund our centers, but also attends to academic and personal needs of those who utilize our centers. Assessment is at the core of our work, but we must be careful that assessment is not the end goal. Rather, we must merge our narratives of assessment with the lived experiences of all who engage within our centers. We must not privilege one narrative or one goal over the central mission of writing center work. We must find avenues for assessment that respond to the multilayered needs of students, writing specialists, faculty, colleges, and deans.

But I know full well that half of what I have "revised" in my mind is disconnected from the document back home that I am revising. My ideas for revision will likely be lost as soon as I sit down to watch Felix perfect his tumbles, wave and give him a thumbs up as he looks to make sure I'm not working on my laptop instead of watching him.

SCENE TWO: THE JOURNEY OF REVISING MY IDENTITY
It's a typical weekday evening. Everyone is in bed, and I'm sitting on the couch as old episodes of *Project Runway* flicker on the television while I blearily finish feedback on student essays. I sigh in relief and slam down my laptop. Finished! I glance at the clock; how is it already 1:00 a.m.? I'm so tired and yet can't get my mind to stop spinning. Days have turned into weeks, and I have barely touched my grant. A sense of dread hangs over me, paralyzing me. Often, instead of revising, I stare blankly at the page, trying to ignore that every nerve in my body seems exposed and my eyes burn from lack of sleep and staring at a screen sixty-plus hours out of the week. I rub my eyes and refocus. I'm at a place in my revisions where I need to delete sections of data that are no longer needed, but I am finding it difficult to cut out entire sections. It's not only that I spent two years crafting and writing up my findings but also the fear and pain of letting that version go. I push my emotions aside and instead sift through the multiple charts; my finger hesitates over the highlighted section that I'm about to delete. I remember all the work and sleepless nights collecting and analyzing my data, and the time-consuming process of visually representing what is about to be sacrificed. This is hard. And I'm scared. What am I going to put in its place (see figure 15.2)? I force myself to unceremoniously delete it. I suck in my breath. It's done. All that work is gone, just like that. Wearily, I close my laptop and head to bed, convincing myself that I'll figure out a way to replace what I've just lost.

The next day, I sit reflecting on my mixed emotions of aggressively deleting and revising years of my work. I'm jolted out of my thoughts of feeling sorry for myself when my middle son, Spencer, who is twenty, walks into the living room, which is often my office. It has been two years since he was in high school, where our lives were hyperfocused on marching band, jazz band, advanced placement classes, what college he'd attend, etcetera. Even though he still lives with us, I'm still getting used to his new independence, seeing him in fits and stages as he increasingly spends less time at home, shifting the narrative of "when will you be home" to "will you be home," of letting go. Spencer looks at me, smiles, and says: "Still working?!"

We do this every day: he comes home from work and walks past me as he heads to the kitchen to get a snack, or else shouts out a "goodbye" as he heads to hang out with friends. And, every time, we smile and give each other that knowing look as he runs past me and yells: "Still working?!" But, this time, he stops and asks me how it's going. I sigh and show him my grant. He gasps: "Mom, you've, like, deleted over half of

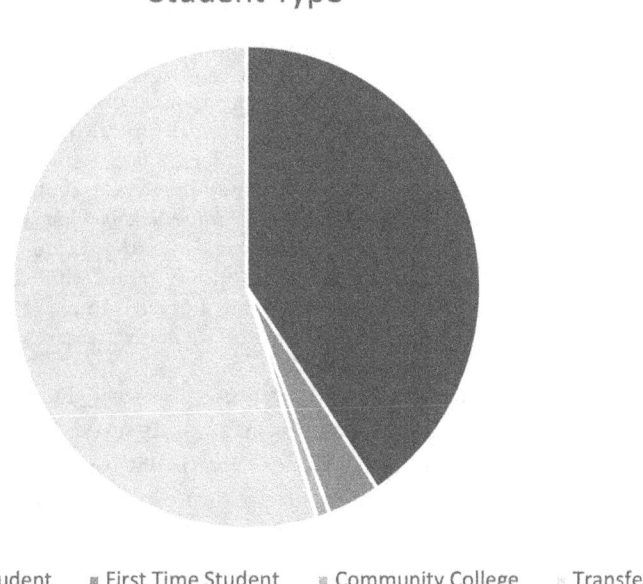

Figure 15.2. Pie chart of student enrollment demographics, deleted.

it! How can you do that!" I laugh and say, "Honey, half of the revision process is deleting."

As I say it, I act nonchalant. I pretend that I am not having trouble with reorganizing, with shifting focus, with deleting my writing. But then I look at him, the sadness and confusion in his eyes, and I say: "But it is hard; it's like how you were once my baby, how this grant was my baby, and I have to let it go, let it be what it is meant to be . . ." And as I trail off, he bends his 6'5" frame down to hug me, smiles, and shoots me an "I love you" as he runs out of the door to explore the world.

With renewed focus, I begin to fill in the gaps that my deletions have left. I place myself into the document. I voice my pain of constantly trying to prove that what I do matters. I narrate my goals and dreams for supporting students and faculty at our university, which have been constantly juxtaposed by an ongoing battle for establishing buy-in and budgetary needs that are rarely met. The revisions I make allow me to share the struggles that so many writing center directors face when tasked with quantifying data that refuses to be quantified. And as painful as it is, I'm revising so that I can share my experience and own up to both my professional and personal purposes for conducting outcome-driven data of students. The new passages give voice to the goals behind the research I conducted as well as my overwhelming desire to prove that the work I do as a writing center director matters, at any cost:

> WSU's diverse student body necessitates that we provide a wide range of support for our students. My goal, then, was to create a writing center that offered free writing, research, and technology assistance to students in all degrees and levels of study. I wanted the writing center to be a place that moved beyond the narrative of "remedial, lacking, or humanities focused." I wanted to expand the writing center to provide support for all WSU students, in all departments, at all levels, and with varied levels of academic needs. And to me, that meant I needed to play a new game of research to make these changes; one of qualitative research.

As I struggle with owning and narrating my story, the phone rings. It's a call from my oldest son, Gavin, who's twenty-seven. Gavin struggled to find himself after high school. Convinced that his only path to success was college, he fell into a deep depression when it didn't pan out. He's since found his own way, brims with confidence and joy, and is immensely successful in the coding and technology field.

In one of the most concrete examples of leaving the nest, he's recently bought his own house and lives with a wonderful and supportive partner. But as a mom, I still worry about him. I hope that his new life isn't too overwhelming. And I deeply miss the time we had together when he lived with us. We'd often stay up until 3:00 a.m. discussing theories of existence, quantum physics, and the universe. With his new life, he's become increasingly preoccupied and rarely calls. So, assuming the worst, I pick up the phone and blurt out: "What's wrong? Is everything okay?"

Gavin chuckles and says: "I'm fine mom, I was just thinking of you and wondering how you were doing. I miss you. Plus, I wanted to see if we could come over for dinner this Sunday. I've been wanting to hear more about your research and your book chapter. How's it going?"

I sigh in relief and tell myself, *See! He does think of you! Maybe he hasn't left me completely!* We chat for a bit and set plans for Sunday dinner. As we say goodbye, he gives me some encouragement: "Love you. You've got this!"

As I put down the phone, I begin to cry. As a mother, every atom in my body, every decision I have made, has been influenced by my children. But then, at first slowly, and then almost in the blink of an eye, they no longer needed me in the same way. They started to develop their own identities beyond me. They began to build and explore their own trajectories in life. Along the way, they stumbled, they fell, they made mistakes. That process is necessary but so incredibly painful. I've yet to come to terms with how empty it feels to unravel the protective shell I've encased them in, trusting that they will be alright, that I'll be alright. Doing so has inevitably left gaps within my own identity and has required me to redefine who I am. The process of revising my grant, I realize, is very similar. I labored over that grant, fussed with it, perfected it, and stood proudly as I viewed its final iteration. But now, I realize that I have stumbled, made mistakes. I must come to terms with the reason I found it necessary to engage in numerical research, if I'm to revise in a thoughtful and personal way. And so, while painful, engaging in those revisions has allowed me to reflect on the purpose and goals of my academic work honestly and truthfully. I've found, as Tellez-Trujillo did in her reflection of an "abandoned" project (chapter 16), that rather than being negative, it has started a journey where I am beginning to form a new identity of myself, of my research goals, and of my grant.

SCENE THREE: ACCEPTING THE PERSONAL AND TRANSFORMATIVE NATURE OF REVISION

There is a cacophony of noise all around me, and I want to scream. Everyone in the house seems hell-bent on ensuring that it's impossible for me to get any revisions done. Felix is madly banging the keys of the new keyboard I bought him for his birthday. *Awesome decision, Jule. So worth the potential cognitive gains of integrating music into his life . . .* Mike, my husband, is singing along to AC/DC while making dinner, pots and pans clanging in time with Felix's "music." Behind me, the wall, which divides the living room I'm currently sitting in and Spencer's room, vibrates with a mix of a video game sounds, music, and screams of "Get him! Go left! Oh NOOOO! I died."

Internally, I hear myself saying, *I swear I'm going to throw that PlayStation out the window.* Tonight is the night. I'm furious. This is personal. I yearn for a room of my own. I now know, intimately, what Virginia Woolf meant. Fed up, I jump up from the couch and yell: "Are you kidding me?! I specifically told everyone that I needed one hour, one hour of peace and quiet for my revisions. I feel like I am going crazy. There is not ONE place in this house that I can go to without constant interruptions! You do realize that my work is important, right?! That it's not just a hobby?! That this matters to me?!" I crumble into the couch and begin to sob.

Slowly, everyone comes into the room, staring at me wide-eyed. Spencer mumbles a "sorry," retreats to his room, and begins turning down his devices. Felix runs up to hug me and whispers in my ear: "I'm sorry mommy, I was trying to make beautiful music for you to help you with your work." My husband also bends down and hugs me, promising he'll keep the noise to a "minimum."

They all slink away from me and I feel even worse. Well, that's settled, I'm a horrible academic and an even worse mom and wife. While I am fully aware that there's no simple disconnect between my life as mother, wife, and academic, for some reason I still attempt to separate them into well-defined boxes. I'm constantly playing a game of balance between research and teaching, career and personal. What would happen if I began to accept and expose the never-ending battle? What if I began considering a truce between my academic and personal self? Fiona Hurd and Smita Singh (2021) bravely explore the raw, personal, and scattered nature of academic existence. Focused on creating spaces of self-care for well-being, they reflect upon categories of struggle that many academics face: "the balancing of academic life with family and relationship complexities, grief, loss and the raw humanness of life" (Hurd and Singh 2021, 348). It seems fitting that I find myself at a section of my grant that hides incredible pain and raw emotion. A reader would never guess the trauma lurking in the shadows, but when I read the section, it takes my breath away. At the midpoint of writing my original grant, I was mistakenly removed from the status of full-time faculty member to alumni for three months because of a clerical error. No one could tell me how my status was changed, and I didn't find out until I lost access to secure data I had been collecting and analyzing for my grant.

Reading the passage where I describe the "limitations" to the study, I can feel how strained the academic voice was that I was trying to present. The genre of the document refused any personal or emotional narrative seething in the background. I remember the anger and the sense of complete loss during that period. It was not simply the fact that my family struggled to pay our bills, couldn't utilize healthcare services, or access therapy for Felix. It also impeded my work as an academic. I was unable to use the library database system or analyze my data, and I lost my research assistant. And in the process of those long three months, I felt like I had lost my identity; I was no longer able to care for my family or do my job. As my finger hovers over the "delete" key, I tear up. This section no longer matters, yet it is a powerful reminder of how my life has become intertwined with my professional identity:

> However, Jule Thomas lost access to COGNOS data until April 2019. Troubleshooting of data collection and export of data was not completed until 6/25/19. The research assistant, Poonam Yadav, used her allotted

hours training Jule Thomas in SPSS and data analysis until her graduation in May 2019. Jule Thomas continued analysis of data, with support from her husband, during the remaining assessment grant timeline.

As I look at this section of the grant, I again realize that it is impossible to disassociate my identity into "well-defined" categories of existence; I must find a way to become whole again. I no longer wish to conceal my multiplicities; instead I must learn how to honor and integrate them into all aspects of my life. And if that means that my life is emotional, painful, and personal—if it means that the work that I do requires openness, reflection, and ongoing revisions—so be it. I'm done fighting a losing battle.

Just now, as I struggle to complete my thoughts and plod through never-ending revisions, Felix runs in. I am sitting in his room—the only place in the house that has a desk where I can close the door and work in a state of quasi peace and quiet. He states quite seriously: "I have a very important question to ask."

I feel myself tense up. Where is my husband? Didn't I say I had to get some revision done tonight? I mean, why am I the only one who can answer all the questions and deal with all the meltdowns? I count to five, turn to him, and smile: "And what might your question be, love?"

"Is God a girl or a boy?" he asks with seriousness.

"I think God is a girl. Only girls can grow babies. They have superpowers, so God must be a girl, right?"

He's been going to mass with his Granny and Grandpa when he spends the night on weekends. So, while we don't speak much about religion in the traditional sense, I begin to understand where his questions—and his newfound notion of gender—are coming from. We've also been having conversations about what boys or girls can or can't do. He's just started kindergarten; so, the narratives of gender he's been taught at home don't seem to align with those at school. I take him into my lap and kiss him.

"That is a very good point! But I think that maybe God isn't a boy or a girl, they just are." He looks at me, puzzled.

"But you are either a boy or a girl, mommy, so which is God?"

I sigh; he's five, but when is the appropriate time to discuss my own views on gender, identity, and religion? Trying to figure out the right response, I notice my husband standing in the doorway. His eyes say, "I'm sorry" and "I've got you." He crouches beside us, and we begin to describe our views on deity and gender. It is simplistic and ends with the possibility of being more than just a boy or a girl. I look at my husband, who flashes me the look I know so well, the look of "We have no clue what we are actually doing, but I hope its okay. That we aren't messing up." Felix interrupts: "Life is so confusing!"

We laugh as he jumps from my lap and sprints out of the room, yelling, "Catch me if you can!"

My husband looks at me and bends down to kiss me. "I've got this; get back to work!"

Chuckling, I say, "You better! This mommy is going to be pissed if I'm interrupted again!" But this is our life; this is how we navigate our work: in fits and stages where life always seeps in. My husband closes the door as I pull up my grant and, once again, dive into the revisions.

As I do so, I can't help thinking about the conversation we had with Felix. I too am still struggling to navigate my own identity as a mother, woman, professor, researcher. Even after thirteen years in the field, I still feel like I'm faking it half of the time. I still have this lingering fear of presenting my work as reflective and ethnographic in a world where women must always fight to be seen as good enough, valid enough. I struggle with owning up to the fact that my grant research might have been one-sided or one-dimensional. Yet, this process of revision has taught me that there is no "right" path I must take. That I, and my identities, will always become interwoven into the work that I do. Instead of fighting against who I am, I must choose to embrace the often terrifying and transformative experience of pushing past traditional expectations of my field. I'm beginning to come to peace with the realization that revision means grappling with new paths, goals, and purposes. I delete the introduction of the grant and begin constructing a new interpretation that is honest and places myself within the pages. I voice the very personal and often brutal nature of academia, the struggle to be valued and seen. And in doing so, I finally acknowledge the very reason that I embarked on a quantitative research journey. From the start, I had to prove that I was competent, knowledgeable, capable, and rational, not a silly, emotional girl. Yet now, I have the courage to tell my story:

> I found that many faculty, specifically those in the English department, were furious about my placement as the director. Previous faculty that I had taken classes from, had sat for hours in their office working through theoretical frameworks, refused to look at me, say "hello" back, or would simply cross the street just so they didn't have to engage with me. I had known that I had a hefty task in front of me, but I had not anticipated the extent of that task. My chair and I would spend countless hours drafting diplomatic email replies to faculty who sent complaints about a student of theirs that had visited the center and was still unable to "write well" after one session. Faculty who sent a scathing diatribe of an email about how they disagreed with the mission or approach of our student-driven

tutoring approach. Or simply sent hurtful and personal post about my inexperience and inadequacies in the position to our listserv.

Looking back on revisions of my life, of my work, that is still ongoing, I have begun to understand that my identities as an academic, wife, and mother can't be separate but are always intertwined, always evolving. Through revising, I have come to realize that our work holds incredible joy, pain, and doubt. Yet, in the midst of it all are the possibilities to reinvent, to retell, to share our journey of revising and reinterpreting who we are between the pages—and the comments in the margins—that we write.

REFERENCES

Hurd, Fiona, and Smita Singh. 2021. "'Something Has to Change': A Collaborative Journey towards Academic Well-Being through Critical Reflexive Practice." *Management Learning* 52 (3): 347–63.

Pantelides, Kate. 2018. "Embracing Interruptions in the Personal and the Professional." In *WPAs in Transition*, edited by Brian Ray, Courtney Adams Wooten, and Jacob Babb, 101–11. Logan: Utah State University Press.

Salem, Lori. 2016. "Decisions . . . Decisions: Who Chooses to Use the Writing Center?" *Writing Center Journal* 35 (2): 147–71.

16

"THAT'S WHERE IT SLEEPS"
What I Say When I Point to My Abandoned Project

Karen R. Tellez-Trujillo

The box shown in figure 16.1 is marked "Mom's." Stored in my garage, the box holds two stacks of white paper and numerous reminders of time spent in Prague, Czech Republic, during the summers of 2010 and 2011 while I was researching the underground dissident literature movement, samizdat. In these stacks sleep scholarly articles written by Jiřina Šiklová, Czech sociologist, author, and political activist; a proposal for an international research scholarship; and various versions of a short story titled "Boxes," part of a larger collection titled *The Back Room*. Also asleep in the box are notes scribbled on half-sheets of white paper; a 3" bright red crepe paper flower (a gift from Šiklová); and a thin book, *Samizdat*, a gift from another Czech author, Vilém Prečan. I saved a folded and deeply creased cartoonish map of Prague on the left side of the box that my then husband, Jakob,[1] and I used to get around the city, as well as two jump drives containing sound files, short bursts of film, and B-roll still photos taken during interviews with dissident authors Šiklová, Prečan, and Ivan Klíma. Despite the number of artifacts in this box and the attempts to revise the multiple projects surrounding them, I have not been able to assemble these treasures into a cohesive project, regardless of how much work I put into it.

I mention work, because hard work plays a lead role in my relationship with the research project I write about in this chapter, but not the role I thought it might at the project's beginning. In 2009, when I initially proposed *The Back Room*, a collection of short stories, I felt that I was ready to take on research and writing commitments, reliant on a formula I was taught in real estate broker training as a way of achieving success. I, in fact, knew very little, most importantly that I would need Institutional Review Board (IRB) approval. It would take many years before I would figure out a formula for enduring encounters with the failure and exhaustion that are inextricably tied to work, particularly

"That's Where It Sleeps" 207

Figure 16.1. Box of artifacts, asleep in my garage.

the academic work I was tasked with when I returned to my local state university to complete my undergraduate degree in 2008.

Early during my return to college, I considered revision to be a natural part of the process that goes into producing a finished, successful product worthy of sharing. Reflection and revision were introduced together in the English program at my university, supporting the idea that "reflection can stimulate effective revision because it often prompts metacognition" (Lindenman et al. 2018, 582). I held dear, early on, what I felt was the promise of revision. If I put reflection toward what needed revising and combined reflection with hard work, I would end up with a piece of writing that I felt was successful. Upon reading Kathleen Blake Yancey's words in *Reflection in the Writing Classroom* about reflection as a part of revision, I realized that reflection would help me to "know my work, to like it, to critique it, to revise it, to start anew" (Yancey 1998, 201). I thought, "There it is! Do that and you can't go wrong." While I know that Yancey is right, and my faith in reflection has seen me through many writing trials, I have yet to figure out how to use revision as a way of waking an abandoned project from sleep, regardless of how much work, love, critique, and reflection I put into it.

I say that my project is sleeping, because it is the alternative to accepting that the project is dead and will never come out of the box where it is held. Each time I open the box and remove its contents, I believe that revision, or reseeing the project, is what will help it thrive again, but I always end up putting it back in the garage, out of sight. I have reseen the project in many ways. It began as a research project proposal in 2009, then went on to become a collection of short stories that I envisioned would fulfill my Honors College requirement for graduation, and then took a new form as the final product promised in my research proposal. When the collection of stories didn't come together, the project became one published short story in an online literary journal. Even after producing one story, I revisited the project with plans for developing a thirty-minute documentary that ultimately didn't go as planned. Its last iteration was six minutes of documentary footage just before the project was put to its longest slumber.

It has been difficult to find the words to express the exasperation that comes with having a story inside that doesn't come out right or come out at all. I have tried explaining my attachment to samizdat and to my research but feel that I come up short. The heart of what I feel has been written by Alejandra Hidalgo in "Consulting Editor to the Rescue: Seeing Storytelling Anew through Veteran Eyes" (chapter 2) as she shares the many approaches she's taken to telling the story of her father's disappearance. Hidalgo writes, "none of those iterations captured the rich, messy essence of what I wanted to say. [. . .] In 2016, I decided to tell it as a feature documentary, but even with three cameras and five mics pointed at her, my story continued to run circles around me" (30). I think my story of samizdat was also running circles around me, but rather than gain control, I put it to sleep. It has been reassuring to know I am not alone in my struggle, or in my numerous approaches to waking my project, for as Hidalgo also notes, "I believe many things about my story, but trying to articulate them into a sentence proved onerous" (34). I would find myself looking deep into the eyes of anyone who asked me why this project was important, hoping that they could see what I was feeling but couldn't say.

In writing this chapter of failed revision, I have learned that I had a tremendous amount of faith in myself and in the revision process, as a lifelong hard worker who believed that time, reflection, and numerous attempts and approaches to the project would yield stories worthy of publication. I have also learned that there are some things revisions can't fix and underpreparation is one of them. As an undergraduate, I had no prior research experience and hadn't yet been published at the time I proposed this project. It wasn't until I wrote this chapter that I realized that while I would be able to revise *The Back Room*, or recreate a later documentary attempt, I could not revise the experiences that informed the larger project. It has taken the writing of numerous drafts of this chapter to discover that there is still hope and possibility within the box, that all is not lost. The contents of the box are only asleep, not lifeless as I'd often feared.

THE BACK ROOM: A COLLECTION OF SHORT STORIES (2010)

The Back Room was meant to be three stories, set in the post–World War II lead-up to Prague Spring.[2] The proposal for this collection was written as part of the application for an undergraduate research travel award.[3] My conception of the stories was not so much concerned with war itself as with the difficulty writers experienced during this time of censorship when authors participated in samizdat, a form of self-publication through underground copying and distribution of state-banned literature in former communist countries of Central and Eastern Europe.

In my proposal for *The Back Room*, I outlined a series of stories that would unfold from the perspective of the protagonist, Sarah Allan, who finds journals and manuscripts in boxes, belonging to her aunt and uncle, Milena and Vilém Kris, both Czech authors. Milena's journals would detail the work she, her husband Vilém, and her friend Petr Skala did as operators of a samizdat press in the back room of their home. I envisioned that—using typewriters, onion paper, and carbon paper—the authors wrote, copied, and distributed illegal texts. I had also decided that by the end of the story collection, Sarah would learn more about how her Aunt Milena ended up in the United States following Vilém and Petr's deaths, as well as the details surrounding the tragedy of their demise.

It was also my vision that this collection would center on censorship and the lengths that an author will go to express their thoughts despite fear of imprisonment, exile, and even death. It would explore the ways publication can change our world, and how we view literature in online settings. I saw this project as an attempt to write fictional stories about efforts made by members of the samizdat movement, particularly Central and Eastern Europeans, to maintain normalcy in constant proximity to persecution and execution for freedom of expression. I was in over my head from the start.

As part of my commitment outlined in this research proposal, I also applied for and was accepted to a summer writing residency, the Prague Summer Program, to be held in 2010 at Charles University, a public university in Prague. The Prague Summer Program offered a month-long writing workshop under the mentorship of American author Stuart Dybek and was based on ideas surrounding writing on the internet and what that action means for modern day self-publishing. At the time, it felt like I'd been set up to complete my project with ease, as the workshop topic of producing revolutionary, self-published literature overlapped with the samizdat movement: both asked that I think about the ends to which authors will go to share their art and to disseminate illegal written information regardless of the dangers. But while in Prague, I didn't write about the movement, which meant I didn't take advantage of Stuart Dybek's expertise. I chose to write about anything but. This failure to make use of my opportunity was not due to negligence or lack of desire to write about samizdat; rather it was in response to learning of the overwhelming weight and palpable danger experienced by all working members within the samizdat movement. I felt that I could not represent the experiences of movement members, as an American raised at considerable distance—cultural, geographic, and temporal—from the samizdat movement.

During the 2010 trip, the first of two I would make to Prague, I learned about the history of underground activities at Charles University through lectures and presentations that gave me political perspectives on samizdat and introduced many of the authors affiliated with the Prague Summer Program. Even though I was physically in the place where the movement had occurred, I still felt unable to represent the experiences of the people involved. Each time I attempted a draft of a short story to fulfill the promises I'd made in my research proposal, I feared essentializing life under communist rule. This writing paralysis left me without content, and it added pressure to the existing stress I felt regarding responsibility to members of the samizdat movement, to either write about their experiences in an expert manner or not at all.

During my first stay in Prague, I revisited my research proposal too many times to count, with hopes that I would find a spark of confidence or guidance for where to begin writing. Although I had clearly envisioned the characters Sarah, Milena, Petr, and Vilém before I ever reached Prague, I could no longer access what I had imagined for them, and I had not given enough detail about them in the research proposal to write and revise them. As each day ended in Prague, I reminded myself that I had flown almost six thousand miles, and was away from my home and three young sons, on the promise of producing three short stories. The success of this collection was dependent on putting to work my plans for revision, but by the time I left Prague, I had only lecture notes and photos to carry home. I had nothing to work with that I felt could be revised into a product that reflected the time, money, and emotional investments I'd made.

THE BACK ROOM: AN HONORS THESIS (2011)

Upon returning home from Prague, the deadline to submit the short story collection to the Honors College came more quickly than I'd anticipated. I had outlined and conceptualized all three stories prior to leaving on my research trip, which ended up being helpful to me, as I was able to modify my plans for three stories down to one. I broke the sole story down further, into three different stories, meeting the requirements of the Honors Thesis to produce a three-story collection. The collection, *The Back Room*, became three new stories titled "Visit," "Boxes," and "Home." I revised the original storyline from a short story about a niece, aunt, and uncle to a story about a mother and daughter who fled from Prague to Milwaukee, Wisconsin, in the late 1980s following the death of the family patriarch at the hands of the ŠtB, or secret police in communist Czechoslovakia. I also added new characters, Jahoda and Radek. These additions helped me to remove myself from the anchors I had to the original proposal. Removing that weight helped me to reduce some of the fear I held that I would do the members of the samizdat movement a disservice by misrepresenting the gravity of living under occupation and disseminating illegal information.

The second of the stories in the collection, "Boxes," was published in my campus's online literary journal, *Din*, in December 2011. I was proud of the success of "Boxes" and believed at the time that if I re-visioned the project into something other than a story, I could make something more of my 2010 experience. But I would need to do something different than story writing, as I was not willing to revise the three stories I'd written to fulfill my proposal. I'd developed an aversion to them, knowing that they were not what I had envisioned, and more importantly, that I still did not feel I had the knowledge that I needed to represent the people of the samizdat movement in story. So, I took a new approach.

THE DOCUMENTARY (2011)

The second major re-visioning of the project continued in June and July 2011. Jakob and I returned to Prague again, although this time with a group of documentary students from my university. The goal was to conduct interviews with three samizdat authors, Ivan Klíma, Jiřina Šiklová, and Vilém Prečan, to learn more about samizdat and to hear firsthand what these authors' experiences were under communist oppression. I intended to combine this interview footage with my notes and the writing from 2010 into a short documentary, as a way of completing the project I had started. I wanted to hold myself responsible to the people

Figure 16.2. Karen and Ivan Klíma in Klíma's home office (Trujillo, J., 2011).

whom I had written about prior. I did not anticipate at the time of this second trip that caring about this movement was not enough.

The basic plans Jakob and I had for filming this documentary were to interview Klíma, Šiklová, and Prečan; to visit the Czechoslovak Documentation Center; and to take as much B-roll footage as possible so that we would have enough material to complete a thirty-minute documentary. Jakob was responsible for carrying and setting up the filming and recording equipment for the interviews and for taking as many photos and films of Prague as he could. He also asked me questions to help prompt what I wanted to know from the authors, because I often struggled with communicating why the project was important to me (I was only able to emphasize, it seemed, that it *was* important to me). My responsibilities were to set up and conduct the interviews, which were made possible through a friend I had made in Prague in 2010.

I was able to schedule three interviews, the first with Klíma, the second with Šiklová, and the last with Prečan. Of the many unexpected acts of kindness I received during the interview process, one of the greatest was when Klíma took control of his interview when he realized that I lacked interviewing experience. He explained the process of samizdat to me in his home office, as seen in figure 16.2, before I properly asked. While doing so, he pulled books from his shelves that he had written during the time of Soviet occupation of Prague and post–Prague Spring.

After we spent some time discussing books, Klíma walked Jakob and me around his office and showed us photographs of other Czech authors, all while telling stories of his experiences with samizdat, about secret meetings in homes, and how authors disseminated packages of written information, carried in the middle of the night by people (mostly women) who would be least suspected of moving information. One of the things he said during the interview that has stuck with me was that "it was a stupid time," referencing Prague's occupation by Soviet forces. He said this while shaking his head, looking to the large window in his sitting room. Klíma smiled occasionally and welcomed Jakob's requests to take photos of his office and items displayed on shelves. I am grateful that Jakob took pictures of Klíma's books and of his writing tools, like his reading glasses. Klíma was tired but gave us more of his time than we had expected, in an interview that lasted nearly two hours. I learned more about the samizdat process than I had anticipated and about authors whose names I hadn't seen during prior research.

At my next interview, with Šiklová, my inexperience with interviewing was more apparent, because I'd failed to create a list of questions, believing that I could approach Šiklová's interview as a conversation about her tenure at Charles University, her involvement in the samizdat movement, and her time in jail in 1981. I thought I could follow the same organization of my meeting with Klíma; although clumsily approached, the interview had gone well. But it wasn't until I began to review sound files from the interview with Šiklová that we could see the need for extensive editing to cover up my lack of preparation. Reviewing the sound files took numerous attempts, because I would start, cringe, and not return to listening again for months.

During our interview in her lifelong home, Šiklová did not let me off as quickly as Klima did. Within the first few minutes after welcoming Jakob and me into her home, she accused me of being a journalist who was interested in getting a story for financial benefit, rather than a student who was meeting with her to learn more about samizdat. My poor preparation was apparent. She was right to be upset. However, after learning more about the project through my insistence that my curiosity came from an attraction to stories of resistance and resilience, rather than out of interest in getting a story into a newspaper or magazine, she too allowed us to film, record, and take notes and photos. I was so worried about seeming unprofessional, as I had felt during my interview with Klima, that I at first came off as cold and impersonal. It wasn't until I relaxed with Šiklová that she could see and believe that I asked for the interview out of interest and care for the experiences of those involved in samizdat.

Figure 16.3. Jiřina Šiklová in her home (Trujillo, J., 2011).

After nearly forty-five minutes (although it felt like hours), Šiklová had not only explained the samizdat process but also given us a tour of her flat, stopping to pull books from their shelves and to share unframed photos she'd tucked in random places. In figure 16.3, she is pulling a book from her personal collection to show me an example written by a friend who had been in exile. She gave me numerous articles she'd written and encouraged me to refocus my interests from samizdat to the women of exile. I wish I had heeded her advice; not doing so is one of my greatest regrets, as it meant another re-vision possibility that I neglected. Had I followed Šiklová's recommendation, I would have likely come away with a different project, but it might have resulted in a completed project guided by a fresh approach.

Ultimately, what began as an interview with a rocky start turned into an afternoon conversation, as Šiklová served Jakob and me dark coffee with cream and sugar cubes. She placed dainty slices of warm apple cake she had baked the morning of the interview on delicate dessert plates. As we ate, I became less interested in samizdat as a movement and more interested in the people involved, particularly the women who carried manuscripts in prams and worked as secretaries at embassies, with the intent of moving texts across borders. The danger associated with samizdat became less important to me than Šiklová's work as a founder of the Prague Gender Studies Center, the first feminist organization in the

Czech Republic, and that she had lived in the same flat her entire life. I wish I had thought to record the time we spent at her kitchen table but also believe it might have ruined the mood of the conversation.

Before Jakob and I left Šiklová's flat, she handed me a red paper flower that had been stuck in the buttonhole of one of her adult son's childhood coats hanging near her front door. She hugged both of us and wished us well on our project. I was never able to reach her again. I felt like I left this interview with many gifts I didn't deserve, tangible and otherwise. The shame, from poor preparedness, and regret, over a missed opportunity to handle the privilege of interviewing these people with more preparation and knowledge, brings wishes for another chance, even now. However, this encounter cannot be revised. Jiřina Šiklová passed away in May 2021.

My final interview of my second trip to Prague was with Prečan, the director of the Czechoslovak Documentation Center (ČSDS), which houses artifacts of anti-totalitarian resistance in Czechoslovakia and abroad during the Communist era. Coincidentally, among the photos in Šiklová's home were photos of Prečan with author and former president of the Czech Republic, Václav Havel. I was excited to learn of the close friendships between Havel, Šiklová, Klíma, and Prečan during our interview, which reinforced the feelings of closeness between the authors, which I had missed during my first trip.

I met Prečan at the ČSDS, and rather than explain the samizdat process and movement, he opened my world to the importance of the documents that had been produced under occupation, explaining that what could appear as a simple, small book could be an imaginative story that would carry someone through the monotony of days under occupation and the weight of oppression. As I walked into the ČSDS for the second time, having visited it during my first trip to Prague, the number of samizdat documents stored at that location caught my breath. I had not had the chance on my 2010 visit to see all that I was encountering on this second trip. Prečan showed me samizdat artifacts ranging from small, 3" by 3" bound books to larger volumes like *Charter 77*, housed in sturdy white cardboard boxes. *Charter 77* criticized the Czech government for failing to protect the political, civil, and human rights of the people by the communist regime. The document is named after the best-known dissent group, with signatories that were important to postcommunist government. Figure 16.4 shows Prečan reading from a book of samizdat artifacts while I take notes. I examined simple flyers, as well as boxes containing volumes of fiction and nonfiction, and other historical documents such as those held in the rooms of the ČSDS, one of which can be seen in figure 16.5.

Figure 16.4. Karen and Vilém Prečan at the ČSDS (Trujillo, J., 2011).

Figure 16.5. A small samizdat library in the ČSDS (Trujillo, J., 2011).

After noticing that my attention had been drawn to a photo of him and Václav Havel (one that I had also seen in Šiklová's home), Prečan gave me a book titled *Samizdat*, which began with a short introduction written by Havel. I felt that he wanted to give me something I could take away from my time spent in the ČSDS. Prečan expressed that he was pleased with my interest in Havel, because although Havel was the former president of the Czech Republic, Prečan described Havel as a "good man." He shared this detail with a thoughtful smile. This comment has stuck with me, in the same way that Klíma's description of communist occupation as a "stupid time" had. Although they were only brief comments, the expressions on these men's faces as they spoke gave me the feeling that there would never be enough time or words to convey what they really wanted to say about that time in history or the people who had experienced it. That book Prečan gave me sleeps in the box and reminds me of the risks the samizdat authors took and of the relationships they formed with other authors. Most recently, it is a reminder that work that is worthwhile requires patience and discomfort, even when it seems physically and emotionally impossible to find a way forward.

By the end of this trip, even though I had finally followed my plans from the original international scholarship proposal, to dedicate weekday afternoons to visiting historical institutions and national archives in Prague and to review personal letters and diaries written by authors during that period, I still could not put my finger on the best way to approach this project and move it forward. I had interview footage, voice files, still photos, and written artifacts (mine and those I collected from the authors I had interviewed), but I did not know what to do with them. I could not piece together what I had gathered on this trip into a draft of a documentary, with or without Jakob. It was a different version of the feelings I had in 2010 when I could not write the short stories. In this case, I lacked the knowledge and training to do these authors a service by putting together a sensitive, informed, and sound documentary. I had learned about samizdat from three different dissident authors and had come away feeling more attached to the movement and people within the movement than before but still lacked confidence that I should be the person to do this work.

Each time I opened the old files on my computer containing drafts of *The Back Room*, I would soon close them, still not knowing what to do to fix them or make them better. The documentary felt like it was my only hope. However, in the end, the documentary process was rife with shortcomings, the most obvious being my inexperience as an interviewer, and the less obvious our lack of editing skills as well as a lack of a strong rhetorical approach for organizing the material. In Jakob's final edits to complete the short documentary, he did the best he could with the material we had gathered.

This is another aspect of my project that revision cannot fix; the fragile relationship between interviewer and participant was part of my education in feminist research, as was the understanding that I must disclose and be aware of my positionality. However, my understanding of the relationship between interviewer and participant stopped there. Neither I nor Jakob had received training on the university-issued recording and filming devices, and we learned after arriving in Prague that the camera only recorded in five-minute increments. Additionally, I did not get IRB approval for this project, because I did not know I needed to. Beyond the lack of IRB approval being a barrier to disseminating the documentary, the IRB process was another lost opportunity: it could have helped me anticipate or avoid some of my challenges. I only knew I was passionate about the topic and deeply interested in others' stories, but I could not put into words why samizdat had grabbed me in such a way that I needed to write, speak, or ask others about their experiences in it. Only now, upon writing this chapter, am I grateful for what I didn't know, because I might have decided against the visits to Prague and the interviews altogether. I might have talked myself out of the opportunity to fail; seeing my past attempts at revising the initial proposal, I am, for the first time, truly glad for this project.

When I returned to the United States at the end of the summer 2011, I reverted to engaging in revision the only way I knew how. I made reflective journal entries and edited the original story, "Boxes," again for grammatical error. I became afraid of listening to my interviews, for fear of reliving my embarrassment and in avoidance of an emotional response I had to the content. In 2012, I was asked to produce and show a shortened version of a documentary for faculty of the College of Arts and Sciences at my university as a way of encouraging other faculty to sponsor trips abroad. Halfway through the process of meeting the expectations of the request made by my college, I became frustrated and shifted my attention to the short story, while Jakob completed the abbreviated documentary using minimal footage and text pulled from my proposal, notes, and each of the interviews. The product was a ten-minute documentary that uses songs from the Brno Philharmonic Orchestra to fill the moments where we relied on images to tell the story of what we learned about samizdat and its authors.

Revisiting the documentary felt like I was on the path once again to seeing the written portion of my original project through. However, I soon hit another obstacle when I read the first few chapters of Madeleine Albright's 2012 book, *Prague Winter,* and again when I read Molly Antopol's 2014 book, *The UnAmericans.* Both books had similar characters, or situations dealing with boxes, to what I had already written. Shifting focus would depend on energy that I didn't have. It is interesting to me that in retrospect, issues that felt like major obstacles to the success of my project are not as grand as they once appeared.

A BIT ABOUT THE BOX

The box that holds the artifacts from my samizdat project has moved from seven houses into seven different garages between two states, New Mexico and California. During our marriage, Jakob and I moved twenty-four times, mostly because we loved to move and felt replenished by the process of getting rid of the old to make space for a new dwelling. Our three sons are now accustomed to moving, and when the younger two have lived in the same home for longer than two years they often ask, "When will we move again?" After flooding from a rainstorm, the original box that held my research artifacts and had "Samizdat" written on it had to be thrown out due to water damage, and my middle son, Nicolas, moved the contents to an empty book box. As I relabeled the box, we joked that I should write "Mom's" on the top, because everyone knew that the box was mine and that it was to go wherever we went, no matter what happened. Boxes are very much a part of my life in that I have moved often, both as a child and as an adult.

In the same way I am concerned with this box of artifacts that I anticipate continuing to carry with me until I do something meaningful with its contents, the protagonist of "Boxes," Sarah, is concerned with the contents of the boxes her mother, Milena, left behind. When I envisioned the story originally, I wanted Sarah to have a way to get to know more about Milena, from whom she was closed off her entire life, and could think of no better storage to hold Milena's story and treasures than a box. When coming across my Prague box, I always say, in my head or aloud, "That's where it sleeps," as if the project is the garage dragon or a fearsome creature that should not be disturbed. When packing for my most recent move to Southern California, I placed my sleeping "Mom's" box into the back of my car for the long drive to my new home, for fear that something would happen to it in the moving van. I now see this as a sign of commitment and hope that I still have revisions for the project left in me.

There have been many moments of frustration at not knowing where to go next with this project, but knowing I have the box that holds all its pieces has been reassuring, because the box signifies the possibility that something will come of the project someday. I have reminded myself on numerous occasions that this project's eternal hold is less a reflection of my lack of interest or willingness to work hard at it and more about lack of practice, training, and emotional and professional preparedness. In this project's earliest days, I was an emerging creative writer and an immature researcher, and, although well-intentioned, I was unsure of the most respectful way to represent wartime and postwar stories in writing or film. Now, thirteen years after writing the initial proposal, I understand that revision doesn't have a time frame.

I can't revise my initial inexperience or make up for my early lack of guidance, and I, to a fault, have made self-directed choices, have not narrated my progress deliberately, and have not received commentary or guidance from a teacher or researcher more experienced than myself, as Lindenman and coauthors (2018) recommend. It is fair to assume that had I received outside support, the project might be completed. But even that is doubtful, because revision of this project needed education, practice, and experience that can only come about with time. Only now can I see the possibilities for revision that were either overlooked for more than a decade or that I previously saw as obstacles rather than opportunities.

One of the most important of the many lessons I have come away with is that the writer must also be emotionally prepared to find out all that they do not know about a place, a people, and history. If the author chooses to write about all that they learn, they must have a defensible reason to do so, especially as an outsider. This is where I feel that revision and time are in a relationship, in that I am geographically and temporally further from the Czech Republic than I have been since the beginning of this project, but this distance contributes to, more than impedes, possibilities for revision.

I can still research women of exile and their role in the samizdat process, as Šiklová suggested. I'm caught off guard by unexpected emotions at present, realizing that it has taken numerous revisions of this chapter to see that what I have believed to be lost in this project is not lost because I still care deeply about samizdat as a movement, the authors who participated, and the people for whom the written word meant survival. This chapter has roused the possibilities that have been sleeping within the box all along. I still hold the voice files and recordings of the interviews with the potential for revisitation and revision. I hold the short stories in my head and in print. I am alive and able to return to Prague, should I choose, or not, to complete the documentary on my own if I were moved to do so. I've abandoned my long-held formula for success and ask myself as I type through writerly waves of discovery, relief, and curiosity, "Is writing about what we are convinced cannot be revised a path to opportunities for revision?"

I have come to know revision in a new way, respecting that it cannot be rushed and that sometimes, while opportunities for revision are right in front of our faces, we may not yet be ready to see them. I'm still okay with the idea that revision is hard work and one must be willing to put a significant amount of effort into revision to see it through. This chapter has brought about many emotions like frustration with my past self or sadness at opportunities that I won't have again, but I am moved to the heart by the surprises that have come from writing about my abandoned project. I am filled with curiosity for what else might be in the box, in the sound and image files, in the articles and book I was gifted, and wonder might happen if I pull the box open to let the light in and whisper, "You've been asleep long enough. It's time to wake up."

NOTES

1. Jakob is the name my ex-husband has chosen for this chapter.
2. From January 5, 1968, to August 21, 1968, the Czechoslovak Socialist Republic experienced a period of mass protest and liberalization from political oppression. This was ended when the Soviet Union and Warsaw Pact countries invaded the country to suppress reforms taking place toward democratization and freedoms granted in the way of speech, media, and travel, among others.
3. I received the Honors College Undergraduate Scholarship for International Research in 2010 at Southwest US Border university. The financial award from this travel scholarship funded my research trip to Prague, Czech Republic, in the summer of 2010. The proposal for this award was completed and submitted in the fall semester of 2009.

REFERENCES

Albright, Madeleine Korbel, and William Woodward. 2012. *Prague Winter: A Personal Story of Remembrance and War, 1937–1948.* New York: Harper.

Antopol, Molly. 2014. *The UnAmericans: Stories.* New York: W. W. Norton & Co.

Lindenman, Heather, Martin Camper, Lindsay Dunne Jacoby, and Jessica Enoch. 2018. "Revision and Reflection: A Study of (Dis)connections between Writing Knowledge and Writing Practice." *College Composition and Communication* 69 (4): 581–611.

Shaughnessy, Mina P. 1976. "Diving In: An Introduction to Basic Writing." *College Composition and Communication* 27 (3): 234–39.

Trujillo, Karen. 2011. "Boxes." *Din.* Online Magazine.

Yancey, Kathleen Blake. 1998. "Reflective Texts, Reflective Writers." In *Reflection in the Writing Classroom*, by Kathleen Blake Yancey, 185–205. Logan: Utah State University Press. https://digitalcommons.usu.edu/usupress_pubs/120.

17

DRAWING A BLANK
Illustrating the Revision Process

Ian Golding

Just as the cover shows the often looping, slow progress of revision, the journey of creating the comic followed a similar—often frustrating— path.

Right from the beginning, the first step to starting the comic was a stumble. When I went to draw revision in action, I wasn't sure how to actually show it. Compared to other aspects of composing, revision is often overlooked in illustrations. The (rest of the) writing process is rich with visual clichés: the lightbulb over the head signifying an idea; or a person hunched over, typing furiously showing productivity. But revision doesn't have a clear illustrative translation. Sure, there is the pile of crumpled paper by the waste bin, but that is about making no progress, about the frustration of being unproductive. While creating this cover would result in *a lot* of crumpled paper, I wanted to show how revision is—if nothing else—an extremely productive process of transformation and growth.

In my search for illustrative cues, two famous depictions emerged. First, the surreal 1953 *Looney Tunes* cartoon *Duck Amuck*, in which the animator—a hidden Bugs Bunny—is constantly harassing Daffy Duck by revising every element of a cartoon in a fourth-wall-breaking experience. The enduring image of the animation—that of Daffy Duck as a four-legged, polka-dotted, flower-faced creature complete with "screw ball" flag—perfectly displays the drastic nature that revision can take. The other, the children's book *Harold and the Purple Crayon*, follows the titular character as he revises the landscape on his journey home. While Harold might be limited to crayon, his illustrations bend the white space around him, creating shapes that exist as foreground, background, and, well, the ground beneath his feet.

Both visualize the ever-changing outcome of revision that Joseph Harris discusses in "On Choosing Not to Revise" (chapter 1). Just as he articulates how revision creates "new lines of thought" that lead his work to be "quite different from the one [he] imagined at the start" (23), the illustrated characters are rarely able to predict where revision will lead them.

But I felt as though something was missing in both *Duck Amuck* and *Harold and the Purple Crayon*. The composers constantly alter their creations but are traveling ever-forward. The characters solve their problems by continuing their journey without reflecting or returning back to change their past work—a trait I find vital to revision.

The cover of this collection was born from a desire to depict that crucial yet unseen step. I wanted to portray revision as an imperfect and ongoing process of returning back to earlier work, making small uncertain changes in hopes of improving the overall piece. To accomplish this, I decided to have the comic loop, repeating a singular pattern throughout. But there was one large problem: I had no idea how to pull it off. Quickly, I learned that creating a flawlessly looping comic would take numerous rounds of revision to solve what felt like a brain-melting puzzle.

Any change to one panel would repeat through the whole thing, throwing off the rest of the comic. In an early draft, for example, the comic looped every five panels. But soon I found that I had three initial "reaction" panels, which meant the fourth panel needed to quickly tie everything together before the loop started again. To correct that issue, the opening needed to be streamlined. Fine. But, in achieving a faster pace at the start, I realized that the third panel arrived abruptly—which then cascaded to the logic of panels four and five. Of course, all of these changes also needed to perfectly interact with the row below and above. Numerous times, I made "improvements" only to realize they ruined the visual loop of the entire page, negating any progress I thought I'd made. My desk was covered with indecipherable doodles as I tried to find the right pattern. I continuously looped back to each panel, making small nudges to get the overall comic timing right. And, just when I thought I'd figured it out, some forgotten detail would arise and send me to the beginning of the loop. It was, honestly, infuriating.

Somehow I completed a draft. This first version followed a similar flow as the final but looked vastly different. I'd spent so much time perfecting the looping pattern that the actual illustrations were left underdeveloped. And by that I mean ugly.

The editors appreciated the draft and were kind enough to not point out how silly the bird looked. They did, however, have a number of suggestions about the looping pattern . . . the perfect looping pattern that

Figure 17.1. Early lumpy bird.

I'd spent so much time getting just right. Sprinkle a few things there, move that one panel here, it'd be great to see more of this feature and less of that one. Reading their input, I felt an anxious twitch in my eye. Did they have any idea just how complex their suggestions were? That the whole illustration was precariously balanced already? I wanted to say that their requests were unreasonable—nay, impossible—and that if they wanted the changes so much, maybe they should try and draw it themselves. I took a breath. I told them, "Sounds great! I'll see what I can do!"

I went back to the drawing board with a sigh. I'd already expected to revise the look of the bird and had practiced new potential models (figure 17.1), but now I also had the whole new list of changes from the editors. I didn't think there was any way to accommodate their requests. It'd be a waste of time, a futile attempt to appease them. But soon, I made one small change and then another, and then, taking a step back, I was able to see how much better the looping pattern became through their feedback. In this collection, William Duffy examines the collaborative timeline, and in this project I was able to experience a similar development firsthand. The insights, ideas, and vision of the editors

Drawing a Blank 225

Figure 17.2. One of many sketch pages of awkward birds.

differed from my own, but through collaboration the updated version improved dramatically.

As I finished the next draft, I grew emboldened by the improved looping. Why stop with just a new bird and the feedback from the editorial team? I could improve everything! For reasons unknown, I wanted to streamline the illustration, narrowing the endless loop into a mere six panels. It would be clean and to the point. Rather than build off the previously revised versions, I wanted to present what I thought was a vastly improved vision. Instead of discussing this with the editors, I went rogue and redrew the comic from scratch (figure 17.2).

I thought it was a pretty slick revision, but the editors were, logically, a bit confused. This was not the comic we'd discussed. Sure, the character looked better, but they weren't editing a book on cartoon birds. Where was the revision? The looping? The frustration? The constant hard work? Good questions. I'd focused on one aspect to the point where I'd thrown aside the rest. In my excitement to make it look better, I forgotten the overall purpose of the comic.

So, just like the character in the comic, I looped once more, altering past work while adding new. Moving forward by looking back, I

Figure 17.3. The comic, sped up a bit too fast.

combined the new character with the original layout, my ideas blurring with the editors' insights. Revision is largely skipped over as a blank space when visualizing a composition, but it is vital. And, ultimately, the final comic as it appears on the cover depicts the ongoing, often unpleasant process of revision while being very much a product of it.

REFERENCES

Johnson, Crockett. 1955. *Harold and the Purple Crayon.* New York: HarperCollins.
Jones, Chuck. 1953. "Duck Amuck." Los Angeles: Warner Brothers.

LOSSES, LEAVINGS, REMAKINGS
An Afterword

Jessica Restaino

> *Like air, revision seemed to fill all the available space.*
> —Christina M. LaVecchia, Allison D. Carr,
> Laura R. Micciche, Hannah J. Rule,
> and Jayne E. O. Stone

There are those things—mysteries, dreams, even memories—that consume us and yet remain out of reach. We keep trying to crack the code, anticipating a flood of recognition, some *that's it!* wave of clarity. *We'll know it when we see it,* we assure ourselves. Revision can occupy our writerly imagination in a similar way, a fixture of sorts: familiar as a process, potentially obsessive, always aspirational, that text we have almost produced but, alas, not yet. Even when we "arrive," in a sense, meeting traditional markers for successful revision—an essay lands in print, a book manuscript moves forward—most of us suspect that another round could yield a still better text. Perhaps one more citation, perhaps a cleaner sentence here or there, will matter in some meaningful way. But this is where we must tangle with revision's bigger realities, its "relationality to everything else," as our editors note in their introduction. Indeed revision *does* move into our sense of ourselves (i.e., "I am a hard worker"), our notions of what we value and why, our sense of what is possible, toward some prize on which we fix our ever-straining eye. And here our editors are, I think, right again to describe revision as "kinetically, existentially, emotionally" fluid, seeping well beyond our very pages (10).

As I was working on this piece, I noticed something I've had so long pinned to the corkboard on my wall that I sometimes forget its existence. Every time I (re)discover it (and I do, routinely), I read it multiple times. It's an email exchange between me and one of my most essential mentors, Eli Goldblatt, dated October 30, 2007, with the subject line "Revision hell." I was working on early revisions of my first book, *First Semester: Graduate Students, Teaching Writing, and the Challenge of Middle Ground*, and I sent Eli a panicked email. What did I have to offer, really, by way of conclusion? I did not have a simple fix nor some grand reveal. Responding to my worry that it seemed the best I could do was revise my way toward more questions about graduate students' experiences as writing teachers, Eli writes this: "Do your questions point to doors where people only see walls now? That would do."

I imagine myself in the present, looking at a door. Indulge me for a moment in unpacking the obvious: a door is both a possibility and a limitation all at once. We do not necessarily know what's on the other side; we don't know that walking through it will transport us to anything better than our current location. For the most part, though, we know what doors can do, how they work. We know they open and they close. Of course, possibility isn't guarantee: and while the very idea of a door suggests there is something and somewhere else, we all face moments where we must contend with our losses, our failed projects, our hopelessness. As someone whose work has taken up terminal illness, death, and grief, I understand that there are indeed some things that can't be simply revised and, too, that there are some doors that might be visible to us, but walking through them to some new location is not an option, even if we wish desperately for transport, for some new way to be. What does this mean for revision in our work? What does our work become, and how might we integrate the limits, even the failures, of revision into our scholarly lives?

Revising Moves carves out a wide space in which to contend with the practice and idea of revision as both possibility and limitation. "Some things," the editors write, "cannot be revised" (13). We must begin here, I think, because we typically only reach a traceable, immovable limit after we have garnered change where it's been possible and, conversely, struggled against the currents of resistance for long enough. This is quite different than the decision *not* to revise, one we can make—as Joseph Harris does in this collection—as an expression of our own convictions and beliefs, our recognition that the very thing we have created is exactly what we want, regardless of the opinions of editors or reviewers. There is a kind of freedom there, for sure. But the impossibility of more traditional approaches to revision drives some of our most radical innovations and new ways of being, our greatest revisions—perhaps we might call them "overhauls." It is at these moments that we show others and, most importantly, ourselves the door. In Aja Martinez's "Alejandra Chooses Life: Revising the Resignation Letter toward Counterstory as Epistle," we witness a failure of structure, form, relationship: the performance of a public-facing email, glossed in professional niceties that obscure all institutional ills. The move, as Martinez casts it, is to respond not in-kind but differently, in ways that both show us another institution entirely, not the one "the chair" originally projects, and also declare this professional relationship beyond repair. Alejandra, in Martinez's counterstory, is moving on, leaving, finding a new space and a new set of relationships, and she will not be waiting around to find out if her former institution is able to revise its structural oppressions. Along the way, Martinez the scholar-writer also offers us—drawing on an approach informed by critical race theory—a text that lives outside the confines of a scholarly genre most shaped by predominantly cishet, patriarchal, white academic norms.

Many of us, for all kinds of reasons, will find ourselves ill-fitted for the most traditional corners of the academy, its values and its most exalted venues. Along the way, we may get to see ourselves more fully, but often not until we have tried painfully and earnestly to augment what we do into a mold not made for us. As Christina M. LaVecchia writes of the second set of essays in this collection, "many of the professional practices we often approach as transactional (getting a job, keeping and advancing in a position, or supporting the searches of others) also construct, and revise, our *identities*" (49). In "Revision as Protecting What Is Important," Cruz Medina describes it this way: "Writing this is hard, perhaps in part because revision can be hard, but more so because returning to the reviewers' comments is also painful. Reading reviewer feedback can often be nerve-wracking, but looking at reviewer suggestions from a journal that was not meant for my work feels more like peeling off a bandage that covered a scar from unnecessary surgery" (131). To observe a scar we have no means of valuing—we can't trace the history of this wound to anything we ever needed—is the stuff of grief. There is no narrative arc here that ends in a kind of triumph, a resolution where the parts that at one time did not fit together suddenly do. Instead, Medina's efforts at revision are about finally coming to see that what we have held tight, what we have perhaps even coveted, is not good for us, doesn't know or value us, is not, ultimately, *for* us at all. Medina describes this process as "the messiness of continually working to resist what we have been inculcated to believe that we desire from our work" (134). To the extent that desire is personal, that it might come from within us, stretching outward, the work of contending with the external manipulation of our belief systems and, thus, desire, stands to unseat us from our very selves. This is not about whether we have installed a recognizable IMRaD format (and indeed Medina tries that) but about learning to step into our own ways of making sense, of connecting, of cultivating meaning. Our frameworks do not always match those that have come before us, but that does not mean they lack value. The questions are: Where are they valued? Who values them? How can we find each other? Our most essential belief systems in such moments of searching need to be about having the courage to look elsewhere. We open the door even when we are unsure of where it leads, because we have assessed our current location and we know: nothing grows here.

In looking elsewhere we have to leave things behind. Drawing on Kathleen Blake Yancey's call for reflection in the revision process, Karen R. Tellez-Trujillo writes in this collection, "While I know that Yancey is right, and my faith in revision has seen me through many writing trials, I have yet to figure out how to use revision as a way of waking an abandoned project from sleep, regardless of how much work, love, critique, and reflection I put into it" (207). Tellez-Trujillo's words resonate with some of my own understandings of loss itself, the very foundation of my work in *Surrender: Feminist Rhetoric and Ethics in Love and Illness*, where what my collaborator and friend, Susan Lundy Maute, and I did in searching for a rhetoric, a way with words for her experience of dying with terminal breast cancer, was to language our way into silence itself, irretrievable loss. Sue died before I could write *Surrender* in its fullest form, and so I spent most of my time awash in our transcripts and audio recordings, grieving and writing alone. Revision of the manuscript that became *Surrender* had to happen without my friend and collaborator. In many ways, the person I was with her—in hospital rooms, at the chemo clinic, propped on her couch at home, always eager for what she might want to say—was also gone. That version of me existed in relation to Sue. The writer I was for *Surrender* had to look upon that past self while also charting a path forward alone, as a kind of grieving outsider, no longer cocooned in the very relationship that had been so generative and, indeed, alive. Reflecting on her own inability to revive an abandoned project, Tellez-Trujillo writes, "I have learned that I had a tremendous amount of faith in myself and in the revision process, as a lifelong hard worker who believed that time, reflection, and numerous attempts and approaches to the project would yield stories worthy of publication. I have also learned that there are some things revisions can't fix" (208).

When our belief systems, our practices, even our attachments are upended, we find ourselves in the present in a way that is stark and painful. Here we are to wonder and to act amid longing and loss, without any means by which to trace our threads backwards beyond this very moment. There is no redoing or recasting, no way of making things turn out differently. Tellez-Trujillo's inability to wake her project seems tied to this sort of failed history. In my case, as I think about *Surrender* there are at least two past selves now gone: the one in relation with Sue while she was alive, and the one who wrote the book alone after her death. While I could never imagine casting *Surrender*—or anything I've ever written—out into the world as anything other than imperfect, *Surrender* is perhaps unique in that the very core tenets of the work involve taking up in words that which language can never fully convey; it's always at least in part a failed project. It's an experience of *missing* something. This is perhaps more profoundly true because the roots of the book are grounded in friendship and love. When I was "getting it right" as a writer of that book, I could always feel its slippage, and I think the revision work back then, for me, was to just try not to edit that messiness, that sense of fruitless reaching, out of the text.

So, while I accept *Surrender* as published, I've also always been aware of the loneliness of that book. Grounded in a relationship that is no longer available to process itself, the book—and my presence in it—has felt in the years since its publication somewhat isolated. Of course, because many of us have lost people we love to illness, I have had the honor of hearing from readers about the book's impact on them, about the ways in which it resonates with something that they know. In that regard, I have been privy to a good deal of conversation around the work, and I'm very grateful for it. But it was only recently that I have been able to take up *Surrender* in a reflexive, critical, collaborative way, where I have been able to engage the version of me in the book who is a complicated figure, the friend and ethnographer bound up in one. Timothy Oleksiak's 2022 essay, "Composing Consent as a Response to the Challenge of Openness," which considers consent in the context of argumentative texts and the writer-reader relationship, gave me a fresh frame for revisiting ideas about consent and subsequently the desire for connection as a praxis in feminist research methodologies. We agreed to write together and, without spoiling that forthcoming piece, I will say that I was able to see myself newly through the lens of Timothy's work. With a writing partner to talk to and co-compose with, I also found myself uncomfortable: as we worked to explore the dynamics of my research relationship with Sue, I had to see myself as a more fraught figure than who I wished I had been at certain hard moments when Sue was alive. While I can't do any of it differently now, Timothy and I worked to carve out a new set of considerations—the methodological manifestations of drive, desire, fear, uncertainty—for how we assess our own orientation to our research relationships, opening up a deeper commitment to reflexivity in our work than what I was able to do on my own as I was writing *Surrender*. For this new path, this next door, I am grateful, even as I know I must live with what essentially "can't be revised": a past version of me, a beloved friend, a relational dance, a writing process, all now far from my reach.

I wish *Revising Moves* well in the world and trust that it will offer our field a much-needed breath of fresh air. In it, scholars show up with bravery and vulnerability in ways that will serve us all as we think about the work we do, why we do it, and how we can make it better (or perhaps, sometimes, leave it behind for something better). And on this last point, I think the editors anticipate what revision can most honestly, most fully offer us: "This is where we have landed, for now. Not stasis, not the final word, rather, a temporary calming of the tides or tremors activating revising's *moves,* just enough to scan the horizon for the next wave" (14). That is good enough, worthy of our embrace.

REFERENCES

Oleksiak, Timothy. 2022. "Composing Consent as a Challenge of Openness." *College English* 84 (2): 429–46.

Restaino, Jessica. 2019. *Surrender: Feminist Rhetoric and Ethics in Love and Illness.* Carbondale: Southern Illinois University Press.

INDEX

Locators with an *f* indicate a figure, locators with a *t* indicate a table, and locators with an *n* indicate a footnote.

able-bodiedness, representations of, 71
abstract ideas, 81, 185
academia, 11, 61, 161, 194, 195, 196, 204
academic labor, 26, 50, 55, 81, 180
academic life, 73, 194
academic programs, 166, 169, 172
Academies for Writing, 170
accessibility, discussing, 98–100
accountability, 102, 111, 113
accreditation documents, 85, 170
acculturation, 53, 113
Across the Disciplines, 151
adjacent possible, 181–82
Adler-Kassner, Linda, 166
administration, 49, 59, 74, 84, 87, 89, 163; writing program, 12, 57
Adobe Audition, 97
agency, 64, 71, 72, 79, 82, 86, 109, 121, 122
Ahern-Dodson, Jennifer, 155
Albright, Madeleine, 218
Alexander, Jonathan, 14*n1*
Allan, Sarah, 209, 210, 219
allatonceness, 91, 92
Ana, 67, 69; applications by, 68; letter of recommendation for, 68
Anderson, Joyce Rain, 14*n1*
Androids (Dick), 24, 25
annual review, 81–83, 83–89; revising, 79, 86
"Anti-Racist Scholarly Reviewing Practices: A Heuristic for Editors, Reviewers, and Authors," 119
antiracism, 12, 138, 147–48, 149; as concept, 141; pieces on, 142; writing center, 174
antiracism statement, 143, 144, 147, 148; components of, 142; writing, 141, 145, 146, 149–50
Antopol, Molly, 218
Anzaldúa, Gloria, 34
Arbery, Ahmaud, 139, 153
artifacts box, 207*f*; described, 219–20; assessment, 118, 171; narratives of, 197; writing, 163–64, 172, 173

Assessment Institute, 172
Association for Writing Across the Curriculum, 174
Atom, 100
Auburn University, 163, 164, 173; core curriculum at, 172; SACSCOC accreditation for, 170; writing plan initiative of, 169
audiences, 135; backlash from, 150; content and, 143–46
audio, 95; revising, 96–97, 100–101
authorship, 122, 174; collaborative, 181, 185
autoethnography, 130
awareness, 10, 76, 130, 160; growing, 149, 180; meta-, 114; shared, 107, 113

Back Room, The, 206, 209–10; drafts of, 217; as honors thesis, 211; revising, 208
Ball State University, 69, 75
Ballenger, Bruce, 79
Bartholomae, David, 8, 129, 130
Basgier, Christopher, 13, 138, 139
Bauer, Dan, 102
Bazerman, Charles, 9
Becker, Anne, 9
Becker, Cameron, 12, 50, 65; disability of, 70, 71; feedback for, 76, 77; letter of recommendation for, 67, 69–74, 75–77
behavior: dickish, 120, 121, 123; good, 119; modeling/fostering, 119; revisionist, 15*n3*
Belanoff, Pat, 15*n4*
belonging, 51; path toward, 91
Berlant, Lauren, 94
Berlin, Isaiah, 57
Bernhardt, Stephen A., 102
Berthoff, Ann, 8, 91, 92
Best of the Journals of Rhetoric and Composition 2020 (Medina), 128, 134–35
Beyond Conversation (Duffy), 181, 189
bias, 64, 67; exposure to, 68; implicit, 75
Big Feelings, about revision, 8
birds, sketch page of, 225*f*
Black Lives Matter (BLM), 154

Blade Runner, 25
Blewett, Kelly, 12, 68; letter of recommendation by, 65–67, 69–74, 75–77; rhetorical choice of, 71
Bowler, Nathaniel, 30
"Boxes," 206, 211, 218, 219
Boyd, Katie, 172, 174
Brackets, 100
Bratta, Phil, 122
Breitbart News, 144, 147
bridge-building, 58, 61
Brno Philharmonic Orchestra, 218
Brodkey, Linda, 14*n2*
Brooks-Gillies, Marilee, 122
Brothers Grimm, 24, 25
Brown, Stuart C., 14*n2*
Bugs Bunny, 222
Burnett, Rebecca E., 68, 72, 75

Canagarajah, A. Suresh, 130
Cannes Semaine de la Critique, 30, 32
Canvas, 70, 73
Carr, Allison D., 227
Carrasco, Cristina, 30, 31, 35, 36, 38, 39; collaboration with, 33; feedback from, 34; film theme and, 33; personal film and, 32
CCC. See *College Composition and Communication*
CCCC. See College Composition and Communication Conference
CE. See *College English*
censorship, 209
Ceraso, Steph, 106
Césaire, Aimé, 24
CFP, 3, 11, 152, 185
changes, 112, 131, 135; making, 52; program, 86 stylistic, 60
characters, 32; composite, 46*n1*, 49; counterstory, 47*n2*
Charles University, 209, 210, 213
Charon, Rita, 14*n3*
Charter 77, 215
Chauvin, Derek, 153, 157
Chignoli, Andrea, 32, 34, 35, 38; collaboration with, 33; on feedback, 39; narration by, 36–37; suggestions by, 37
Cicchino, Amy, 167, 171; feedback from, 165, 168–69; revision and, 174
Ciccotta, Joseph, 144
civil rights, 215
claims, actions and, 143
CLAS. See College of Liberal Arts and Sciences
coauthorship, 39, 182, 184; asynchronous, 139; pedagogical value of, 190

Code Pen, 101
CodeCanyon, 101
coding, 96–97, 99, 100, 104; revising, 101–2
collaboration, 8, 13, 39, 68, 71, 72, 74, 92, 110, 121, 122, 123, 151, 154, 161, 169, 174, 179, 180, 183–85, 225; community and, 195; complications of, 186, 187; defining, 182, 183, 186–87, 188, 189; expanding, 160; framework for, 181; impact of, 33, 190*n2*; interdisciplinary, 54–55; low-stakes, 184; pursuing, 187; retheorizing, 183; revision and, 11, 75, 93, 159, 178; rhetoric and, 187; student-teacher, 3; understanding of, 182; writer-candidate, 12; writing, 154, 169
collaborators, 14, 31, 189; feedback from, 29, 34; relying on, 39
College Composition and Communication (CCC), 109, 115, 187, 188, 189
College Composition and Communication Conference (CCCC), 4, 130
College English (CE), 96, 98, 107, 108, 188, 189
College of Liberal Arts and Sciences (CLAS) (WSU), 192, 193
Comi, Dana, 12, 62*n1*, 114, 123, 161; feedback for, 30; feedback from, 107, 108, 109, 110; imposter syndrome for, 91; mentoring by, 115, 161; revision story of, 92
comics, 178, 222, 226; looping, 223; reviewing, 225; sped up, 226*f*
commitments, 21, 55, 72, 74, 106, 123, 138, 144, 145, 146, 148, 149, 150, 161, 164, 174, 180, 219, 231–32; to inclusive practice, 147; liberal arts, 54, 56, 57; personal/professional, 61; research, 166, 206; writing, 206, 209, 219
communications, 72; technical, 119, 189; written, 77
communities: building, 170; collaboration and, 195; fostering, 77; marginalized, 61
communities of color, resistance by, 145
communities of practice, 91, 170
Comp Tales (Haswell and Lu), 5
competition, 93, 118, 127
"Composing Consent as a Response to the Challenge of Openness" (Oleksiak), 231
composition, 3, 65, 119, 151, 172; collaboration and, 187; digital, 54; discipline of, 141; history of, 24; options, 94; pedagogical work of, 165; plans for, 175; print-centric, 94; teaching, 24; visualizing, 226
composition courses, 58, 126

Composition Studies (Medina), 115, 132–33, 134
composition theory, 54, 57, 186
Constellations: A Cultural Rhetorics Publishing Space (Powell), 122, 123
content, 142; audience and, 143–46
contexts, 4, 11, 32, 55, 59, 65, 72, 74, 87–88, 124, 125, 129, 130, 133, 142, 159, 160; composite, 46*n1*; epistemological, 92, 126; interdisciplinary, 6; scholarly, 102; socially tense, 139
conversations, about revision, 91–92, 113, 184
cooperation, 118, 120, 122, 123, 134
copy-pasting, 50, 94, 97
Council for Writing Program Administrators (CWPA), 87, 88
counterstory/counterstories, 4, 11, 41–42, 47*n2*, 49, 229; composite, 46*n1*, 47*n2*; critical race, 41; as epistles, 42–46. *See also* story
Counterstory: The Rhetoric and Writing of Critical Race Theory (Martinez), 117, 118
COVID-19 pandemic, 13, 34, 153, 156, 159, 194, 195; lockdowns, 154, 160
Craft of Revision, The (Murray), 9
crap draft, 152
Creative Commons license, 97, 98, 99
Creative Writing, 37
critical capacities, 185
critical race theory, 143, 229
Cruel Auteurism: Affective Digital Mediations toward Film-Composition (kyburz), 94
ČSDS. *See* Czechoslovak Documentation Center
CSS, 101
Cultural Rhetorics Conference, 122
Cultural Rhetorics Consortium, 122
culture, 69, 122; academic, 12; popular, 129; writing, 82, 85, 86
curriculum, 72, 86, 87, 138, 230; redesigning, 170; surveillance of, 144; WE, 164, 165, 166, 171
Czechoslovak Documentation Center (ČSDS), 212, 215, 216, 216*f*, 217

Daffy Duck, 222
Daily Wire, The, 144
Danielewski, Mark Z., 102
data: analyzing, 202, 203; COGNOS, 202; collecting, 130, 131, 152, 171, 202; multimodal, 95; numerical, 193; outcome-driven, 199–200; qualitative, 95; quantitative, 194
"Decolonial Potential in a Multilingual FYC" (Medina), 128, 134

decolonialism, 129, 130, 133, 134
definitions, 142, 188; developing, 184, 185; stale, 177
DeRocher, Patricia, 76
dialogue, 68; back-and-forth, 92; revision and, 184
dick, term, 119–20, 123, 127
Dick, Philip K., 24
dickishness, 119, 124
digital archives, 129
Digital Archives of Literacy Narratives, 5
digital books, 94, 95; print books and, 96*t*; production of, 102; time for, 99
digital media: companions, 96; revising, 100, 104; scholarship on, 94, 95, 100, 104
digital publication, revising for, 103
digital texts, frustrations with, 31
Din (journal), 211
disabilities, 64, 70, 71; concealing/eliding, 72; disclosing, 72, 73
discourse, 166; objects of, 187, 189; scholarly, 177
dissertations, 108, 121, 181; crafting, 39
documentaries, 30, 36, 208, 211–19, 220; revisiting, 218–19; social justice, 31
documentation, 87, 103, 104
documents: final, 174; professional, 55, 82; releasing, 143; revising, 51
Doing Emotion: Rhetoric, Writing, Teaching (Micciche), 85
Dolmage, Jay, 63, 64
doomscrolling, 153
drafting, 114, 128, 146; back-and-forth, 152; revision and, 149
drafts, 63; development of, 181; feedback on, 25; final, 177; first, 146; producing, 143; writing, 146–49; zero, 142–43, 146
Drexel Writing Center, 146
Duck Amuck (cartoon), 222, 223
Duffy, William, 177, 178, 179, 224
Dybek, Stuart, 209, 210

editing, 12, 104, 135, 157, 217; back-and-forth, 152; minor, 156; ruthless, 158
editor: consulting, 30, 32; journal, 108, 112–13, 125, 128, 130, 134–35, 156; press, 19, 23, 25–27, 92, 95–99
education, 37; higher, 140, 144; inequities in, 145; interdisciplinary, 56, 57, 58; promoting, 67; reform movement, 163
Egri, Lajos, 33, 34, 38, 39
Elbow, Peter, 15*n4*, 124
"Embracing Interruptions in the Personal and the Professional" (Pantelides), 196

engagement, 9, 67, 122, 164, 166, 178, 182; community, 59
English studies, 55, 56
Enos, Theresa, 14*n*2
enrollment demographics, 199*f*
epistemology, 6, 92, 120, 126; Indigenous, 4
ePortfolio Project, 166, 170
equity, 138, 140*n*2, 143, 153, 157, 159
Erwin, Cathleen, 164, 168, 169, 171; revision and, 174; writing plan initiative and, 167
Espinoza, Hannah, 122
essays: analytic, 26; video, 30; writing, 26
ethics, 7, 68, 92
ETS HEIghten, 172, 173
"Evaluating the Intellectual Work of Writing Administration" (Wenger), 87
evaluations, 58, 88, 124, 172
existence, 36, 85, 168, 227; categories of, 203; theory of, 200, 202
experiences, 4, 102, 119, 130; academia, 195; breadth of, 59; embodied, 6; historical, 169; humanizing, 134; revising, 10, 15*n*3, 179; tracking, 163; transformative, 103, 204; writing, 167, 168

FaceTime, 154
faculty: BIPOC, 4, 11, 42, 45, 46, 74; development of, 164; marginalized, 41; non-tenure-track, 89; WE, 170; writing, 89
Family of Stories, A, 36, 39
feedback, 25, 29, 31, 33, 56–60, 71, 72, 85, 99, 102, 106–10, 111–14, 121, 133, 134, 157, 164, 165, 171; anti-racism, 138; audience, 38; audio, 156; constructive, 61, 92, 132; contradictory, 178; editorial, 186; endless loop of, 39; importance of, 12; interpreting, 19, 34; marginal, 205; positive, 73; providing, 62, 69; reviewer, 131, 179; revision and, 12, 19, 93; toxic, 52; types of, 162; using, 52, 55, 156, 158
fiction, 29, 30, 33, 36, 215
films: personal, 32; political, 31; reshaping, 32
First Semester: Graduate Students, Teaching Writing, and the Challenge of Middle Ground (Restaino), 228
first-year composition (FYC) course, 128, 142, 183
Flash, Pamela, 171, 173, 174
Floyd, George, 153, 154
Framework for Success in Postsecondary Writing, 83
framing, 4, 27, 64, 68, 88, 92, 109, 132
Frigo, Stefanie, 19, 108, 138, 139, 194; collaboration and, 13; radical adaptability and, 177
Fulford, Collie, 19, 108, 138, 139, 154, 156, 194; collaboration and, 13; equity and, 153, 159; presentation and, 153; publication process and, 160; radical adaptability and, 157, 159, 177; on radical vocabulary, 157; revision and, 155; writing program and, 152
Function of Theory in Composition Studies, The (Sánchez), 121
FYC. *See* first-year composition course

Gallagher, John R., 99
Garcia, Mike, 12, 13, 137, 138, 139; revision and, 173–74; zero drafts and, 81
gatekeeping, 73, 117, 118, 119, 122
gender, 3, 68, 203
gender studies, banning, 140*n*1
General Studies Composition Committee, 81, 82
genres, 79, 80, 81; institutional, 174; occluded, 75; revision and, 174; self-help, 181
Gershon, Ilana, 60, 61
Gilyard, Keith, 14*n*2
GitHub, 95, 104
Glasby, Hillery, 14*n*1
Godwin, Norman, 163, 164–65, 166, 167, 168, 169, 170, 173; revision and, 174; WE courses and, 172; "writing-enhanced" courses and, 164
Goldblatt, Eli, 227
Golding, Ian, 6, 13, 177, 178; artist statement of, 21; on revision, 180
Google, 15*n*5, 100, 103, 104, 154
Gradin, Sherrie, 14*n*1
graduate studies, 61, 63, 67, 113
"Grammar Is Racist? You Bet It Is, You Racist" (Curl), 144
grant writing, 31, 193, 195, 202, 204
Greenfield, Laura, 145
grindstone terms, 71
Gubele, Rose, 14*n*1

handbooks, 9, 24, 85
Harold and the Purple Crayon, 222, 223
Harris, Joseph, 11, 13, 19, 20, 21, 91, 92, 132, 162, 222, 228
Haswell, Richard H., 5
Havel, Václav, 215, 216, 217
HB7 ("Stop WOKE" Act) (2022), 137, 140*n*1
HBCUs. *See* historically Black colleges and universities
headnotes, 12
Health Administration, 168, 169

HF 802. *See* House File 802
Hidalgo, Alexandra, 12, 14*n1*, 20, 21, 96, 122, 208, 229; narration by, 38
Hidalgo, Miguel, 29, 37
high-impact practices (HIP), 163, 166, 172
Hispanic-Serving Institution (HSI), 65
historically Black colleges and universities (HBCUs), 151, 152, 154
holding space, 66–67, 165; as conscious act of being, 80; as mindful revision, 80–89
"Home," 211
Horning, Alice, 7, 9
Horwitz, Howard, 121
House File 802 (HF802), 137, 144
House of Leaves (Danielewski), 102
How Writing Faculty Write (Tulley), 9
HTML, 101; code, 96, 97; web pages, 94
HTML5UP.net, 96, 99
humanities, 118, 182, 193
Humanities Center Faculty Fellow, 45
Hurd, Fiona, 36, 202
hyperlinks/hypertexts, 102

identity, 49, 55, 57, 61, 63, 64, 151, 179, 184, 203, 205, 229; academic, 60, 72, 195, 196; administrative, 88; cultural, 69, 75; ethics of, 68; formation of, 3, 49, 54, 83–84, 194, 200, 202, 210; gaps in, 201; interdisciplinary, 58; liberal arts, 59; linguistic, 69, 76; navigating, 204; as ongoing individual project, 62; possibilities of, 53; revising, 10, 49, 54, 60, 74, 79, 92, 198–201; revision and, 10, 60, 79, 92; self-, 58; specialist, 59; WPA and, 50, 79, 83–84, 85, 86, 87. *See also* professional identity
ideobody, 110, 112
ideology, 46, 120; language, 163; monolingual, 129, 130, 132
imagination, revision and, 185, 227
"Imagining Coauthorship as Phased Collaboration" (Duffy and Pell), 185, 186, 187
IMRaD format (Introduction, Method, Results, and Discussion), 132, 133, 229
inclusion, 17, 71, 75, 122, 128, 138, 143, 145, 157; identity and, 72; revision and, 73
innovation, 99, 197; radical, 228
Inoue, Asao B., 137, 144, 145, 146, 147
Inside the Subject (Sánchez), 121
insights, 49, 51, 54, 71, 74, 106, 151, 178, 187, 190, 197, 224, 226; generating, 5, 9; sharing, 103
Institutional Review Board (IRB), 155, 206, 218

institutions, white-dominant, 20–21, 41
instruction, 9, 113; designing, 59
interactions, 67, 70, 77, 125, 187, 188, 195; progressive, 181, 189
interdisciplinarity, 6, 55, 56, 60
Interdisciplinary Studies program, 152
internships, recommendations for, 63, 68
intervention: institutional, 75; mutual, 181, 189
"Inventing the University" (Bartholomae), 129
invention, 182–87
IRB. *See* Institutional Review Board
Itchuaqiyaq, Cana Uluak, 134

JavaScript, 101
Jennings, Catheryn, 14*n1*
job documents, 55, 59, 60; revising, 52–53, 61, 62, 139
job letters, revising, 21*n1*, 91
job market, 12, 52, 53, 54, 60, 114
John, 34; on narration, 36
Johnson, Steven, 181–82, 189
Journal for the History of Rhetoric, 4

Kabat-Zinn, John, 80, 86
Kairos: A Journal of Rhetoric, Technology, and Pedagogy, 94, 97, 99–100, 104
Kelly, Devin, 138
Kelsky, Karne, 53
Kerschbaum, Stephanie L., 14*n1*
King, Lisa, 14*n1*
Kirklighter, Cristina, 133
Kitchen Cooks, Plate Twirlers and Troubadours: Writing Program Administrators Tell Their Stories (Bramblett and Knoblauch), 5
Klíma, Ivan, 206, 211, 212, 212*f*, 213, 215, 217
knowledge: base, 92, 126; decolonial, 131; making, 5, 129, 132; productive, 86; underlying, 10
Kolosseus, Beverly, 102
Kris, Milena, 209, 210, 219
Kris, Vilém, 209, 210
kyburz, bonnie, 94
Kynard, Carmen, 14*n1*, 42, 46

language: biased, 68, 75; boilerplate, 65; bold, 148; choices, 71; difference, 69; fluidity of, 182; racist, 144; response to, 130, 148–49; service, 164–67
LaVecchia, Christina M., 227, 229
leadership: administrative, 87; collaborative, 83, 89
learning, 94; service, 59; trajectory, 62
Learning from Adult Learners, 151

letter writing: practices, 50, 66, 69; translingual approaches to, 67
letters of recommendation: past, 69–74; personalizing, 68; reading, 65–67; reflecting on, 75; revising, 66, 67, 72, 91; text, 75–77; time/labor for, 63
liberal arts, 57, 59, 60; commitment to, 54, 56
lies: family, 36; storytelling and, 35; as theme, 37
Lindenman, Heather, 220
linguistic diversity, 72, 130
linguistic homogeneity, 129, 131
linguistics, 64, 69, 146, 149, 151
liquid networks, term, 181
literacy, 14n1, 117, 128, 129, 130, 131, 134; study of, 120
literary theory, 59
literature, 59, 64, 76; banned, 209; dissident, 206; self-published, 210
literature review, 110, 118, 119, 170
Lockridge, Tim, 95, 104
Looney Tunes, 222
looping pattern, 222, 223, 224, 225
Lu, Min-Zhan, 5
lumpy bird, early, 224f
Luther College, 137–38

Machado, Natalia, 32
Mad at School: Rhetorics of Mental Disability and Academic Life (Price), 72
Madhu, 4
"Madwoman in the Basement," 85
make-believe, 36
Maraj, Louis M., 118
Markdown, 97
Martinez, Aja Y., 4, 20, 117, 118, 119, 125, 228; counterstory by, 49, 229; personal/political stories and, 11
Mary Jo, 108, 109, 110, 112
Matheson, Breeanne, 134
Mayberry, Bob, 15n4, 133, 134
Mays, Chris, 20, 21n1, 52, 179
McGee's ideograph, 112
meaning, 49; cultivating, 230; making, 75
Medina, Cruz, 12–13, 76, 91, 92, 122, 138, 148, 229
memoirs, 14n1, 30, 32
memories, 32, 36, 227
mentoring, 64, 66–67, 71, 75, 92, 110, 122, 127, 209; collaborative, 113; horizontal, 106, 107, 113, 114–15; revision and, 123; vertical, 106
Mernit, Billy, 33
metanoia, concept of, 178
metaphors, 20, 125, 165

methodologies, 5, 108, 132; decolonial, 130, 131, 133; feminist research, 231; justifying, 107; majoritarian, 4
Mexican American Studies, 132
Micciche, Laura R., 8, 85, 133, 134, 227
microrebellions, 72
Microsoft Word, 104
Miller, Susan, 121
mindful revision, 80–89
mindfulness, 80, 81, 84, 86, 165
models, 122; shortage of, 141
Monberg, Terese Guinsatao, 122
monolingualism, 132
Mukavetz, Andrea Riley, 122
Muldoon, Andrea, 19
multiculturalism, 76
multilingualism, 128, 129, 132
multimedia, 69, 99
multimodality, 55, 56, 57, 58, 77, 95; incorporating, 87; pedagogy of, 54
multiple marginalized or underrepresented (MMU), 68
Mündel, Ingrid, 15n3
Murray, Donald M., 9, 14n2, 49
Myers, Kelly, 79, 178
mythologies, 4, 36, 38

narratives, 7, 11, 36–37, 112, 138, 139, 186; ethnographic, 194; institutional, 41; literacy, 128, 129, 131, 134; personal/emotional, 202; revisions to, 41; structure of, 20; *testimonio*, 76
narrator, voice of, 36–38
National Council of Teachers of English (NCTE), 92, 128, 129, 130, 133
National Public Radio (NPR), 98, 197
navigation links, 99, 103
NCCU, 153, 156
NCTE. See National Council of Teachers of English
"Neustros Refranes" (Medina), 133
Newkirk, Thomas, 14n2
No! (Chignoli), 32

obligations, ethical/professional/moral, 120
OBS. See Open Broadcaster Software
Office of Academic Assessment (Auburn), 172, 173
Office of Equity and Inclusion (UWT), 145
Oleksiak, Timothy, 231
Olson, Gary A., 121
Op. Cit. (book proposal), 24, 25
Open Broadcaster Software (OBS), 95, 103
open-access, 95, 183
open-source, 103, 121

Ordinary Plots, 138
O'Reilley, Mary Rose, 14*n*2
organizational structures, 10, 11, 58
orientation, 231; affective, 95; changing, 80; methodological, 5
Osorio, Ruth, 14*n1*

pacing, 97
Pantelides, Kate, 196
Parks, Steve, 124–25
participation, 71, 72, 73, 74, 218; cultivating, 169
past, recognizing, 167–69
Peck, Wayne, 7
pedagogy, 54, 76, 109, 165, 185; composition, 57; limits of, 10; multimodal, 58; online, 89, 98; public, 109
peer review, 93, 106, 111, 119, 122, 125, 126, 170, 172, 185, 190*n*2; anonymous, 160; process, 127; scholarly, 118, 121
Pell, John, 182, 183, 184, 185, 186, 187, 190*n*2; collaboration and, 189
performance, 19, 37–38; ranking, 66; writing and, 36
personal branding, 60
personal information, removing, 155
personal life, 7, 194, 196
personal notes, screenshot showing, 197*f*
personal statements, reviewing, 63
perspectives, 120–23
Petr, 209, 210
phrasing, 25, 131, 143, 144, 146, 147
planning, 102, 163, 169, 171, 172, 174, 175; assessment, 164. *See also* writing plans
PlayStation, 201
poetry, 26, 38
politics, 3, 25, 46*n1*, 71–74, 85, 145, 221*n*2; campus, 163; English-only, 129
positionalities, 7, 218
postmortems, 95
Pough, Gwendolyn, 122
Powell, Malea, 117, 118, 119, 122, 124, 125; revise/submit and, 123; on stories, 4
power, 17; imbalance, 113
practices, 118, 119; multiple, 117; revising, 51
Prague, 21, 206, 210, 211, 215, 217, 218, 219, 220; Soviet occupation of, 212, 213
Prague Gender Studies Center, 214–15
Prague Spring, 209, 212
Prague Summer Program, 209, 210
Prague Winter (Albright), 218
Prečan, Vilém, 206, 211, 212, 215, 217
prejudice, 67, 68
premises, well-formulated, 33–36
Present Tense, 111, 112

Price, Margaret, 72
Prieto, Alejandra, 11, 47*n*2; counterstories and, 41; resignation letter from, 43, 49
print articles, web revision for, 97*f*
print books, digital books and, 96*t*
professional identity, 12, 61, 79, 106, 161; building, 53, 57, 80; revision of, 53–60
professional practices, 49, 92, 229; focusing on, 51; revising, 50
Professor Is In (Kelsky), 53
projects: defining, 143–46; institutional, 174
proposals, 24, 84, 85, 122; call for, 151; revising, 95–96
Proposition 63, 132
prototypes, 96, 100; submitting, 98
Psenka, Carolyn, 68
public service, 80, 81, 83, 84
publication, 123, 208; language around, 159; process, 160, 193
publics, 114; creating, 107
publishing: difficulties with, 107–10; process of, 188

Qualley, Donna, 189, 190*n1*; influence of, 186–87
Queer, 15*n*3
queer-erasing legislation, 140
QuickTime, 103

R&Rs, 112, 155, 156, 187, 188
racism, 41, 44, 138, 145; challenging, 148; defining, 150; legacy of, 137; naming, 147*f*; Standard English and, 148; statement against, 146; structural, 146; whiteness and, 146
radical adaptability, 13, 138, 153, 155, 159, 177; term, 157, 158
radicalism, 155, 158
reactions, 36, 70, 71, 109, 155; community, 138; "hot take," 126; negative, 145, 146
reader reports, 6, 189
reading, 93, 102; critical, 24
recommendations, 49, 67, 69, 70, 74, 76, 126, 131; anonymous analyses of, 64; approaches to, 75; devaluing, 63; pursuing, 125; revising, 63; self-examination of, 65; space of, 73; uploading, 63. *See also* letters of recommendation
references, checking, 159
Reflection in the Writing Classroom (Yancey), 207
Reflections (Medina), 133
reflexivity, 184–85, 189, 190*n1*, 232
Reiff, Mary Jo, 106
rejections, 32, 122, 161; desk, 107, 108, 109

RELATE Lab, 15n3
relationality, 4, 6, 75, 118, 122, 227
relationships, 34, 123, 125, 228; building, 87; changing, 140; editorial, 96; hierarchical, 106; interpersonal, 163; mentoring, 12, 74; research, 231; working, 151; writer-reader, 231
reminders, screenshot showing, 197f
representation, 64, 71; accurate, 179; conversions about, 74
research, 55, 56, 76, 80, 103, 138, 194, 200, 206, 208; activist, 15n3; funds, 31; multimodal, 58; process, 46; qualitative, 200; quantitative, 193, 204; skills, 67; teaching and, 202; undergraduate, 151, 152, 155
research teams, 151, 152
resignation letters: practice, 49; retelling, 49; text of, 42–43, 43–46; writing, 41–42
resilience, 64, 114; stories of, 213
resistance, 14n1, 28, 213; revision and, 7; strategies of, 7
Restaino, Jessica, 14
resubmission, revision and, 133, 155, 159, 188
resumes, reviewing, 63
retelling, 41; revision and, 192–97
review process, 14, 111, 123, 125, 171, 185
reviewers, 52, 121–22, 134, 160, 187, 188; comments by, 132; experience of, 102; railing against, 159
revision: acts of, 7, 62; aggressive, 198; destabilization through, 52–53; drawing, 222, 224, 225; failed, 162, 208; helping with, 98–99, 100–101, 112; holistic quality of, 6, 10; large-scale, 42, 85, 114; motivation for, 82, 193; outcome of, 222; perpetual/ongoingness of, 13, 14, 21, 62, 120, 173, 177, 205, 223; personal/transformative nature of, 201–5; possibilities of, 220, 221; as recalibration, 139–40; refusal as, 20; revisitation and, 220; rules for, 146; screenshot showing, 197f; as self-generative process, 86; struggles with, 11, 12, 39, 178, 179, 199, 222; as tale of discovery, 33; talking about, 27–28; teaching, 8, 21; thinking about, 3, 121, 178, 182; time frame for, 220; vitality of, 3-4, 20; work of, 8–9, 12, 23, 51, 149–150, 182, 186, 203, 204
ReVision Centre for Art and Social Justice, 15n3
Revision: History, Theory, and Practice (Horning and Becker), 9–10

revision process, 9, 82, 126, 129, 134, 138, 139, 143, 149, 169, 179, 204, 208, 226; complexity of, 89; described, 10
revision stories, 6, 7, 11, 177
Rewriting: How to Do Things with Texts (Harris), 11, 23, 25, 26, 27, 28
Reynolds, Kim, 137
rhetoric, 24, 41, 54, 65, 66, 76, 110, 117, 122, 124, 126, 142, 172, 174; collaboration and, 187; Indigenous, 14n1; pedagogical work of, 165; public, 106; social dimensions of, 181; study of, 120
Rhetoric Society of America (RSA), 111
Rhetoric Society Quarterly, 108, 109
rhetorical ecology, 182, 185
rhetorical ecosystems, 80, 190
"Rhetorical Hiccups" (Vidali), 64
Rhodes, Jacqueline, 14n1, 125
Ribero, Ana Milena, 14n1
Rice, Carla, 15n3
Rickert, Thomas, 9
Roen, Duane H., 14n2, 166
Rogers, Carl, 124
Rose, Mike, 14n2
Rosenblatt, Adam: feedback from, 156, 157, 158
rubrics, 170, 171, 172
Rule, Hannah J., 36, 179, 227
Russell, Alisa, 12, 62n1, 91, 114, 115, 123; feedback from, 30, 92, 110, 111, 112–13; mentoring by, 110, 161
Ryerson, Rachael, 14n1

Salem, Lori, 192
samizdat, 206, 208, 209, 214–15, 217, 218, 219, 220; experiences with, 213; movement, 210, 211; Library, 216f; process, 212, 213, 214
Samizdat, 206, 216
Sánchez, Fernando, 11–12, 50, 53, 54, 55, 59, 60, 61–62, 82, 106, 139; feedback from, 57
Sánchez, Raúl, 12, 19, 50, 92, 93, 121, 134
Schaefer, Erin, 122
Schrodinger's Texts, 21
Scott, Ridley, 24
screen grabs, 6
Screencastify, 103
screenings, focus group, 32, 34–33, 38–39
Scrivener, 100
self-care, 44, 202
self-examination, 65
self-expression, 26, 79
service, defining, 167
Sexton, Anne, 24, 25
sexual minorities, 74

Shakespeare, William, 24
shared vocabulary, developing, 131
Shivener, Rich, 12, 35, 36, 39, 91, 92, 96; digital texts and, 31
Šiklová, Jiřina, 206, 211, 212, 214*f*, 220; death of, 215; interview of, 213; samizdat and, 214–15
Silicon Valley, 129, 130
Silicon Valley (HBO), 130
Sills, Ellery, 11–12, 50, 53, 54–55, 82, 106, 139; cover letter from, 57*f*, 59*f*; feedback from, 56–60; job document of, 60; multimodality and, 55, 56
Singh, Smita, 202
sirdefenition, 119
Skala, Petr, 209
Skype, 30
slippages and swells, 95, 103–4
slow hunches, term, 181
social justice, 31, 76, 148, 174
Social Justice Center Faculty Fellowship, 45
social media, 192
Social Sciences Feminist Network Research Interest Group, 74
Sohan, Vanessa Kraemer, 12, 50, 71, 74; advocacy by, 72; approach of, 67–69; letters of recommendation and, 65–67
Sommers, Nancy, 7, 9, 51, 178, 179
soundbites, 148
sound files, reviewing, 213
space, 73, 84; academic, 72, 91; digital, 70, 71; epistemological, 4, 6; physical, 70, 71; relational, 75; for revision, 79; textual, 86; work, 88. *See also* holding space
Spooner, Michael, 23, 27
Squarespace, 100
Stack Exchange, 101
Standard English, 141, 144, 147; evaluating with, 145; racism and, 148
Steff, 153, 154, 155, 156; equity principle and, 159; publication process and, 160; radical adaptability and, 157; writing partnerships and, 152
STEM, 56–57
stereotypes, 4, 46*n1*
Stewart, Kathleen, 94
Stone, Jayne E. O., 8, 227
"Stop WOKE Act," 137, 140*n1*
story, 4–6, 29–30, 39; as decoloniality, 132; as methodology, 117–18. *See also* counterstory
storytelling, 4, 30, 31–32, 33, 36, 118, 129, 132; lies and, 35; queer, 14*n1*; revising, 41; as theme, 37
structural issues, 52, 229

Stuart, Heather, 167, 169, 174
submissions, 3, 52, 99, 108, 118, 130, 132, 155, 179, 183, 184, 188; preparing, 102–3; revised, 100; systems, 63
Substack, 138
Surrender: Feminist Rhetoric and Ethics in Love and Illness (Restiano and Maute), 230, 231, 232

Tales (Brothers Grimm), 24
Taylor, Breonna, 153
teacher-scholars, 5, 9, 15*n4*, 75
teaching, 59, 80, 94; online, 153; research and, 202; as service, 85
teaching philosophies, 53, 58
technical terms, 119–20
technology, 91, 192, 200
Tellez-Trujillo, Karen R., 13, 21, 34, 161, 177, 178, 201, 212*f*, 214*f*, 216*f*, 230, 231
Tempest (Shakespeare), 24
tenure, 26, 46, 49, 86, 87, 103, 213; files, 74; pressures of, 160; support for, 42
texts, creative reuse of, 24–25
textual change, 9, 20, 49, 52, 96–97
"Theorizing Rhetorical-Affective Workflows: Behind the Scenes with Webtext Authors" (Shivener), 96
theory, 54, 59; courses, 58; framework, 182
"They Say/I Say" or Ways of Reading (Graff and Birkenstein), 26
"Three Tips for Training Your Voice" (NPR), 98
Tobias, Ronald B., 33
track changes, 104, 158
training, formal/informal, 119
transformation, 45, 103; process of, 180, 222; revision and, 80
translingualism, 67, 69, 79, 128, 129, 130
traumatic brain injury (TBI), 64
Trimmer, Joseph, 14*n2*
Trix, Frances, 68
truths, 4, 30, 35, 38, 145; relationship with, 36
Tulley, Christine, 9
Turning Point USA, 137
Turns of Thought: Teaching Composition as Reflexive Inquiry (Qualley), 186, 189
tutorials, 31, 100, 101, 102
Twitch, 103

Ulysses, 97
UnAmericans, The (Antopol), 218
Universal Design for Learning (UDL), 72
"University of Washington Declares Proper Grammar Is Racist" (Ciccotta), 144

University of Washington–Tacoma (UWT), 137, 144, 145
University Writing (Auburn), 163, 164, 165, 167, 171, 173; ePortfolio Project and, 170; plan by, 166; success for, 170; WE courses and, 166, 168
University Writing Committee (UWC), 163, 164, 167, 169, 171, 172, 173; writing plans by, 168
UWC. *See* University Writing Committee
UWT. *See* University of Washington–Tacoma

VanHaitsma, Pamela, 106
Van Ittersum, Derek, 95
Vidali, Amy, 64, 65, 67, 70
video segments, 95
Villanueva, Victor, 4, 14n2, 117, 121
violence: colonial, 5; police, 139, 154; racial, 154
"Visit," 211
voice-overs, 97, 98
Vygotsky, Lev, 182

W3Schools, 101
WAC. *See* Writing Across the Curriculum
WAC/WID courses, 50, 54, 56, 57, 58, 59, 60; teaching/administering, 55
Waldrep, Tom, 5
Wallis-Thomas, Jule, 13, 21, 100, 161, 177, 178, 179, 194, 201, 202, 203
Wayne State University (WSU), 192, 200
WE. *See* Writing-Enhanced courses
WE Write, 164, 166, 172, 173, 174; process of, 169–70, 171
web design, 96, 98–100
Webflow, 100
WEC. *See* writing-enriched curriculum
WEC Institute, 174
Wenger, Christy I., 12, 50, 165, 174
Where Good Ideas Come From (Johnson), 181
white, term, 138, 147
white supremacy, 41, 42, 49, 142, 147, 148, 174
whiteboards, using, 141, 142, 146
whiteness, 138, 142, 145; addressing, 146; naming, 146, 147f; racism and, 146

Women's Ways of Making It in Rhetoric and Composition (Lutkewitte, Kitchens, and Scanlon), 5
WPA, 13, 65, 80, 81, 82, 139; identity and, 50, 79, 83–84, 85, 86, 87; work as, 84, 85, 87, 88–89
WPA Addendum, 86, 87, 88
WPA Outcomes Statement, 83
Writers on Writing (Waldrep), 5
writing: advanced, 54; article, 113–14; belonging through, 91; collaborative, 181, 182; critical, 24; developmental, 54; interdisciplinary, 59; nature of, 194, 195; performance and, 36; practices, 100, 117; professional, 59; projects, 177, 187; questioning, 159; student, 129, 134; support, 185; technical, 59. *See also* letter writing
Writing Across the Curriculum (WAC), 56, 82–83, 165, 171; programs, 139, 163; scholarship in, 164; theory, 166
Writing Center (UWT), 144, 146
writing centers, 141, 142, 144, 146, 148, 194, 195; changes for, 150; personal nature of, 193; student retention and, 192
Writing-Enhanced (WE) courses, 164, 166, 167–68, 170; creation of, 171; effectiveness of, 173; planning, 172; promoting, 168
writing-enriched curriculum (WEC), 164, 166, 171; impact of, 165; philosophy for, 172
writing groups, 111, 113, 152
writing plans, 165, 167, 168; collaboration on, 169
writing process, 9, 46, 82, 95, 143, 183, 222; ownership of, 173
writing programs, 7, 12, 54, 82, 85, 100, 141, 152, 174; creation/maintenance of, 88; revisions of, 88; as university programs, 84
Writing Spaces, 183, 184, 185, 186
writing studies, 7, 9, 56, 172; knowledge-making in, 4; pedagogical work of, 165
WSU. *See* Wayne State University

Yadav, Poonam, 202–3
Yancey, Kathleen Blake, 207, 230

ABOUT THE AUTHORS

Christopher Basgier is Director of University Writing at Auburn University. In that role, he works with departments to integrate writing throughout undergraduate and graduate curricula, particularly in support of high-impact practices like writing-intensive courses and ePortfolios. His research, which spans writing across the curriculum, genre, threshold concepts, and digital rhetoric, has appeared in venues like *Across the Disciplines*, *WAC Journal*, *Composition Forum*, and *Studies in Higher Education*. He is also active in national organizations like the Association for Writing Across the Curriculum, the Conference on College Composition and Communication, and the WAC Clearinghouse.

Cameron Becker is a doctoral candidate in Rhetoric and Composition at Ball State University. She received her bachelor of arts from Indiana University–Kokomo in humanities with a minor in English literature. Her master of arts in English with a certificate in composition studies is from Indiana University East. Cameron's research interests are in disability studies, critical embodiment pedagogy, and decolonial theory. She also studies digital writing, rhetorics of craft, and information literacy.

Kelly Blewett is assistant professor of English at Indiana University East, where she also directs the writing program and teaches courses in writing and writing pedagogy. Her research on the social contexts of writing and feedback has appeared in *College English*, *JAEPL*, and *Journal of College Literacy and Learning* as well as several edited collections.

Allison D. Carr is associate professor of rhetoric and Director of Writing Across the Curriculum at Coe College, where she teaches courses in rhetorical theory, writing studies, cultural studies, and creative nonfiction. Her research engages affective conceptualizations of failure in the writing classroom and beyond, appearing in *Composition Forum*, *Pedagogy*, Ball and Loewe's *Bad Ideas about Writing*, Adler-Kassner and Wardle's *Naming What We Know*, and elsewhere. Most recently she coedited with Laura Micciche *Failure Pedagogies: Learning and Unlearning What It Means to Fail* (Peter Lang 2020). Her nonfiction has appeared in *The Rumpus*, *Apple in the Dark*, and *CRAFT Literary*.

Dana Comi is an assistant professor at Utah Valley University, where she teaches technical communication and first-year composition. Her latest research on infrastructure, access, and genre can be found in *Communication Design Quarterly* and *Writing the Classroom* (Stephen Neaderhiser 2020).

William Duffy is an associate professor of English at the University of Memphis, where he teaches in the Writing, Rhetoric, and Technical Communication Program.

Stefanie Frigo is an associate professor at North Carolina Central University. She teaches English language and linguistics classes and serves as the coordinator of the Interdisciplinary Studies Program. Her publications can be found in *SAGE Research Methods Cases*, *Across the Disciplines*, and the *Journal of Student Success in Writing*.

ABOUT THE AUTHORS

Collie Fulford is associate professor and director of the Academic and Professional Writing Program at the University at Buffalo–SUNY. She previously worked at North Carolina Central University, where she conducted the collaborative research about and with adult students that informs her chapter in this collection. Her publications on writers and writing programs can be found in *Pedagogy*, *WPA: Writing Program Administration*, *Composition Studies*, and *Across the Disciplines*.

Mike Garcia is associate professor of English and Writing Director at Luther College. In this capacity, he directs the Nancy K. Barry Writing Center; coordinates writing instruction in Paideia, the common first-year course sequence; and contributes to faculty development in writing instruction across the disciplines. He teaches rhetoric, professional and technical writing, and courses on the English language for future middle and high school teachers. His research focuses on writing pedagogy across the disciplines, writing assessment, and rhetoric. His work has appeared in *Kairos*, an NCTE anthology of activities for first-year composition, and an upcoming collection on failure(s) in writing, among other venues.

Ian Golding is assistant professor of English at the University of Cincinnati–Blue Ash. His work has appeared in *Pedagogy*, *College English*, *Composition Studies*, and other journals.

Joseph Harris currently teaches composition part-time at the University of Pittsburgh. Previously, he directed the first-year writing programs at Pitt and Duke University. His books include *A Teaching Subject*, *Rewriting*, and *The Work of Teaching Writing*.

Alexandra Hidalgo is an award-winning Venezuelan writer, filmmaker, theorist, memoirist, and editor. She is the recipient of From the Heart Productions' inaugural Carole Joyce Award for Excellence in Documentary Storytelling. Her videos and writing have been featured in *The Hollywood Reporter*, *IndieWire*, *NPR*, *The Criterion Collection*, and *Women and Hollywood*. She is associate professor and Crow Chair of English at the University of Pittsburgh. Her video book *Cámara Retórica: A Feminist Filmmaking Methodology for Rhetoric and Composition* received the 2018 Computers and Composition Distinguished Book Award. Her scholarship has been published in *Kairos*, *Composition Studies*, *Enculturation*, and *Peitho*, among others. She is cofounder and editor-in-chief of the digital publication *agnès films: supporting women and feminist filmmakers* and of the peer-reviewed journal *Constellations: A Cultural Rhetorics Publishing Space*.

Christina M. LaVecchia is an assistant professor of English at the University of Cincinnati. Her research spans multiple disciplines: in rhetoric and composition, her work on contemporary composing theories, writing pedagogies, digital literacies, and professional practices appears in *College English*, *Composition Forum*, and *Composition Studies*, among others. Her healthcare collaborations with Mayo Clinic's Knowledge and Evaluation Research (KER) Unit on patient-clinician communication, shared decision-making, and making care fit appear in *Patient Education and Counseling*, *Health Expectations*, *BMJ Open*, and *Mayo Clinic Proceedings: Innovations, Quality and Outcomes*.

Aja Y. Martinez is associate professor of English at University of North Texas. Her award-winning scholarship, published nationally and internationally, makes a compelling case for counterstory as methodology through the well-established framework of critical race theory (CRT).

Cruz Medina is associate professor of rhetoric and composition at Santa Clara University. He has been faculty with the Bread Loaf School of English since 2016. His monograph *Reclaiming Poch@ Pop: Examining the Rhetoric of Cultural Deficiency* was published in 2015 by Palgrave. In 2018, he coedited *Racial Shorthand: Coded Discrimination Contested in Social*

Media with Octavio Pimentel for Computers and Composition Digital Press. His forthcoming book *Sanctuary: Exclusion, Violence, and Indigenous Migrants in the East Bay* (OSUP) applies decolonial methods and CRT to research based on experiences in a volunteer English program with predominantly Indigenous Guatemalan students.

Laura R. Micciche is professor of English and Director of the Rhetoric and Composition Graduate Program at University of Cincinnati. Her research focuses on composing processes, feminist pedagogies, and affect. Recent books include *Failure Pedagogies: Learning and Unlearning What It Means to Fail* (Peter Lang 2020), coedited with Allison D. Carr, and *Acknowledging Writing Partners* (Parlor 2017). For six years, she served as editor of *Composition Studies*, an independent journal in rhetoric and composition, and is currently coeditor, with Chris Carter, of the WPA Book Series for Parlor Press.

Jessica Restaino is professor and Chair of Writing Studies at Montclair State University. She is the author of two monographs: *Surrender: Feminist Rhetoric and Ethics in Love and Illness* (SIU 2019), recipient of the 2020 CCCC Outstanding Book Award, and a runner up for the 2020 RSA Book Award; and *First Semester: Graduate Students, Teaching Writing, and the Challenge of Middle Ground* (SWR/NCTE 2012). She is coeditor (with Laurie Cella) of *Unsustainable: Re-imagining Community Literacy, Public Writing, Service-Learning, and the University* (Lexington 2012). Her essays and book chapters have appeared in numerous venues. She is also the cofounder, with Jacqueline Regan, of Text Power Telling Inc., a nonprofit organization that offers writing workshops for sexual trauma survivors.

Hannah J. Rule is associate professor of English in composition and rhetoric at the University of South Carolina, where she teaches graduate and undergraduate courses in first-year writing, writing and embodiment, and the teaching of writing. Her scholarship focused on questioning commonplaces in writing pedagogies appears in venues including *CCC*, *Composition Forum*, *Composition Studies*, and several edited collections. Recent books include *Situating Writing Processes* (WAC Clearinghouse / University Press of Colorado 2019) and *The Material Culture of Writing*, coedited with Cydney Alexis (Utah State University Press 2022).

Alisa Russell is an assistant professor in the Writing Program at Wake Forest University, where she also researches and facilitates writing across the curriculum initiatives. Her most recent projects explore genre access in government writing, and her articles have appeared in publications such as *Written Communication*, *Pedagogy*, and *WAC Journal*.

Fernando Sánchez is associate professor of English at the University of St. Thomas in St. Paul, MN. He has served as head of the professional writing committee; director of the Academic Development Program; and interim chair of the Department of English. His research focuses on participatory frameworks in technical communication; political and policy rhetorics; and writing in health and medicine. His research has been published in multiple scholarly venues in rhetoric, composition, and technical writing and communication.

Raúl Sánchez is an associate professor in the Department of English and an affiliate faculty member in the Center for Latin American Studies at the University of Florida. He is the author of *Inside the Subject: A Theory of Identity for the Study of Writing* (NCTE/CCC/Studies in Writing and Rhetoric 2017) and *The Function of Theory in Composition Studies* (SUNY 2005). He is the coeditor, with Iris D. Ruiz, of *Decolonizing Rhetoric and Composition Studies: New Latinx Keywords for Theory and Pedagogy* (Palgrave 2016).

Rich Shivener is an assistant professor in the Writing Department at York University. His latest research investigates digital media writing practices and emotions, and he teaches courses in the department's digital cultures stream. Rich is also a section editor for *Kairos: A Journal of Rhetoric, Technology, and Pedagogy*.

Ellery Sills is a teaching assistant professor in the Core Writing Program at the University of Nevada, Reno, where he teaches developmental composition, first-year composition, and argument. His research explores how multimodality gets articulated within disciplinary and pedagogical contexts, and his interests include composition pedagogy, information literacy, public and digital rhetorics, and English education. His previous publications have appeared in the *Journal of Writing Assessment, College Composition and Communication*, and the edited collection *Teaching Critical Reading and Writing in the Era of Fake News*.

Vanessa Kraemer Sohan is associate professor of English in the Writing and Rhetoric program at Florida International University, where she also serves as associate director of the Liberal and Interdisciplinary Studies programs. Her research and teaching focus on translingual and transmodal approaches to literacy practices, feminist historiography, and material and cultural rhetorics. She is the author of *Lives, Letters, and Quilts: Women and Everyday Rhetorics of Resistance* (University of Alabama Press, 2020), and her scholarship has appeared in *College English, Pedagogy, JAC, Journal of College Literacy and Learning*, the *Journal of Multimodal Rhetorics*, and several edited collections.

Jayne E. O. Stone is a doctoral candidate in rhetoric and composition at the University of Cincinnati, where she also teaches undergraduate composition and writing classes. Her current research foregrounds revision in first-year writing classrooms and also investigates complex and multiagent writing environments.

Karen R. Tellez-Trujillo is assistant professor of rhetoric and composition at Cal Poly Pomona in the Department of English and Modern Languages. Karen's present scholarship centers on enactments of feminist resilience in the writing classroom. She teaches cultural rhetorics, creative writing, and literacy, language, and cultural practices. Her upcoming work will appear in Steven Corbett's *If at First You Don't Succeed? Writing, Rhetoric and the Question of Failure*, Lynn Lewis's *Pivotal Strategies*, and Fishman, Rosenberg, and Garcia's *Community Listening: Stories-So-Far and Possibilities of New Stories*. She is active in the Conference on Community Writing and the Conference on College Composition and Communication. Karen is also a 2022 recipient of the NCTE Early Career Educator of Color Leadership Award.

Jule Wallis-Thomas is associate professor of rhetoric and composition at Wayne State University in the Department of English. Her current research and curriculum design focuses on STEM, AI and ethics, and international co-teaching courses. She directs the Composition Learning Community program and teaches services learning courses that partners with 826Michigan. She is the recipient of six grants, a College of Liberal Arts and Science Assessment award, and received two Presidential Awards for Excellence in teaching. Her current professional development is the completion of a third master's in Learning Design and Technology.

Christy I. Wenger is Dean of Education and Liberal Arts and professor of Writing and Rhetoric at Lake Superior State University. She was previously Director of Writing and Rhetoric for eleven years at Shepherd University. She has long researched the implications of non-Western rhetorics and contemplative practice on the pedagogy and practice of writing. Her latest research focuses on emotional labor and inclusive leadership in higher education. Her previous publications have appeared in *WPA: Writing Program Administration, Journal for the Assembly of Expanded Perspectives on Learning*, and *The Things We Carry: Strategies for Recognizing and Negotiating Emotional Labor in Writing Program Administration*.

www.ingramcontent.com/pod-product-compliance
Lightning Source LLC
Chambersburg PA
CBHW052135070526
44585CB00017B/1833